D1161957

Psychoanalysis and Male Sexuality

PSYCHOANALYSIS

AND

MALE SEXUALITY

Edited with an Introduction by

DR. HENDRIK M. RUITENBEEK

COLLEGE & UNIVERSITY PRESS · *Publishers*

NEW HAVEN, CONN.

Library of Congress Catalog Card Number: 66-14819

TO THE MEMORY
OF
ALFRED KINSEY

MANUFACTURED IN THE UNITED STATES OF AMERICA BY
UNITED PRINTING SERVICES, INC.
NEW HAVEN, CONN.

105208

Acknowledgments

The International Journal of Psychoanalysis granted permission to reprint the following articles:

Melanie Klein, "Early Stages of the Oedipus Conflict," Vol. IX, 1928.

Karen Horney, "The Dread of Woman," Vol. XIII, 1932.

Felix Boehm, "Femininity Complex in Men," Vol. XI, 1930.

Franz Alexander, "The Castration Complex in the Formation of Character," Vol. VI, 1923.

Rudolph Loewenstein, "Phallic Passivity in Men," Vol. XVI, 1935.

Otto Fenichel, "The Psychology of Transvestism," Vol. XI, 1930.

Ralph Greenson, "On Homosexuality and Gender Identity," Vol. XLV, 1964.

Heinz Lichtenstein, "The Role of Narcissism in the Emergence and Maintenance of a Primary Identity," Vol. XLV, 1964.

M. Masud R. Khan, "Foreskin Fetishism and Its Relation to Ego Pathology in a Male Homosexual," Vol. XLVI, 1965.

With the permission of the *Journal of the American Psychoanalytic Association*:

Robert Bak, "Fetishism," Vol. I, no. 2, April 1953.

With the permission of *The American Journal of Psychology*:

Glenn V. Ramsey "The Sexual Development of Boys," Vol. 56, 1943.

With the permission of *The American Sociological Review*:

Clifford Kirkpatrick and Eugene Kanin, "Male Sex Aggression on a University Campus," February 1957.

With the permission of Holt, Rinehart & Winston:

J. W. M. Whiting, R. Kluckhohn, A. Anthony, "The Function of Male Initiation Ceremonies at Puberty," in *Readings in Social Psychology*, edited by Maccoby, Newcomb, and Hartley. New York, 1958.

Contents

Introduction

I

It has been said that sexuality in the United States will never be the same since Kinsey published his reports on the sexual behavior of the American male and the American female. The specific results of Kinsey's research—impressive though they may be—are less significant than the bringing of sexuality out into the open for all to discuss and evaluate.

Slowly, the study of sexuality has begun to detach itself from the stigma of "psychopathia sexualis" as that was presented by Iwan Bloch, Magnus Hirschfeld, and George Hirth. Today we tend to look at sexuality and its varied manifestations in a more matter-of-fact way. We are still aware of the pathological ramifications of contemporary sexuality, but we are learning to see sexuality itself as but one mode of our total existence. The neo-Freudians have de-emphasized libido theory in psychoanalysis, but it is the existentialist school which has given a new dimension to our thinking about sexuality. In *Phenomenologie de la Perception*, the French existentialist Merlau-Ponty writes:

> Sexuality, it is said, is dramatic because we engage in it our entire personal life. But precisely why do we do so? Because our body is for us a mirror of our being, not only because it is a natural self, a stream of given existence, of a kind in which we never know whether the forces which support us are theirs or ours—rather because they are neither theirs nor ours entirely. There is no excelling of sexuality as there is no sexuality closed upon itself. No one is saved and no one is entirely lost.

Building upon Binswanger's *Daseinanalyse*, the existentialist school stresses that being in love represents a new modality of existence in which the individual is no longer ruled by sexual libido alone, but in which he confronts another individual in a new form of human relatedness. In a remarkable study of

9

sexual perversions, Medard Boss has observed that "Dasein-analysis" sees perversions as results of specific concealments and restrictions of possibilities for loving.

Rollo May brings Boss's observation closer to the theme of this anthology when he observes that many contemporaries experience their bodies as alien; hence they tend to exploit their bodies—including the sexuality they see as part of the body—as if they were machines. "The Victorian person," May says, "sought to have love without falling into sex; the modern person seeks to have sex without falling into love."

Love is the most risky of human relations and desire to avoid risk seems a compelling factor in the response which many contemporary Americans make to life. The wish to avoid risk is an expression of insecurity and anxiety, and the American male appears both anxious and insecure in respect to his sexuality. He questions his own masculinity and feels under constant pressure to show that he is a man. American society, with its demand for success and performance, makes him feel challenged each time he enters his office, shop, or classroom. A confident sense of masculinity gains little support from our other-directed society. And he no longer can feel certain of getting at home from mother, sister, daughter, or wife what the world outside so often refuses, namely, recognition of, and support for, his awareness of being a man. Continual challenge and failure of accustomed support have produced a crisis for the contemporary American male. He responds to that crisis by neurotic aggressiveness or neurotic submission, compulsive pursuit of money and women, or an equally compulsive retirement into the safe enclosure of family life and the economic womb of the large corporation. Or he may avoid the issue entirely, refuse sexual relations with the women whom he sees as an element in a threatening social context, and turn to homosexual expression.

American society demands that men succeed: that they make money and show themselves good sexual performers. In the formative adolescent years, the boy is called upon to play a role at a pace dictated by the environment rather than by his own needs. He cannot look to other young people for help since they are apt to experience similar pressures and share like anxieties. Failure to "date" when most of his classmates do, for example, can injure a boy's status among his peers and can distort his psychosexual growth. Sexuality is no longer considered a private affair; friends and relatives show concern with any departure from what they consider appropriate behavior. Among adults, the blatant sexual chatter which is so common nowadays makes the male feel peculiarly exposed.

The contemporary concern of the male with power, especially economic power as measured by income, reflects the relationship between his perception of his sexuality and his conception of his total existence. Infatuation with sports, gambling, and money are but a few examples of how the American male demonstrates that he has a penis. Karen Horney has pointed out that castration-anxiety *per se* does not concern itself with the penis alone but also involves the male's self-respect. Where his self-respect and sense of self are diminished or lost, the male may experience a variety of sexual disturbances. Sometimes, as in the instance of male homosexuality, this variant sexual behavior becomes quite institutionalized. In other cases, such as impotence, exhibitionism, and fetishism, the sexual disturbance does not enter into a reasonably acceptable life-pattern and hence is more apt to be treated in psychoanalysis.

The male's sexual confidence and identity are threatened by two important sociological factors: the change in the position of women and the development of an other-directed society. These have helped create the crisis in male identity which may well lie at the root of the problems which some of the essays in this anthology discuss in greater detail.

Women no longer depend on fathers, brothers, and husbands for their livelihood. They earn their own way and even compete with men in many business and professional situations. They acknowledge their own sexuality, as middle-class women in earlier generations were at least not supposed to do, and require that the men in their lives satisfy their sexual needs. At the same time, women have assumed a new role in the family. Instead of being a sort of unpaid servant who soothed her husband's ego while she fetched his slippers and darned his socks, the American wife is now copartner and even ruler in the home. Advertisers judge that it is the approval of women which makes goods seem desirable—women's pictures adorn advertisements for everything from oatmeal to heavy lubricating oil; moreover, agreeable wives are essential to successful political campaigning. In popular fiction—especially as presented in comic strips and on TV—"mother" has common sense and poise, whereas "father" is almost invariably fatuous or unable to handle people, even when he is right.

The American boy (of white Anglo-Saxon or Jewish origin, it might be noted; Italian and Slav families are more male-dominated, whereas the Negro family is female-dominated in an entirely different context) is expected to treat his mother as "boss" of the household. He has doubts of asserting himself against her, doubts that are often reflected in his behavior with other women toward whom he may assume a posture of defense or aggression. The initial castration-anxiety which the boy may experience in his early relation with his mother is reinforced by later experience and may be expressed in sexual impotence or in passive attitudes in other aspects of his life.

American women are said to be peculiarly aggressive and possessive, but those traits have been encouraged by male tendencies toward passivity. Passivity, meanwhile, is certainly not lessened by the growth of other-direction in American society which is directed and dominated by large-scale economic organizations. The male is only too aware that he must meet the expectations of the people in his environment and that little independent choice is actually allowed him. He finds it difficult to take refuge in the male company which once was a sublimation for latent homosexuality; the old-fashioned barbershop and saloon have disappeared as respectable, or even disreputable male refuges, and only the relatively prosperous can belong to clubs. Society apparently gives less and less approval to expressions of male intimacy. Coeducation makes increasing inroads upon male comradeship at school. Early marriage allows the young man fewer opportunities to incorporate his discovery of sexuality into his life design. Earlier sexuality is a fragmentary experience which he cannot set into its proper place as he forms his life patterns. Even in adolescence he may be trapped into the routine of dating which is often followed by the currently fashionable early marriage. Contemporary America seems to have no room for the mature bachelor. As a colleague of mine once remarked, a single man over thirty is now regarded as a pervert, a person with severe emotional problems, or a poor creature fettered to his mother. By emphasizing sex and by making its sublimation in the classic Freudian sense unfashionable, our society is imposing imperatives which many men find it impossible to obey. Hence we witness what Abram Kardiner calls "the flight from masculinity." That flight is evidence of the failure of many American men to establish a firm sense of identity, personal or sexual.*

Although numerous studies are made of the shift in the position of American women and its accompanying problems, changes in our society have affected American men even more deeply. The male's role and his prestige have been more strikingly attacked than have the female's, and he seems to be losing psychological status. Currently, many historians are inquiring into the relationship between movements for social change and groups which have lost, or fear to lose, prestige in the community. If the American male thinks he belongs to such a group, it is scarcely extraordinary that he should show by sexual impotence his loneliness, anxiety, and insecurity. The high level of sexual disturbance indicates that certain problems can no longer be understood in a merely psychoanalytic context, informative as that is; sociological backgrounds and issues are increasingly important in any study of the changing sexual role of the American male. And such studies, incidentally, are greatly needed if we are to have the information needed for coping with our problems.

II

The first essay in this anthology gives us some interesting material on the sexual behavior of pre-adolescent and adolescent boys. The 90 per cent masturbation figure is not surprising, but the rates of homosexual play reported (38 per cent in the pre-adolescent group and 30 per cent in the adolescent group) are of peculiar interest because this study antedates the Kinsey report.

In "The Function of Male Initiation Ceremonies at Puberty," J. W. M. Whiting and his colleagues reach some interesting conclusions: in effect, initiation ceremonies break up the close relationship between mother and son and allow him to assume a place in the community of men. As far as our society is con-

* For fuller discussion of the identity problem as it appears in our world, see my book, *The Individual and the Crowd: A Study of Identity in America* (New York: Thomas Nelson & Co., 1964). Some ramifications of contemporary male homosexuality in America are discussed in my essay, "Men Alone: The Male Homosexual and the Disintegrated Family," in *The Problem of Homosexuality in Modern Society*, Hendrik M. Ruitenbeek, ed. (New York: E. P. Dutton, 1963).

cerned, they conclude that many social problems among contemporary adolescents are related to an increase in the exclusiveness of the mother-child relationship and a decrease in the authority of the father. Most sociologists and psychoanalysts have recognized the danger in the absence of a strong father and the subsequent appearance of a dominating and possessive mother. Direct links between this situation and the appearance of impotence and homosexuality are evident. "Male Sex Aggression on a University Campus" by Kirkpatrick and Kanin continues the developmental discussion of Ramsey's essay.

Melanie Klein, well known for her psychoanalytic work with children, contends that the Oedipus complex comes into being sooner than is usually supposed. She feels that the sense of guilt which is clinically associated with pregenital fixation is certainly the direct result of the Oedipus conflict. Karen Horney examines man's fear of woman. She agrees with Freud that his initial fear is with the vagina itself, but Horney believes that anxiety goes beyond mere dread of the vagina; it is the fear of repulsion that really lies behind fear of the female. Dread of being rejected and derided by women, Horney contends, is "a typical ingredient in the analysis of every man."

Our knowledge of and particular insight into the phenomenon of homosexuality is still fairly limited. Recent publications have not always helped to clarify our concepts and interpretations on this point. While Irving Bieber's study, *Homosexuality*, and Daniel Cappon's *Toward an Understanding of Homosexuality* are a case in point, we should make an exception for Judd Marmor's excellent anthology, *Sexual Inversion*, which is a most valuable contribution to a better understanding of contemporary homosexuality. In this anthology we selected Ralph Greenson's essay on homosexuality and gender identity, which is a further clarification of some of the clinical ramifications of homosexuality. Heinz Lichtenstein's article on the role of narcissism fits well in this collection, since narcissism has always been an important link between sexuality and identity.

Felix Boehm's essay acquires new pertinence when we see it in relationship to the plight of the American male. As the negative Oedipus complex develops, Boehm thinks, boys do not simply hate the mother; they envy her and are jealous of the part she plays with the father. Freud says, "a boy has not merely an ambivalent attitude towards his father and an affectionate object relation to his mother, but at the same time he also behaves like a girl and displays an affectionate feminine attitude to his father and a corresponding hostility and jealousy towards his mother."

Franz Alexander, one of the most distinguished figures in the history of psychoanalysis, is represented here with an essay on the castration complex and its impact on character formation. The castration complex is a fundamental element in Freudian theory and Alexander defends the concept as he describes the analysis of a particular patient.

Sandor Ferenczi was one of Freud's most illustrious pupils. Here, he discusses the cure of psychosexual impotence with the aid of Freudian methods of treatment. Ferenczi thinks that impotence is always the symbolic expression of repressed memory traces of infantile sexual experience, of the unconscious wishes striving for their repetition, and of the mental conflicts thus provoked. He also agrees with Freud that incestuous fixation and sexual shame in childhood are of great significance in understanding impotence.

Rudolph Loewenstein's essay on phallic passivity in men also discusses the problem of impotence. He, too, puts the castration complex at the center of the picture and goes on to deal with the problem of *passive* homosexuality, which he thinks is associated with phallic passivity in males.

In describing the psychology of transvestism, Otto Fenichel relates this perversion to fetishism and passive homosexuality. Transvestism has a twofold significance: it is object-erotic (fetishistic) and narcissistic (homosexual). In transvestism, identification with the mother is obvious, but the transvestite also identifies himself with a creature of fantasy, the woman who has a penis. Female fetishists are extremely rare, Fenichel points out; female transvestites are merely women who covet the penis and have therefore identified themselves with men.

Robert Bak's essay on fetishism, found primarily among males, is one of the few brief treatments of this pattern of behavior. The fetish acts as a safeguard against the danger of castration. As Freud pointed out, fetishism is the direct result of the castration threat. Often, one may note here, fetishism, like homosexuality, may be an outcome of the male's horror at the sight of a creature who might be himself, and yet has no penis.

In addition to Bak's article on fetishism, we concluded this collection with an essay by M. Masud R. Khan on the relationship between fetishism, ego pathology and homosexuality. The literature on the relationship between fetishism and homosexuality in males is extremely limited and Khan presents us in this essay with a most complete and insightful interpretation of the relationship between fetishism and homosexuality. The introduction of ego pathology in the discussion of fetishism and homosexuality was a heretofore new element and its inclusion and subsequent discussion by Khan is most valuable for our understanding of this problem.

The essays presented here give only a fragmentary picture of male sexuality, but that picture is sufficiently varied and complex to show the range of the problem and the serious need for further research into the ways in which sexuality expresses itself as part of the total existence of the contemporary American male.

Psychoanalysis and Male Sexuality

I

The Sexual Development of Boys*

By Glenn V. Ramsey

This study is concerned with the sexual development, physical and behavioral, of pre-adolescent and adolescent boys. The results reported here are drawn from 291 complete sex histories,[1] as obtained by the author in personal interview. The ages ranged from 10 to 20 years; 85% from 12 to 16. Five of the boys were Negro and 286 white. Approximately three-fourths of the group were Protestant, 7% Catholic, 3% Jewish, and 15% with no religious affiliation. The population was primarily from the middle and upper-middle socioeconomic levels of a Midwestern city of over 100,000 people. One-half of the boys (146) constituted the entire seventh- and eighth-grade male population in a junior high school of the city. This sample afforded a measure of the adequacy of the whole series. The remainder of our subjects (145) was a random sample drawn from organized neighborhood-groups that met in various sections of the city. The present results provide interpretations of the boys studied, but further information is needed before generalizations can be drawn for boys at large.

I Physical Development

The phases of development here considered are nocturnal emissions, growth of pubic hair, change of voice, first ejacula-

---

* From the Department of Zoology, Indiana University. This study was directed by Dr. A. C. Kinsey.

[1] For a study of the sex education of this group of boys, see G. V. Ramsey, "The Sex Information of Younger Boys," *J. Orthopsychiat.*

tion, breast knots, and the erotic and non-erotic stimuli to which these boys responded.

Table 1 gives the results obtained in the onset of ejaculation, pubic hair growth, voice-change, and nocturnal emissions. The percentages show the number of boys that first reached each of these stages in development at each indicated age. The accu-

TABLE 1. *Percentage at Every Age-Group Showing Phase of Sexual Development*

Age-group (in yr.)	Ejacula- tion	Voice- change	Nocturnal emission	Pubic hair
10	1.8	.3	.3	.3
11	6.9	5.6	3.7	8.4
12	14.1	20.5	5.3	27.1
13	33.6	40.0	17.4	36.1
14	30.9	26.0	12.9	23.8
15	7.8	5.5	13.9	3.3
16	4.9	2.0	16.0	1.0

mulated percentages of those experienced in each of these items are presented graphically in Fig 1.

Ejaculation. Ejaculation is, perhaps, the most important event in the sexual development of the male; yet there is a paucity of information concerning its onset. The boys were asked to report the age at which ejaculation first occurred. The results show the lower limit for the experience to be at 10 years and the upper limit at 16 years. The median for the first ejaculation is at 13.8 years. First ejaculation occurred in masturbation in 75% of the cases; in nocturnal emissions in 22%; while homosexual relations or heterosexual intercourse provided the first source of ejaculation for the remainder.

Pubic hair and voice-change. The age-range for the first appearance of pubic hair and voice-change is from 10 to 16 years. The median age of onset is at 13.6 years for pubic-hair and 13.4 years for voice-change. The accumulative experience curves (Fig. 1) for these two characters show a remarkably close relationship. The voice-change was the first indication of a deepening of the voice, and not the final breaking and conspicuous loss of control which is usually completed two to four years after first ejaculation (according to Kinsey's unpublished data), and which ushers in the final pitch of the average white male's voice.

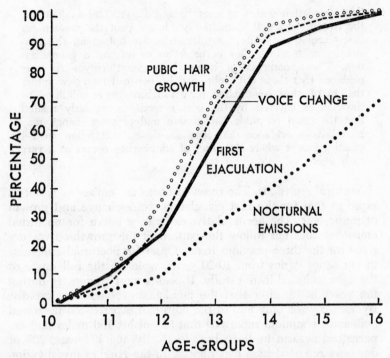

FIG. 1. ACCUMULATIVE EXPERIENCE CURVES OF SEXUAL DEVELOPMENT

Kubitschek has published photographs of the development of pubic hair in a group of 730 boys ranging from 11 to 18 yr.[2] These photographs show a variation in age of onset that is essentially the same as that exhibited in the present study. In an earlier paper by Crampton the median age for first appearance of pigmented hairs in the pubic area is given as approximately 13.6 yr., which is exactly the same as that found in the present study.[3]

Our results show that hair-development and first voice-change precede first ejaculation by a fraction of a year, except when

[2] P. E. Kubitschek, "Sexual Development of Boys with Special Reference to the Appearance of the Secondary Sexual Characters and Their Relationship to Structural and Personality Types," *J. Nerv. & Ment. Dis.*, 76, 1932, 425-51.

[3] C. W. Crampton, "Physiologic Age: A Fundamental Principle," *Amer. Phys. Educ. Rev.*, 13, 1908, 146.

first ejaculation occurs at ages 10 and 11 yr. The medians for the two items are 0.2 and 0.4 yr. lower than the median for first ejaculation. While the differences are not great, the consistency with which they occur seems to warrant a generalization. The smoothness of these three growth-curves is some evidence that these data, obtained by personal interview rather than by physical examination, have a high degree of validity. The three items covered by the curves seem so regularly related that the onset of pubic hair-growth and of voice-change may be taken as evidence that first ejaculation will follow in 2-4 months, except where the onset of adolescence occurs at a very early age.

Noctural emissions. The onset of nocturnal emissions is not as rapid as that for the first ejaculation, voice-change and growth of pubic hair. The accumulative-experience curve for nocturnal emissions does not follow the pattern of the growth-curves derived for the three previous items. Onset for nocturnal emissions in our series varies from 10-20 years, which is the full range of the ages included in the study. It occurs most frequently during the years 12-16; after that the incidence declines very rapidly. By age 15 years only half of the boys had experienced nocturnal emissions. Hamilton reported[4] that 55% of his 100 males had experienced orgasm in sleep by age 15. By age 17 years, 73% of our boys reported such experiences. In the Hughes investigation 81% of the boys reported[5] nocturnal emissions before leaving high school (i.e., at 17 and 18 years of age). Achilles[6] found that 397 (i.e., 82.5%) of a group of 482 boys had experienced their first nocturnal emissions before 18, and (as in the present study) the incidence of onset was highest during the years 12 to 16. Thus our data and those from previous studies are here in striking agreement. Nocturnal emissions constitute one of the several possible sources of sexual outlet for the male, and any consideration of their frequency should involve a consideration of the total outlet for each individual involved. In the present study the onset of nocturnal emissions was observed to precede, appear concurrently with, or follow, the beginning of other

[4] G. V. Hamilton, *A Research in Marriage*, 1929. p. 313.

[5] W. L. Hughes. "Sex Experiences of Boyhood," *J. Soc. Hyg.*, 12, 1926, 267.

[6] P. S. Achilles, *The Effectiveness of Certain Social Hygiene Literature*, (Amer. Soc. Hyg. Assoc.), 1923, 49.

forms of sexual outlet. In respect to its frequency, it was noted that it would increase, decrease, or remain the same as the frequencies of other sources of outlets were developed, terminated, or altered. Thus it appears that its incidence or frequency cannot be determined or predicted by the incidence or frequency of other sexual outlets that appear in any particular history. The average frequency of nocturnal emissions for those experiencing the phenomenon was slightly less than two a month. The range in frequencies for the group was from a single experience in a whole history to a regular rate of 4.5 a week, and a maximum of 13 in any single week. Peck and Wells[7] reported an average frequency of one a month for a group of college men and Hughes[8] reported an average rate of two a month for a group of younger boys. The frequency-rates for two lone individuals over a period of some years are reported by Nelson[9] and anonymously.[10] In the Nelson report the average frequency was 5.3 a month for a 3½-year period, and in the anonymous report 3.43 a month for a period of 8 years. In both reports the frequencies showed wide variations.

Breast knots. Subareolar nodes or breast knots appearing in the male have received only brief mention in the published literature. A previously published record on the incidence of this phenomenon was made by Jung and Shafton in 1935.[11] Their physical examinations of the subareolar areas of 169 boys showed a high incidence of the knots at age 14 years, after which time they rapidly decreased in number and size. In approximately one-third of their cases they found extremely enlarged knots. In the present study, approximately one-third of the boys reported breast knots, and this group is probably the equivalent of the similarly-sized group in which Jung and Shafton found the most enlarged knots. For the majority of our boys, the knots caused little or no difficulty, though a few of the boys reported them as quite painful over extended periods of time. The knots

[7] M. W. Peck and F. L. Wells, "On the Psycho-Sexuality of College Graduate Men," *Ment. Hyg.*, 7, 1923, 706.

[8] Hughes, *op. cit.*, 1926, p. 267.

[9] J. Nelson, "A Study of Dreams," *American Journal of Psychology*, 1, 1888. 399-401.

[10] Anonymous, "Nocturnal Emissions," *ibid.*, 15, 1904, 104-106.

[11] F. T. Jung and A. L. Shafton, "The Mammary Gland in the Normal Adolescent Male," *Proc. Soc. Exper. Biol. Med.*, 33, 1935, 455-58.

were usually reported as appearing at ages 12, 13, and 14 years. Of the boys reporting breast knots, 47% remembered them as lasting less than two weeks, 47% for two to twelve weeks, and 6% for three to twenty-four months. So transitory are these knots that very few males in their late teens or older have had any memory of their occurrence, as Kinsey has discovered in the case-history study which he made of older males.[12]

Erotic responsiveness. An approach to the study of the erotic nature of each individual was made by asking the boy to rate his response to each item in a list of possible erotic stimuli, indicating his reactions as "never," "sometimes," "often," or "almost always." A score of 0, 1, 2, 3 . . . was assigned to each response. Fifteen items were checked on each individual. The total erotic score of each individual was obtained by adding the score for all the items involved. The erotic nature of the individual was thus indicated by a figure which took into account the number of items that elicited response and the degree of response to each item.

Table 2 gives a frequency distribution of the total erotic scores of 280 of the boys. It shows clearly that there is a wide variation in the erotic responsiveness of these individuals. The range in the erotic scores was greater for the adolescent population than it was for the pre-adolescent group.

TABLE 2. *Erotic Scores and the Number of Individuals Making Them*

Score	No. individuals	Score	No. individuals
0	4	10	18
1	4	11	18
2	7	12	17
3	7	13	14
4	19	14	6
5	24	15	5
6	24	16	1
7	36	17	3
8	36	18	3
9	31	19	2
		20	1

[12] A. C. Kinsey, unpublished data on sex-histories (Indiana University, Bloomington, Ind.).

The following list of 13 items is arranged in a descending scale of scores received by each item. The scores for two age-groups are shown for comparison.

Ages 11-14 yr.	Ages 15-18 yr.
Sex conversation	Female nudity
Female nudity	Day dreaming
Obscene pictures	Obscene pictures
Motion pictures	Motion pictures
Day dreaming	Sex conversation
Burlesque or stage shows	Burlesque or stage shows
Nude art	Dancing
Motion when riding	Nude art
Literature	Motion when riding
Own body	Own body
Male nudity	Literature
Dancing	Male nudity
Music	Music

Conversation involving sex matters, pictures in which nudity or sexual behavior was evident, daydreaming on sexual matters, observation of the female, and motion pictures were the strongest erotic stimuli for these boys. Observation of the sex-anatomy and the sexual behavior of animals was also a source of considerable erotic stimulation. The older group of boys responded to a greater number of these erotic items and to a greater degree than did the younger boys. They also rated dancing and sexual daydreams considerably higher than the boys of the younger group, while their rating on sex-conversation was decidedly lower than that given to that item by the younger group.

Non-erotic stimuli. About 50% of the boys reported erections resulting from some type of non-erotic stimulus. These responses were most frequently reported for ages 10, 11, and 12 years. The incidence and frequency of the phenomenon decrease rapidly after age 12 years, and, according to Kinsey's unpublished data,[13] adults seldom recall these pre-adolescent and early adolescent responses to non-erotic stimuli. The situations in which non-erotic responses occurred usually involved elements

[13] *Ibid.*

of fear, excitement, or other emotional situations. A partial list of the items reported as non-erotic stimuli is given here:

Carnival rides
Accidents or near accidents
War motion pictures
Marching soldiers
Airplane rides

Cops chasing him
Playing musical solo
Falling from garage, etc.
Losing balance when on heights
Fast sled or bicycle riding

Being late to school
Reciting before class
Watching exciting games
Fast elevator rides
Playing in exciting games

A radical change in environment
Band music
Grade card
Hearing "extra paper" called
Fear of punishment

Big fires
Fast car-driving
Finding money
Electrical shock
Setting a field afire

Punishment
Seeing name in print
Long flight of stairs
Looking over edge of building
Adventure stories

Angry at another boy
Being alone at night
Watching a stunting airplane
Fear of a big boy
Sitting in class

National anthem
Harsh words
Tests at school
Getting home late
Taking a shower

Boys also reported that the dream-content previous to a period of awakening in which they found themselves in erection often contained non-erotic stimuli. The contents of such dreams included fighting, accidents, wild animals, falling from high places, giants, being chased or frightened, and situations similar to those presented in the above list of non-erotic stimuli.

II BEHAVIORAL DEVELOPMENT

Objective studies of the behavioral aspects of human sexuality have appeared only recently in the published literature. The principal contributions have been made by Hamilton,[14] Davis,[15]

---

[14] Hamilton, *op. cit.*, pp. 1-570.

[15] K. B. Davis, *Factors in the Sex Life of Twenty-Two Hundred Women*, 1929, pp. 1-430.

Dickinson and Beam,[16] Taylor,[17] Strakosch,[18] Landis,[19] Henry,[20] and Kinsey.[21] These studies have been based primarily upon adults, whose memories have supplied the data on pre-adolescent activities. In the present investigation, data concerning this early behavior were obtained by interviewing our group of 291 boys as they were passing through these periods of development. The items reported here include masturbation, heterosexual activities, homosexuality, animal relations, and total sexual outlets.

Masturbation. The boys were asked to report the age of their first intentional stimulation of the external genitalia. The accumulative incidence of such masturbation is shown in Table 3. The percentages in this and in the following tables show how many individuals had experienced the particular phenomenon at the given age or previous to that age.

Data concerning the masturbatory experience of mature males have been reported as follows:

Dickinson and Beam* (1932)	± 100%
Kinsey* (unpublished data)	97% (2,300 men and older boys)
Hamilton* (1929)	97% (100 men)
Peck and Wells (1923, 1925)	86% (187 college men)
Hughes (1926)	85% (1,029 boys)
Merrill* (1918)	85% (100 boys)
Taylor* (1933)	± 70% (40 men)
Achilles (1923)	63% (470 men)
Exner (1915)	62% (53 men)
Brockman (1902)	56% (232 older boys and men)
Bromley-Britten (1938)	7% (592 men)

* Personal interview studies

[16] R. L. Dickinson and Lura Beam, *A Thousand Marriages; a Medical Study of Sex Adjustment,* 1931, pp. 1-482.

[17] W. S. Taylor, "A Critique of Sublimation in Males: A Study of Forty Superior Single Men," *Genet. Psychol. Monog.,* 13, 1933, 1-115.

[18] F. M. Strakosch, *Factors in the Sex Life of Seven Hundred Psychopathic Women,* 1934, pp. 1-102.

[19] Carney Landis, *et al., Sex in Development,* 1940, pp. 1-329.

[20] G. W. Henry, *Sex Variants: a Study of Homosexual Patterns,* 1941 (2 vols.), pp. 1-1179.

[21] Kinsey, *op. cit.*

TABLE 3. *Incidence of Masturbation*

Age-group (in yr.)	No. of boys involved	Percentage with masturbatory experience	Increment at each age-group (in per cent)
6 or less	284	5.3	5.3
7	284	9.5	4.2
8	284	14.1	4.6
9	284	22.9	8.8
10	284	28.8	5.9
11	283	53.5	24.7
12	278	72.6	19.1
13	230	84.8	12.2
14	161	95.0	10.2
15	104	98.1	3.1

The personal-interview studies cited above, when taken along with our study, indicate clearly that masturbation appears at some time in the sexual histories of nearly all of the males in our society. The lower incidences reported in the questionary studies reflect the inadequacy of the questionary as a method for studying human sexual behavior and supply no evidence of the true incidence of masturbation in any population.

The onset of masturbatory experience for the boys is also indicated in Table 1. Three-fourths had their first experience between the ages of 10 and 16 years. Hamilton reported that 48% of his males started masturbation between 12 and 15 years,[22] against 44.4% of our youth. Achilles,[23] and Peck and Wells[24] reported that the modal age for first masturbation in their two studies was at 14 years; in our own it was 12 years. It is clear that masturbation begins for nearly all males during the years immediately preceding, or very soon after, puberty.

In the present study an investigation was made of the common belief that circumcision lowers the incidence of masturbation. Of the 266 boys that answered the question concerning circumcision, 47% had been circumcised and 53% had not. By age 14 years, 90% of the uncircumcised group and 89% of the circumcised group had had masturbatory experience. Apparently circumcision had little effect on the incidence of masturbation in this group.

[22] Hamilton, *op. cit.*, p. 427.
[23] Achilles, *op. cit.*, p. 50.
[24] Peck and Wells, *op. cit.*, p. 704.

The average frequencies of masturbation for the 257 boys that had masturbatory histories are presented in Table 4. The range extends from a single experience to a maximal frequency of over 1,000 per year. Seventy-three percent of the boys showed masturbatory frequencies of 1-4 times per week.

TABLE 4. *Average Masturbatory Frequencies*

Av. frequencies per week at age of reporting	No. involved	Percentage involved
Under 0.25	2	.8
0.25	15	5.8
0.5	16	6.2
1	47	18.3
2	51	20.0
3	53	20.6
4	37	14.4
5	10	3.9
6	9	3.3
7	14	5.5
8 to 14	1	.4
15 or more	2	.8

In the questionary studies of Hughes and of Peck and Wells, the reported average frequency of masturbation was less than one a week. Once again, the questionary studies fail to discover what personal interviews can obtain. Hamilton's personal interviews gave figures much nearer our own. Hamilton reports the following for the 100 men involved in his study:

Never masturbated	3%
Less often than monthly; infrequently	15%
One to three times monthly	22%
Frequently or regularly	8%
One to six times weekly	26%
Daily or more frequently	20%

Seventy-one percent of the 100 boys in the Merrill study,[25] as compared with 49% in our study, reported masturbatory frequencies of three or more per week.

[25] Lilburn Merrill, "A Summary of Findings in a Study of Sexualism among a Group of One Hundred Delinquent Boys," *J. Juven. Res.*, 3, 1918, 257.

Masturbatory frequencies are not independent entities in adolescent histories, but are dependent upon the frequencies of other forms of sexual outlet, upon the health of the individual, upon acquired inhibitions and restraints, and upon the erotic capacities of the individual. During the period of adolescence, masturbation is, for most males, the major source of outlet. As socio-sexual contacts are developed during the adolescent period, the frequency of masturbation usually decreases. A more detailed study is needed that will consider the frequency of masturbation at all age-levels, and its relationship to other forms of sexual outlet.

The average time required to reach an orgasm in masturbation was reported as follows; 2 min. or less, 43%; 3–5 min., 43%; 6–10 min., 10%; more than 10 min., 4%. Manual techniques of masturbation were the ones most commonly employed, but various other techniques were reported including the use of bottles, bedclothes, holes in boxes and boards, clothing, a partially opened door, and femoral contacts.

None of the boys in this study points out any evidence of physical harm that could be considered the outcome of their masturbation. Many of them thought that extended practice would result in such physical and mental injuries as are commonly described in the traditionally moralistic literature. A great many fears, a great deal of worry, and more serious problems were the outcome of their beliefs in the alleged deleterious effects of self-stimulation. Mental conflicts arising from these unsupported beliefs were resopnsible for most of the sexual problems of the boys in this study. As reported by them, the most frequent sources of misinformation on the subject of masturbation were popular lectures on sex and the current literature on sex-education.

Heterosexual activities. The heterosexual activity of a boy may be divided into its pre-adolescent and adolescent periods. The pre-adolescent sex-play with the female involved a variety of forms. Most frequently it was manual exploration that was usually associated with direct observation of reproductive anatomy. Exhibitionistic sex-play was the next most frequent type of behavior. Other forms of play included attempts at intercourse, oral contacts, and various other forms of experimentation. Data concerning pre-adolescent intercourse are presented in a later section of this study. The age of onset of the pre-adolescent sex play and cumulative experience data on this point are given in Table 5.

The frequency of the pre-adolescent heterosexual play as reported by 286 of the boys was as follows:

No experience	34%	16 to 25 times	8%
1 to 5 times	27%	26 to 50 times	7%
6 to 15 times	15%	above 50 times	9%

The number of different females involved with each boy in the pre-adolescent heterosexual play was reported as follows:

No experience	34%	16 to 25 females	5%
1 to 5 females	47%	26 to 50 females	3%
6 to 15 females	9%	more than 50 females	2%

The most common form of heterosexual activity during the adolescent period was that which is commonly termed "petting." In the present study petting was defined as any direct contact that was intended to produce or actually did produce erotic response. During the first few years of adolescence, the petting techniques included kissing, manual exploration, and manipulation by the male of the female breasts and reproductive organs. As the adolescent age-level increased, there was also an increase in the variety of petting techniques employed and in the frequency of their appearance. By age 18 years, approximately 80% of the boys reported kissing, and the more experienced individuals reported such techniques as deep kiss with tongue

TABLE 5. *Pre-Adolescent Heterosexual Play*

Age	No. of boys	Percentage with some experience	Increment at each age (in per cent)
5	286	2.4	2.4
6	286	16.8	14.4
7	286	24.8	8.0
8	286	34.8	10.0
9	286	41.2	6.4
10	286	46.9	5.7
11	280	52.5	5.6
12	235	58.3	5.8
13	122	66.1	7.8

contacts, manual manipulation of male genitalia by the female, oral genitalic contacts, and genitalic apposition without actual intercourse.

Twenty percent of the older boys had petted to climax without having had actual intercourse. Most of them reported that this eliminated such nervous tensions as usually accompany heavy petting in which there is no orgasm.

Approximately 33% of the boys had attempted heterosexual intercourse before adolescence and approximately 44% of the adolescent boys by age 18 years had experienced intercourse. The detailed data on incidence of heterosexual intercourse are presented in Table 6. It should be pointed out that all the data concerning pre-adolescent behavior are based on a period through which most of the boys had passed or had almost completed; while the data concerning adolescent behavior are representative only of those years included in the study.

By age 18 years, over 14% of the males in the Achilles[26] study and 21% of those in the Hamilton[27] study had experienced intercourse. These figures are much lower than those in the present study, and the difference may be explained by the fact that these two studies were based on an older generation. Bromley and Britten (1938) state that approximately half the men in their investigation had had pre-marital intercourse and that two-

TABLE 6. *Heterosexual Intercourse*

	PRE-ADOLESCENCE			ADOLESCENCE	
Age	No. of boys involved	Percent with experience	Age	No. of boys involved	Percent with experience
5	280	1.1	10	5	0
6	280	6.1	11	45	3.9
7	280	10.7	12	145	7.6
8	280	16.1	13	202	16.5
9	280	19.3	14	158	19.6
10	280	22.2	15	105	26.6
11	274	26.3	16	65	30.0
12	230	26.9	17	43	32.6
13	119	35.8	18	25	44.0

[26] Achilles, *op. cit.*, p. 50.
[27] Hamilton, *op. cit.*, p. 347.

thirds of these (about 33% of the total population) were initiated while still in high school.[28] These latter figures agree very well with our own.

The frequencies of heterosexual intercourse for the pre-adolescent and adolescent periods are as follows:

Frequency of intercourse	No. of pre-adolescent individuals	No. of adolescent individuals
6 to 10	18	21
1 to 5	43	61
11 to 25	13	14
26 to 100	6	8
More than 100	5	5

The number of coital partners involved in these experiences was as follows:

Number of females	No. of pre-adolescent individuals	No. of adolescent individuals
1 to 2	48	33
3 to 5	22	16
6 to 10	11	6
More than 10	3	4

The ages of the female partners of the pre-adolescent group were in 80% of the cases within one year of the same age as those of the males; in 11% of the cases the female partners were two or more years older; and for the remaining 9% these partners were two or more years younger. The girls involved were usually neighborhood friends, female relatives, girls met during visits, females of the same family, and occasionally an older girl or woman. The partners of the older boys included companions, pick-ups, prostitutes, fiancées, house-servants, and older women. Approximately 20% of the boys by age 18 had had intercourse with a prostitute and a larger number had visited houses of prostitution. Only four of the boys out of the 69 with experience in heterosexual intercourse had been initiated by prostitutes. Two of the boys had contracted gonorrhea from prostitutes, but none reported the contraction of syphilis.

[28] D. D. Bromley and F. H. Britten, Youth and Sex; a Study of 1300 College Students. 1938. pp. 133, 158.

The most common means of contraception used by the boys was the condom, and the next most frequent method reported was withdrawal. In a few instances suppositories and douches were relied upon. Only a small number of the boys had failed to employ birth-control methods. The boys had obtained the condoms from taverns, filling stations, drug stores, older friends, and occasionally from home. No one of the boys, as far as he knew, was responsible for a pregnancy. The places in which intercourse most frequently occurred were out-of-doors, at the female's home, and in automobiles. Other places reported were abandoned or empty buildings, barns, sheds, box cars, and similar places. The restraints on their heterosexual intercourse included various moral restraints, fear of pregnancy, fear of loss of social status or economic support, fear of venereal diseases, lack of opportunity, personal ideals, and fear of harmful physical effects.

Homosexual activities. In the present study, a pre-adolescent boy was considered to have had homosexual play if he had voluntarily accepted direct sexual stimulation by another male, or if he had sexually stimulated another male by actual contact with him. Adolescent homosexuality included, by our definition, only those contacts between males in which one or both of the individuals had come to full and complete climax. Table 7 presents the incidence of such homosexual activities.

Approximately half the boys who had been involved in pre-adolescent homosexual play had confined their relationships to one other boy. The remaining boys in this group reported from two to ten partners in their play. These partners were, except

TABLE 7. *Homosexual Play and Experience*

	PRE-ADOLESCENT PLAY			ADOLESCENT EXPERIENCE	
Age	No. of boys involved	Accumulative incidence (in per cent)	Age	No. of boys involved	Accumulative incidence (in per cent)
6	215	3	11	45	14
7	215	4	12	143	15
8	215	7	13	204	15
9	215	12	14	160	23
10	209	19	15	108	28
11	209	27	16	68	31
12	169	36	17	46	30
13	75	38			

in rare instances, boys of approximately the same age. The frequency of homosexual play ranged from a single experience to a maximum of over 400 times. Manual techniques were most frequently reported, but oral and femoral contacts also appeared.

Adolescent homosexual relationships were restricted in all but four cases to five or fewer partners. The frequencies of the homosexual relationships were reported as follows:

Frequencies	No. of boys involved
1 to 5	47
6 to 10	18
11 to 25	8
26 to 100	9
More than 100	5

Manual relationships appeared in 93% of the histories reporting homosexual experience. This technique was the one usually involved in the initial contacts. Femoral and oral techniques also appeared, but at much lower frequencies. The more experienced individuals usually employed a wider variety of techniques in their relationships.

Thirty-five of the boys had been approached by adult males that desired homosexual relationship, and eight of these boys had accepted the proposals and had participated in relationships with the older men. All the boys involved were 11 years or more. In 75% of the cases, the adults making the approach were strangers to the boys. In none of the approaches or relationships was any sort of physical force used, but in about a third of the cases the boys were offered some reward, such as money, an automobile ride, or an invitation to a motion-picture show or some athletic event. The approaches were made in schools, on the street, in theaters, at athletic events, in boys' camps, from automobiles, at carnivals, on journeys, and at other similar places and occasions.

Animal relationships. Boys frequently reported that they had been sexually aroused while observing the reproductive anatomy or sexual behavior of animals. Thirty-five out of the 285 boys had engaged in sex play with animals, and eight of these admitted animal intercourse.

Nocturnal emissions. "Wet dreams" or nocturnal emissions constituted another form of sexual outlet for these boys. This phenomenon was considered in an early part of the present study.

Total sexual outlet. The total sexual outlet for each individual during a given period of time was obtained by adding the number of climaxes reported for each of the six possible forms of outlet during the interval. The average weekly rate, therefore, included nocturnal emissions, masturbation, heterosexual petting to the point of climax, heterosexual intercourse, homosexual relations, and animal intercourse. The individual histories showed various combinations and frequencies of these six outlets. In Table 8 representative patterns of outlet are presented.

TABLE 8. *Samples of Total Sexual Outlets*

FREQUENCIES PER WEEK

Case history	Age	Mastur- bation	Nocturnal emission	Animal inter- course	Petting to climax	Hetero- sexual inter- course	Homo- sexual rela- tions	Total outlets per week
1278	14		4.0					4.0
1322	16	3.0						3.0
1164	20							0
1406	16	2.5	1.0	.1	.1	1.0	1.0	5.7
6485	15	3.0					3.0	6.0
1311	13	2.5		2.0		.1	.1	4.7
1188	15	4.5	3.0		3.0	.2	.2	10.9
1185	15	8.0	1.0					9.0
1120	17	.5						.5
1151	14	4.5	.3			−	3.0	7.8
1366	16		2.0					2.0
1313	20	2.0			1.5	1.0		4.5
1102	16	6.0						6.0
1304	20	3.5			3.0	.5		7.0
5480	13	3.0				.5	2.0	5.5

(−) indicates less than .1 per week

It is apparent that the six sources of sexual outlet appear in a wide variety of combinations and frequencies in the histories of these boys. Their total outlets ranged from none in a very small group of adolescent boys to an outlet in one 15-year-old boy that averaged approximately 40 climaxes a week for a period of more than a year. The average total outlet of these boys was between three and four per week.

The principal source of sexual outlet for these boys was, as previously indicated, masturbation. As heterosexual or homosexual activities developed, the frequency of masturbation usually declined, but only in a few cases did either of these two socio-sexual forms of behavior provide the principal source of outlet for a period of a year or more. Nocturnal emissions provided a very small proportion of the total outlet for the group as a whole. Only in a very few cases did animal intercourse appear as a source of outlet, but it is to be remembered that this is an urban population in which there were few opportunities for animal contacts. The limited number of histories on which this study is based does not warrant more detailed analyses of these patterns of total outlet.

SUMMARY

The materials presented in this study were drawn from the complete sex histories of 291 pre-adolescent and adolescent boys. They were obtained by personal interview.

Physical development. The median age for first ejaculation was 13.8 years, while the range was from 10 to 16 years. The range for onset of pubic hair-growth and voice-change was also from 10 to 16 years, with medians at 13.6 years and 13.4 years respectively. About one-third of the boys had been aware of breast knots or nodes which occurred most frequently at 12, 13, and 14 years. They usually were of short duration, but in a few cases they lasted a year or two. Nocturnal emissions were experienced by approximately 75% of the boys by age 18 years.

About 50% of the boys reported erections resulting from non-erotic stimuli. These were most frequent during the years 10, 11, and 12. The situations giving rise to such responses usually involved fear, excitement, or other emotional factors. The erotic responses of these boys showed a wide range of variation.

Behavioral development. Before or soon after the onset of adolescence over 90% of the boys reported masturbatory experience, which in the majority of cases ranged in frequency from one to four times per week. As socio-sexual forms of outlet were developed, the frequency of masturbation usually declined. Worry over alleged deleterious effects of masturbation was the most common sexual problem presented by these boys. The popular literature of sex-education and lectures were primarily responsible for the widespread misinformation on this subject.

Pre-adolescent sex-play with the female appeared in two-thirds of the histories, while one-third of the boys had attempted heterosexual intercourse. By 18 years, approximately 80% of the boys had been involved in petting and 20% of them had petted to climax. By age 18 years, about 44% of the boys had experienced heterosexual intercourse, with frequencies ranging from one to several hundred times. One boy in five had experienced intercourse with a prostitute, but in most cases the coital partners were girls of a comparable social class and of approximately the same age. Intercourse was reported to have occurred most frequently in automobiles, the female's home, and out-of-doors.

Pre-adolescent homosexual experience appeared in approximately 38% of the histories of the boys. At least 30% of the population by age 17 years had been involved in one or more homosexual experiences after the onset of adolescence. In 18% of the cases, the homosexual relationships were restricted to three or fewer companions, with a frequency of 25 or fewer times. Homosexual approaches by adults were reported by 30 of the boys. Eight of these had had homosexual relationships with an adult.

Masturbation, nocturnal emissions, petting to climax, heterosexual intercourse, homosexual relationships, and animal contacts were reported as sexual outlets for these boys. Various combinations and frequencies of sexual outlet were found in the individual histories.

II

The Function of Male Initiation Ceremonies
at Puberty*

By John W. M. Whiting, Richard Kluckhohn,
and Albert Anthony

Our society gives little formal recognition of the physiological
and social changes a boy undergoes at puberty. He may be
teased a little when his voice changes or when he shaves for the
first time. Changes in his social status from childhood to adulthood are marked by a number of minor events rather than by
any single dramatic ceremonial observance. Graduation from
grammar school and subsequently from high school are steps to
adulthood, but neither can be considered as a *rite de passage*.
Nor may the accomplishment of having obtained a driver's
license, which for many boys is the most important indication
of having grown up, be classed as one. Legally the twenty-first
birthday is the time at which a boy becomes a man; but, except
for a somewhat more elaborate birthday party this occasion is
not ceremonially marked and, therefore, cannot be thought of
as a *rite de passage*. Neither physiologically, socially, nor legally
is there a clear demarcation between boyhood and manhood in
our society.

* A cross-cultural study of the function of male-initiation rites involving
some of the variables of this study as well as a number of others was the
basis of the doctoral dissertation of Albert S. Anthony, *A Cross-Cultural
Study of the Function of Initiation Rites at Puberty,* unpublished Ed.D.
thesis, Graduate School of Education, Harvard University, 1956. A version
of this paper was read at the meetings of the American Anthropological
Association in December, 1956.

Such a gradual transition from boyhood to manhood is by no means universal. Among the Thonga, a tribe in South Africa, every boy must go through a very elaborate ceremony in order to become a man.[1] When a boy is somewhere between ten and 16 years of age, he is sent by his parents to a "circumcision school" which is held every four or five years. Here in company with his age-mates he undergoes severe hazing by the adult males of the society. The initiation begins when each boy runs the gauntlet between two rows of men who beat him with clubs. At the end of this experience he is stripped of his clothes and his hair is cut. He is next met by a man covered with lion manes and is seated upon a stone facing this "lion man." Someone then strikes him from behind and when he turns his head to see who has struck him, his foreskin is seized and in two movements cut off by the "lion man." Afterwards he is secluded for three months in the "yards of mysteries," where he can be seen only by the initiated. It is especially taboo for a woman to approach these boys during their seclusion, and if a woman should glance at the leaves with which the circumcised covers his wound and which form his only clothing, she must be killed.

During the course of his initiation, the boy undergoes six major trials: beatings, exposure to cold, thirst, eating of unsavory foods, punishment, and the threat of death. On the slightest pretext he may be severely beaten by one of the newly initiated men who is assigned to the task by the older men of the tribe. He sleeps without covering and suffers bitterly from the winter cold. He is forbidden to drink a drop of water during the whole three months. Meals are often made nauseating by the half-digested frass from the stomach of an antelope which is poured over his food. If he is caught breaking any important rule governing the ceremony, he is severely punished. For example, in one of these punishments, sticks are placed between the fingers of the offender, then a strong man closes his hand around that of the novice, practically crushing his fingers. He is frightened into submission by being told that in former times boys who had tried to escape or who revealed the secrets to women or to the uninitiated were hanged and their bodies burnt to ashes.

[1] The following account is taken from Henri A. Junod, *The Life of a South African Tribe* (London: Macmillan & Co., Ltd., 1927), pp. 74-95.

Although the Thonga are extreme in the severity of this sort of initiation, many other societies have rites which have one or more of the main features of the Thonga ceremony. Of a sample of 55 societies[2] chosen for this study, 18 have one or more of the four salient features of the Thonga ceremony, e.g., painful hazing by adult males, genital operations, seclusion from women, and tests of endurance and manliness; the remaining 37 societies have either no ceremony at all or one which does not have any of the above features.[3]

I HYPOTHESES

It is the purpose of this essay to develop a set of hypotheses concerning the function of male initiation rites which accounts for the presence of these rites in some societies and the absence of them in others. The theory that we have chosen to test has been suggested by previous explanations for the rites, particularly those of psychoanalytic origin.[4] These explanations were modified to fit the problem of this research in two respects. First, certain of the concepts and hypotheses were restated or redefined so as to be coherent with the growing general behavioral theory of personality development,[5] and second, they

[2] The method of sample selection is discussed below.

[3] Seven of these societies have a minor ceremony which generally takes place during adolescence. In these societies the boy's change in status is announced by investing him with some symbol of manhood such as the donning of long pants which played such a role in our society in former years. Specifically these are tattooing—Maori and Ontong Javanese; tooth filing—Alorese, Balinese and Lakher; donning the "sacred thread"—Hindu (Khalapur Radjput). The Kwakiutl fall in a similar category. Their ceremony consists of a potlatch given for the boy by his father. The ceremonies in these societies are so different in sociopsychological import from those to be described below that they will be classed hereafter with those societies which lack puberty ceremonies.

[4] See, e.g., Sigmund Freud, *Moses and Monotheism* (New York: Alfred A. Knopf, Inc., 1939); Bruno Bettelheim. *Symbolic Wounds* (Glencoe, Ill.: Free Press, 1954); Margaret Mead, *Male and Female* (New York: William Morrow & Co., Inc., 1949).

[5] See, e.g., J. W. M. Whiting and Irwin L. Child, *Child Training and Personality* (New Haven: Yale University Press, 1953); Robert R. Sears, Eleanor E. Maccoby, and Harry Levin, *Patterns of Child Rearing* (Evanston, Ill.: Row, Peterson & Co., 1957); and John Dollard and Neal E. Miller, *Personality and Psychotherapy* (New York: McGraw-Hill Book Co., 1950).

were restated in such a way as to be amenable to cross-cultural test, i.e., cultural indices were specified for each variable.

We assume that boys tend to be initiated at puberty in those societies in which they are particularly hostile toward their fathers and dependent upon their mothers. The hazing of the candidates, as well as the genital operations, suggests that one function of the rites is to prevent open and violent revolt against parental authority at a time when physical maturity would make such revolt dangerous and socially disruptive. Isolation from women and tests of manliness suggest that another function of the rites is to break an excessively strong dependence upon the mother and to ensure identification with adult males and acceptance of the male role.

It is to be noted here that the educational and disciplinary functions of the initiation are not limited in time to the actual period of initiation. The boy knows all during childhood and latency about the initiation which he will face at puberty. While he is overtly not supposed to know any of the secrets of the rite, he actually knows almost everything that will happen to him. He is both afraid of what he knows will happen and also envious of the kudos and added status which his older friends have acquired through having successfully gone through this rite. Thus, through the boy's whole life the initiation ceremony serves as a conditioner of his behavior and his attitudes towards male authority, while at the same time emphasizing the advantages of becoming a member of the male group through initiation.

We assume that a long and exclusive relationship between mother and son provides the conditions which should lead to an exceptionally strong dependence upon the mother. Also, we assume that if the father terminates this relationship and replaces his son, there should be strong envy and hostility engendered in the boy which, although held in check during childhood, may dangerously manifest itself with the onset of puberty, unless measures are taken to prevent it.

As we indicated above, the hypothesis is derived from psychoanalytic theory. However, it should be noted that there are some modifications which may be important. First, no assumption is being made that the envy is exclusively sexual in character. We are making the more general assumption that if the mother for a prolonged period devotes herself to the satisfaction of all the child's needs—including hunger, warmth, safety, freedom from pain, as well as sex—he will become strongly dependent upon her. In accordance with this we believe rivalry may be based upon a competition for the fulfillment of any of these needs. Second, we do not propose, as most psychoanalysts do, that Oedipal rivalry is a universal, but rather we claim it is a variable which may be strong or weak depending upon specific relationships between father, mother, and son. Thus, we assume father-son rivalry may range from a value of zero to such high intensities that the whole society may be required to adjust to it.

An illustration of cultural conditions which should intensify dependency of a boy on his mother and rivalry with his father is found in the following case.

Kwoma Dependency. The Kwoma,[6] a tribe living about 200 miles up the Sepik River in New Guinea, have initiation rites similar to those of the Thonga. Examination of the differences in the relationship of a mother to her infant during the first years of his life reveals some strong contrasts between the Kwoma and our society. While in our society an infant sleeps in his own crib and the mother shares her bed with the father, the Kwoma infant sleeps cuddled in his mother's arms until he is old enough to be weaned, which is generally when he is two or three years old. The father, in the meantime, sleeps apart on his own bark slab bed. Furthermore, during this period, the Kwoma mother abstains from sexual intercourse with her husband in order to avoid having to care for two dependent children at the same time. Since the Kwoma are polygynous and discreet extramarital philandering is permitted, this taboo is not too hard on the husband. In addition, it is possible that the mother obtains some substitute sexual gratification from nursing and caring for her infant.[7] If this be the case, it is not unlikely that she

[6] For a description of the Kwoma child-rearing reported here see J. W. M. Whiting, *Becoming a Kwoma* (New Haven: Yale University Press, 1941), pp. 24-64.

[7] This is, of course, difficult to determine and is a presumption based upon the following factors: (1) Kwoma informants reported that mothers had no desire for sexual intercourse as long as they were nursing the infant and (2) clinical evidence from women in our own society suggests that nursing is sexually gratifying to some women at least. See Therese Benedek, "Mother-child, the Primary Psychomatic Unit," *Am. J. Ortho-Psychiatry,* XIX, 1949; Helene Deutsch, *The Psychology of Women* (New York: Grune & Stratton, Inc., 1944-45), Vols. I and II; Sears, Maccoby, and Levin, *op. cit.*

should show more warmth and affection toward her infant than if she were obtaining sexual gratification from her husband. Whether or not the custom can be attributed to this sex taboo, the Kwoma mother, while her co-wife does the housework, not only sleeps with her infant all night but holds it in her lap all day without apparent frustration. Such a close relationship between a mother and child in our society would seem not only unbearably difficult to the mother, but also somewhat improper.

When the Kwoma child is weaned, a number of drastic things happen all at once. He is suddenly moved from his mother's bed to one of his own. His father resumes sexual relations with his mother. Although the couple wait until their children are asleep, the intercourse takes place in the same room. Thus, the child may truly become aware of his replacement. He is now told that he can no longer have his mother's milk because some supernatural being needs it. This is vividly communicated to him by his mother when she puts a slug on her breasts and daubs the blood-colored sap of the breadfruit tree over her nipples. Finally he is no longer permitted to sit on his mother's lap. She resumes her work and goes to the garden to weed or to the swamp to gather sago flour, leaving him behind for the first time in his life. That these events are traumatic to the child is not surprising. He varies between sadness and anger, weeping and violent temper tantrums.

It is our hypothesis that it is this series of events that makes it necessary, when the boy reaches adolescence, for the society to have an initiation rite of the type we have already described. It is necessary to put a final stop to (1) his wish to return to his mother's arms and lap, (2) to prevent an open revolt against his father who has displaced him from his mother's bed, and (3) to ensure identification with the adult males of the society. In other words, Kwoma infancy so magnifies the conditions which should produce Oedipus rivalry that the special cultural adjustment of ceremonial hazing, isolation from women, and symbolic castration, etc., must be made to resolve it.

If our analysis of the psychodynamics in Kwoma society is correct, societies with initiation rites should have similar child-rearing practices, whereas societies lacking the rite should also lack the exclusive mother-son sleeping arrangements and *post-partum* sexual taboo of the Kwoma.

II   TESTING THE HYPOTHESIS

To test this hypothesis a sample of 56 societies was selected. First, the ethnographic material on more than 150 societies was checked to determine whether or not there was an adequate description of our variables: e.g., sleeping arrangements, *post-partum* sex taboo, and initiation rites at puberty. Only half of the societies reviewed fulfilled these conditions. Although we had initially endeavored to select our cases so as to have maximum distribution throughout the world, we found that some areas were represented by several societies, while others were not represented by any. To correct for any bias that might result from this sample, we made a further search of the ethnographic literature in order to fill in the gaps, and we thereby added several societies from areas previously not represented. Finally, to maximize diversity and to minimize duplication through selection of closely related societies, whenever there were two or more societies from any one culture area which had the same values on all our variables, we chose only one of them. Using these criteria, our final sample consisted of 56 societies representing 45 of the 60 culture areas designated by Murdock.[8]

The societies comprising our final sample range in size and type from small, simple, tribal groups to segments of large, complex civilizations such as the United States or Japan. In the latter case, our information has been drawn from ethnographic reports on a single delineated community.

When this sample had finally been chosen, the material relevant to our variables was first abstracted, and then judgments were made for each society as to the nature of the transition from boyhood to manhood, the sleeping arrangements, and the duration of the *post-partum* sex taboo. To prevent contamination, the judgments on each variable were made at different times and the name of the society disguised by a code. All judgments were made by at least two persons and in every case where there was a disagreement (less than 15 percent of the cases for any given variable), the data were checked by one of the authors, whose judgment was accepted as final. Our findings with respect to initiation rites have been tabulated in Table 1 below.

[8] G. P. Murdock, "World Ethnographic Sample," *Am. Anthropol.*, LIX, 1957, 664-87.

We discovered that only five societies out of the total number had sleeping arrangements similar to our own, that is, where the father and mother share a bed and the baby sleeps alone. In only three societies did the mother, the father, and the baby each have his or her own bed. In the remaining 48, the baby slept with his mother until he was at least a year old and generally until he was weaned. In 24 of the latter, however, the father also shared the bed, the baby generally sleeping between the mother and father. The remaining 24 societies had sleeping arrangements like the Kwoma in which the mother and child sleep in one bed and the father in another. Often the father's bed was not even in the same house. He slept either in a men's clubhouse or in the hut of one of his other wives, leaving mother and infant not only alone in the same bed but alone in the sleeping room.

Similarly, the societies of our sample were split on the rules regulating the resumption of sexual intercourse following parturition. Twenty-nine, like our own, have a brief taboo of a few weeks to permit the mother to recover from her delivery. In the remaining 27, the mother did not resume sexual intercourse for at least nine months after the birth of her child, and in one instance, the Cheyenne, the ideal period adhered to was reported as ten years. The duration of the taboo generally corresponded to the nursing period and in many cases was reinforced by the belief that sexual intercourse curdles or sours the mother's milk, thus making it harmful for the infant. In other societies, like the Kwoma, the taboo is explicitly for the purpose of ensuring a desired interval between children where adequate means of contraception are lacking. In these societies the taboo is terminated when the infant reaches some maturational stage: e.g., "until the child can crawl," "until the child can walk," or "until he can take care of himself." For the 27 societies that have this taboo, more than a few weeks long, the average duration is slightly more than two years.

III   RESULTS AT THE CULTURAL LEVEL

Our hypothesis may now be restated in cultural terms as follows: *Societies which have sleeping arrangements in which the mother and baby share the same bed for at least a year to the exclusion of the father and societies which have a taboo restricting the mother's sexual behavior for at least a year after childbirth will be more likely to have a ceremony of transition from boyhood to manhood than those societies where these conditions do not occur (or occur for briefer periods).* For the purposes of this hypothesis, transition ceremonies include only those ceremonies characterized by at least one of the following events: painful hazing of the initiates, isolation from females, tests of manliness, and genital operations.

The test of this hypothesis is presented in Table 1. It will be observed from this table that of the 20 societies where both antecedent variables are present, 14 have initiation ceremonies and only six do not. Where both antecedent variables are absent only two of the 25 societies have the ceremonies. Thus, over 80 percent of the 45 pure cases correspond with the prediction.[9] Though our hypothesis was not designed for predicting the mixed cases, that is, where only one of the antecedent variables is present, it seems that they tended not to have the transition ceremonies.

Although the eight cases which are exceptional to our theory —the six in the upper left-hand column and the two in the lower right-hand column—may be simply misclassified through error of measurement, re-examination uncovers some other unanticipated factor which may account for their placement.[10] This analysis turns out to be enlightening.

Reviewing first the six cases in the upper left-hand column, that is, the societies which have both exclusive mother-son sleeping arrangements and a *post-partum* sex taboo but no initiation, we found that four of them (Khalapur, Trobrianders, Nyakusa, and Yapese) have an adjustment at adolescence which may serve as a psychological substitute for the initiation ceremony. The boys at this time leave the parental home and move to a men's house or a boys' village where they live until they are

---

[9] Even though we made every effort to ensure at least a reasonable degree of independence for our cases, there are many instances of known historical connections among them. A statistical test of significance is therefore difficult to interpret. If the cases were independent, the probabilities are less than one in one thousand that this relationship could be obtained by chance ($\chi^2 > 18$).

[11] B. Malinowski, *Sex and Repression in Savage Society* (New York: *Marriage, Authority, and Final Causes; A Study of Unilateral Cross-Cousin Marriage* (Glencoe, Ill.: Free Press, 1955). It was used most effectively in their cross-cultural study of authority patterns and cross-cousin marriage.

married. Malinowski[11] observed this type of adjustment amongst the Trobrianders in 1927. He wrote:

> But the most important change, and the one which interests us most is the partial break-up of the family at the time when the adolescent boys and girls cease to be permanent inmates of the parental home . . . a special institution . . . special houses inhabited by groups of adolescent boys and girls. A boy as he reaches puberty will join such a house. . . . Thus the parent home is drained completely of its adolescent males, though until the boy's marriage he will always come back for food, and will also continue to work for his household to some extent. . . .[12]

> At this stage, however, when the adolescent has to learn his duties, to be instructed in traditions and to study his magic, his arts and crafts, his interest in his mother's brother, who is his teacher and tutor, is greatest and their relations are at their best.[13]

This account suggests that this change of residence serves the same functions that we have posited for initiation ceremonies, for example, by establishing male authority, breaking the bond with the mother, and ensuring acceptance of the male role. It is important for our hypothesis, also, that there are only two other societies in our sample where such a change of residence occurs. One of these is the Malaita which has one but not both of our antecedent variables; the other is the Ashanti where the boy may move to the village of his mother's brother at or before puberty, but this is not mandatory and only half the boys do so. Thus, if we were to revise our hypothesis such that a change of residence was considered to be equivalent to initiation, the four societies mentioned should be moved over to the right-hand column and the exceptional cases would be reduced from eight to four.

Some comment should be made on the two remaining cases in the upper left-hand column. The Ganda are reported to have an interesting method of child rearing which may or may not be relevant to our theory. For the first three years of his life, a Ganda child sleeps exclusively with his mother and she is subject to a sexual taboo. At this point the boy is reported to be weaned and transferred to the household of his father's brother

[11] B. Malinowski, *Sex and Repression in Savage Society* (New York: Harcourt, Brace & Co., 1927).

[12] *Ibid.*, p. 67.

[13] *Ibid.*, p. 69.

TABLE 1. *The Relationship between Exclusive Mother-Son Sleeping Arrangements and a Post-partum Sex Taboo* and the Occurrence of Initiation Ceremonies at Puberty*

| CUSTOMS IN INFANCY | | CUSTOMS AT ADOLESCENT INITIATION CEREMONIES | |
Exclusive mother-son sleeping arrangements	Post-partum sex taboo	Absent	Present
Long	Long		Azande *hgs* †
			Camayura *hs*
			Chagga *hgs*
			Cheyenne *ht*
			Chiricahua *ht*
			Dahomeans *hgs*
			Fijians *gs*
			Jivaro *ht*
		Ganda	Kwoma *hgs*
		Khalapur (Rajput)	Lesu *gs*
		Nyakyusa	Nuer *hs*
		Trobrianders	Samoans *g*
		Tepoztlan	Thonga *hgs*
		Yapese	Tiv *hgs*
	Short	Ashanti	
		Malaita	Cagaba *ht*
		Siriono	
Short	Long	Araucanians	Kwakiutl *s*
		Pilaga	Ojibwa *t*
		Pondo	Ooldea *hgs*
		Tallensi	
	Short	Alorese	Hopi *hs*
		Balinese	Timbira *hst*
		Druz	
		Egyptians (Silwa)	
		Eskimos (Copper)	
		French	
		Lapps	
		Igorot (Bontoc)	
		Japanese (Suye Mura)	
		Koryak (Maritime)	
		Lakher	
		Lamba	
		Papago	
		Lepcha	
		Maori	
		Mixtecans	
		Navaho	
		Ontong Javanese	
		Serbs	
		Tanala (Menabe)	
		Trukese	
		United States (Homestead)	
		Yagua	

* Both of a year or more duration.

† The letters following the tribal designations in the right-hand column indicate the nature of the ceremony: *h* = painful hazing, *g* = genital operations, *s* = seclusion from from women, and *t* = tests of manliness.

by whom he is brought up from then on. It might be assumed that this event would obviate the need for later ceremonial initiation into manhood. Since several other societies that do have initiation also have a change of residence at weaning, however, this simple explanation cannot be accepted and the Ganda must remain an unexplained exception.

Finally, Lewis[14] reports for the Tepoztlan that there was some disagreement among his informants as to the length of the taboo and exclusive sleeping arrangements. Since again there were other equally equivocal cases, we shall have to accept the verdict of our judges and let this case also remain an exception.

A reconsideration of the two exceptions in the lower right-hand column, the Hopi and the Timbria, which have the type of initiation into manhood required by our theory but have neither exclusive sleeping arrangements nor a prolonged *post-partum* sex taboo, also turns out to be fruitful. In neither of these societies does the father have authority over the children.[15] This is vested in the mother's brother who lives in another household.[16] That these societies should have an initiation rite, again, does not seem to contradict our general theory, even though it does contradict our specific hypothesis. From clinical studies in our own society it is clear that even with the lack of exclusive sleeping arrangements and a minimal *post-partum* sex taboo, an appreciable degree of dependence upon the mother and rivalry with the father is generated. The cases here suggest that, although these motives are not strong enough to require ceremonial initiation into manhood if the father is present in the household and has authority over the child, this may be required if he lacks such authority.

But what of the cases which have but one of the antecedent variables? Taking into account the societies with exclusive sleeping arrangements but no *post-partum* sex taboo, our theory predicts that these conditions should produce dependency and rivalry. However, since the mother is receiving sexual satisfac-

---

[14] O. Lewis, *Life in a Mexican Village: Tepoztlan Restudied* (Urbana: University of Illinois Press, 1951).

[15] A consideration of the influence of authority patterns was suggested by the work of Homans and Schneider, *op. cit.*

[16] This is also true of the Trobrianders discussed above, but of no other society in our sample about which we have information on authority patterns.

tion from her husband, she has less need to obtain substitute gratification from nurturing her infant, so that the dependency she produces in her child would be less intense and the need for initiation should be attenuated. Three of the four cases with exclusive sleeping arrangements but no taboo appear to fulfill these conditions. As we have reported above, the Ashanti and the Malaita practice a change of residence which, it could be argued, is somewhat less drastic than initiation. In any case this is permissive and not required for the Ashanti. When the Cagaba boy reaches adolescence, he is given instruction in sexual intercourse by a priest and then sent to practice these instructions with a widow who lives with him temporarily in a specially built small hut. The boy is not allowed to leave this hut until he succeeds in having sexual intercourse with her. This trial is reported to be terrifying to the boy and it is often several days before he does succeed. This type of initiation, however, does not seem to compare with other societies which like the Thonga have a full-fledged ceremony. The Siriono, on the other hand, do not have any ceremonial recognition of the shift from boyhood to manhood and they must be regarded as an exception to our theory.

The final group of cases to consider are those that have a long *post-partum* sex taboo but not exclusive mother-son sleeping arrangements. For these, our theory would also predict an attenuated need for initiation ceremonies. Although the mothers of this group are presumed to gain substitute sexual gratification from being especially nurturant and loving toward their infants, they have less opportunity to do so than with those of societies where there are also exclusive sleeping arrangements.

As in the previous group of societies the ceremonies are, except for the Ooldea which will be discussed below, mild. The Kwakiutl have a ceremony which consists of a potlatch given by the father for the son. There the boys undergo no hazing or genital operations but are secluded and expected to perform a dance. For the Ojibwa, the boy is expected to obtain a guardian spirit in a vision before he reaches maturity. Thus, generally when he is 11 or 12 years old, he goes alone into the forest where he stays—often for several days without food, water, and generally without sleep—until he either has a vision or returns home to recuperate before trying again. Again neither hazing nor genital operations are involved.

The Ooldea, a tribe situated in southwestern Australia do, however, have a full-fledged initiation rite with hazing, isolation, and a very painful genital operation. This apparently runs counter to our assumption that the rites should be mild if only one determinant is present.

Radcliffe-Brown, however, reports that in many Australian tribes

> . . . the discipline of very young children is left to the mother and the other women of the horde. A father does not punish and may not even scold his infant children, but if they misbehave he will scold the mother and perhaps give her a blow with a stick. He regards the mother as responsible for misbehavior by very young children. When they are a little older, the father undertakes the education of the boys but leaves the education of the girls to the mother and the women of the horde. But the father behaves affectionately and is very little of a disciplinarian. Discipline for a boy begins when he approaches puberty and is exercised by the men of the horde. The big change comes with the initiation ceremonies when, in some tribes, the father, by a ceremonial (symbolic) action, hands over his son to the men who will carry out the initiation rites. During the initiation period of several years the boy is subjected to rigid and frequently painful discipline by men other than his father.[17]

If the Ooldea be one of those Australian tribes described above, they fall, along with the Trobrianders, Hopi, and Timbira, into the class of societies where the function of initiation is to make up for the lack of discipline exercised by a father over the boy during childhood.

A study of those societies without exclusive sleeping arrangements and with a long *post-partum* sex taboo which do not have the rites is interesting. In the first place both the Pondo and the Araucanians are reported to have had initiation ceremonies in the recent past, indicating that they are perhaps near the threshold of needing them. The Tallensi also are interesting. An observer notes that the Tallensi should have invented the Oedipus-conflict theory since they are quite open and conscious of the strong rivalry and hostility between father and son, a conflict which remains strong and dangerous, guarded only by ritualized forms of etiquette, until the father dies and the son takes his

---

[17] Cited from a letter by A. R. Radcliffe-Brown to these authors in Homans and Schneider, *op. cit.*, p. 41.

place. Furthermore, family fissions are reported to occur frequently and the oldest son often leaves the family to establish a new lineage of his own.

Thus, the presence of a *post-partum* sex taboo alone seems to produce tension, which these societies commonly seek to resolve through initiation ceremonies. Societies in this group which do not have ceremonies either had them recently or show evidence of unresolved tension.

Summary. The cross-cultural evidence indicates that:

1. A close relationship is established between mother and son during infancy as a consequence of either (a) their sleeping together for at least a year to the exclusion of the father or (b) the mother being prohibited from sexual intercourse for at least a year after the birth of her child or (c) both of these together have measurable consequences which are manifested in cultural adjustments at adolescence.

2. The cultural adjustments to the presence of the above factors are made when the boy approaches or reaches sexual maturity. These adjustments are either (a) a ceremony of initiation into manhood involving at least one and generally several of the following factors; painful *hazing* by the adult males of the society, tests of endurance and manliness, seclusion from women, and genital operations, or (b) a change of residence which involves separation of the boy from his mother and sisters and may also include some formal means for establishing male authority such as receiving instructions from and

TABLE 2. *The Relationship of Infancy factors to Cultural Adjustments at Adolescence*

Authority of father over son	Exclusive mother-son sleeping arrangement	Post-partum sex taboo	None	Change of residence	Initiation ceremony
		CUSTOMS IN INFANCY AND CHILDHOOD		CULTURAL ADJUSTMENT AT ADOLESCENCE	
Present	Long	Long	2	3	14
		Short	1	2	1
	Short	Long	4	0	2
		Short	23	0	0
Absent			0	1	3

being required to be respectful to the mother's brother or the members of the men's house.

3. If both the factors specified in (1) are present, the consequences at adolescence tend to be more elaborate and severe than if only one is present.

4. The cultural adjustments specified in (2) also occur in societies where the father does not have the right to discipline his son, whether or not the conditions specified in (1) are present.

The evidence for these statements is summarized in Table 2.

IV THE SOCIOPSYCHOLOGICAL IMPLICATIONS

So much for the manifest results at the cultural level. But what is the most reasonable sociopsychological interpretation of these relationships? What are the psychodynamics involved? We are not concerned with the bizarre rites of the Thonga or the peculiar life of a Kwoma infant, for their own sakes, but rather in discovering some general truths about human nature. We therefore wish to state what we believe to be the underlying processes that are involved. These are processes that we have not directly observed and which must be accepted or rejected on the grounds of their plausibility or, more important, on the basis of further research implied by our theory.

We believe that six sociopsychological assumptions are supported by our findings:

1. The more exclusive the relationship between a son and his mother during the first years of his life, the greater will be his emotional dependence upon her.

2. The more intensely a mother nurtures (loves) an infant during the early years of his life, the more emotionally dependent he will be upon her.

3. The greater the emotional dependence of a child upon a mother, the more hostile and envious he will be toward anyone whom he perceives as replacing him in her affection.[18]

4. If a child develops a strong emotional dependence upon

---

[18] If, however, the mother herself is perceived by the child as the one responsible for terminating the early intense relationship, this should lead the boy both to envy her and to identify with her. This should produce conflict with respect to his sex role identity, which initiation rites would serve to resolve.

his mother during infancy, and hostility toward and envy of his father in early childhood at the time of weaning and the onset of independence training, these feelings (although latent during childhood) will manifest themselves when he reaches physiological maturity in (a) open rivalry with his father and (b) incestuous approaches to his mother, unless measures are taken to prevent such manifestations.

5. Painful hazing, enforced isolation from women, trials of endurance or manliness, genital operations, and change of residence are effective means for preventing the dangerous manifestation of rivalry and incest.

6. Even a moderate or weak amount of emotional dependence upon the mother and rivalry with the father will be dangerous at adolescence if the father has no right to (or does not in fact) exercise authority over his son during childhood.

If these sociopsychological hypotheses are true, they have some interesting implications for individual differences in our own society.[19] It has long been known that there is an association between certain types of juvenile delinquency and broken homes.[20] We would predict that the probability of a boy becoming delinquent in such instances would be highest where the separation of the mother and father occurred during the early infancy of the boy and where she remarried when he was two or three years old.

We would further predict that insofar as there has been an increase in juvenile delinquency in our society, it probably has been accompanied by an increase in the exclusiveness of mother-child relationships and/or a decrease in the authority of the father. It is not unreasonable that industrialization and urbanization have done just this, but, of course, this matter should be investigated before such an interpretation is accepted.

[19] In a study of infant training William Sewell reports that "the child who slept with their mothers during infancy made significantly p' showings on the self-adjustment, personal freedom, and family re' components of the California Test of Personality and suffered m² disturbances than did those who slept alone." W. H. Sewell, "Inf' ing and the Personality of the Child," *Am. J. Sociol.*, LVIII, 1'

[20] Compare for example, E. Glueck and S. Glueck, *Unrave'* *Delinquency* (New York: Commonwealth Fund, 1950); V berg and J. J. Balistrieri, "Gang Membership and Juver' *Am. Sociol. Rev.*, XV, December 1950, 744-52.

Finally, if further research shows that juvenile delinquency in our society is in part a function of the early childhood factors that have been described in this paper, then it can be countered either by decreasing the exclusiveness of the early mother-child relationship, increasing the authority of the father during childhood, or instituting a formal means of coping with adolescent boys functionally equivalent to those described in this paper. Change of residence would seem more compatible with the values of our society than an initiation ceremony. The Civilian Conservation Corps camps of the 1930's were an experiment which should provide useful data in this regard. The present institution of selective service would perhaps serve this purpose were the boys to be drafted at an earlier age and exposed to the authority of responsible adult males.

III

Male Sex Aggression on a University Campus*

BY CLIFFORD KIRKPATRICK AND EUGENE KANIN

A person-to-person relationship that is characterized by exploitation and shared stigma provides the conceptual framework for this research. In abstract ideal-typical terms, member B of an AB pair is urged by member A to participate in behavior desired by A but prohibited by primary group and institutional controls. B may develop ambivalent resistance but yield to a point where stigma would be involved with disclosure. With B's apparent reluctance to seek guidance from the primary group or to appeal to institutional protection, the exploitative advantage of A is increased, leading to further overtures. B's involvement and participation further increase stigmatization and isolation from primary group or institutional protection. Illustrations might include incest, homosexuality, sex aggression against children, violence between family members, illegally selling drugs, and procurer-prostitute relationships.

This type of person-to-person relationship was explored by an investigation of sexual aggressiveness in dating-courtship relationships on a university campus. This study was prompted by some case material reporting instances of violent male aggression with reluctance on the part of the offended girls to invoke protection and punishment.

An eight-page mimeographed schedule was distributed to the

* Acknowledgment is made of assistance from the Graduate School Research Fund of Indiana University. Appreciation must also be expressed to Sandra Rubinstein for helpful suggestions.

females in twenty-two varied university classes, the male members being dismissed. In general, co-operation was excellent. Only two girls refused to fill out the schedules. However, the 291 female students whose usable schedules were completely analyzed cannot be regarded as a representative sample from a defined student universe. The responding group was biased in favor of underclassmen, the quota index for freshmen being 131.5 (100 equals proportionate representation), for sophomores 181.3, juniors 85.6 and seniors 49.7. Sorority girls were over-represented as shown by a quota index of 173.7.

The questionnaire distinguished five degrees of erotic aggressiveness, namely attempts at "necking," "petting" above the waist, "petting" below the waist, sexual intercourse, and attempts at sexual intercourse with violence or threats of violence. The reporting of offensiveness by the respondents implied no confession that they were willing participants at any level of erotic behavior. Undoubtedly male behavior often became offensive after willing participation at milder levels of erotic intimacy. In the interest of gaining full co-operation the questionnaire was carefully devised to avoid probing the sex conduct of the female respondents. Instead the basic data were focused on the non-incriminating reports of being "offended" by intimacy level, frequency, and number of men. The girls could have been extremely prudish or could have been offended at the means rather than the erotic goals pursued by the offenders.

I Erotic Offensiveness

Of the 291 responding girls 55.7 per cent reported themselves offended at least once during the academic year at some level of erotic intimacy. The experiences of being offended were not altogether associated with trivial situations as shown by the fact that 20.9 per cent were offended by forceful attempts at intercourse and 6.2 per cent by "aggressively forceful attempts at sex intercourse in the course of which menacing threats or coercive infliction of physical pain were employed." There is no reason to think that offended girls had merely a single unpleasant experience with one partner. The 162 offended girls reported 1022 offensive episodes. While for some girls offensive experience was no doubt trivial, considerable mention was made of fear and guilt reactions.

A seasonal variation may exist in the reported offensive behavior of male students. Since the schedules covered the period
only from September 15, 1954, to May 15, 1955, the full record
of exposure during September and May is not available. If the
number of episodes for September and May are extrapolated by
doubling the episodes reported for half-month periods, then a U-
shaped curve can be drawn from the data indicating a higher
prevalence in fall and spring.

A 3×3 table yielding a Chi-square significant at the .05 level
suggests that episodes of lesser offensiveness are concentrated
in the fall and the more offensive episodes in the spring. The
excess of mildly offensive episodes in the fall may have been
due to imperfect communication between members of newly
formed pairs. The concentration of episodes more seriously
offensive in the spring may have been due to involvement in
continuing affairs in which offensive behavior reflected frustration of sex tensions and perhaps assumed exploitability of the
female because of her emotional involvement.

II CHARACTERS OF OFFENDED GIRLS

The offended girls reported themselves younger than did the
non-offended. The mean age of the offended girls was 18.8 and
the corresponding mean age of the 129 non-offended girls was
19.0 (C.R.=2.5). A 2×3 table relating victims and non-victims
to three age categories yielded a Chi-square $.02 > P > .01$. The
number of semesters of college work is closely related to age.
The mean semester standing of the 162 offended girls was 3.6
while that of the 129 non-offended girls was 4.1 (C.R.=2.0).
The difference could be due either to prudishness of younger
students or to their assumed exploitability.

Frequency of dating is a personal characteristic which might
be associated with differential proneness to be offended in the
course of dating-courtship behavior. In response to a question
concerning total number of dates in April, 1955, the mean figure
given by the offended was 11.6 in contrast to 10.3 for non-
offended girls (C.R.=1.3). The *eta* between number of dates
per month (April) and total number of episodes reported by
offended girls was only .24. Thus it would seem that dating
frequency is an exposure variable which need not be taken
seriously into account in interpreting other findings. Dating

frequency in relation to maximum level of offensiveness reported by the offended girls yielding an insignificant Chi-square (.70>P>.50).

Girls with lower group status characteristics rendering them more exploitable would seem more likely to report themselves offended. A 2×2 table distributing sorority and non-sorority girls as offended or non-offended, however, showed sorority girls in slight excess among the offended (.30>P>.20).

It might still be argued that of the offended girls the sorority members, less exploitable as compared with non-sorority girls, would experience offensiveness at milder maximum levels. A 2×5 table, including the five intimacy levels at which maximum offensiveness occurred, showed such a trend but yielded a Chi-square without statistical significance (.30>P>.20).

The non-significant findings concerning sorority status do not take into account the number of episodes at various levels of offensiveness. In Table 1 it is shown more clearly that the offensive experience of sorority girls is relatively concentrated at the milder levels of offensiveness.[1]

The implications of sorority status in the present context are not clear. It may be that high group status makes such girls offended easily even at mild levels of aggression or it may be that greater dating frequency means exposure to offensiveness at a mild level. The dating frequency of sorority girls who were

TABLE 1. *Offensive Episodes Experienced by Sorority and Non-Sorority Girls by Levels of Erotic Intimacy*

	Sorority	Non-Sorority	Total
Necking and petting above the waist	333	415	748
Petting below the waist	55	136	191
Attempted intercourse and attempted intercourse with violence	28	55	83
Total	416	606	1022

$\chi^2=17.35$; d.f.=2; P<.001

[1] Levels of aggression are telescoped in order to satisfy requirements for Chi square.

offended was 12.4 as compared to 9.5 for offended non-sorority girls (C.R.=3.6). It can be said that the *savoir faire* attributed to sorority girls did not prevent them from getting into situations reported as offensive.

Respondents were asked, "Do you consider yourself religious?" In spite of theoretically greater intolerance of male aggressions, girls answering "yes" seem less likely to report offensive experience (Chi-square at .10>P>.05 level).

The relative academic class standing of offended and offenders was obtained from the schedules. Of the 388 offenders known only as reported by offended girls, 358 were students with known class standing. Of these students 9.5 per cent offended girls one or two years more advanced than themselves, 34.1 per cent offended girls of the same class standing, 43.6 per cent offended girls one class below, and 12.8 per cent offended girls three or four years lower in class standing. The mean difference in class standing in favor of the offenders was 1.2 with a sigma of .05. The evidence shows that offenders tend to be of higher academic class than the offended respondents, but exploitation is not proven since the normal class discrepancies for pairs dating without erotic offensiveness are not known.

Some limited evidence is available concerning relative socio-economic standing of the offended girls and the men whom they described as offenders. Of the 388 offenders, 68.1 per cent were reported as of the same "socio-economic status" as their offended partners, 13.9 per cent were reported as lower and 18.0 per cent reported as of higher status. Ratings of relative socio-economic status probably are lacking in reliability and validity. Offenders could be down-graded because they were offensive or up-graded to soothe a latent guilt feeling at having been involved with offensive behavior.

The proportion of fraternity men among the offenders is high, implying a quota index of 205.8 with reference to the proportion of fraternity men in the male student body. It is possible, however, that fraternity men date more, without being more aggressive per date, than non-fraternity men. A table distributing the female offended and the male offenders by organizational (fraternity-sorority) status shows a rather clear pattern of homogamy rather than supporting a theory that men are especially predatory toward non-sorority girls. It does seem clear that open communication and *savoir faire* attributed to sorority girls and fraternity men does not prevent experiences reported as offensive. There seem to be misunderstandings even among the "Greeks."

Data are available in Table 2 concerning relationship involvement and erotic intimacy level at which offensiveness occurs. Table 2, which includes column percentages, suggests that there is a significant association of offensiveness at a mild level of erotic intimacy with a non-involved pairing and offensiveness at a serious level with "pinned" or engagement relationships. It could be plausibly argued that offensive experience at a mild level of intimacy and involvement is due to misunderstanding while experiences at a more serious level and with greater relationship involvement are due to male exploitation of feminine involvement.

The experience of being offended might be further related to selectivity in information and disruption of courtship relationships. Offended girls may express their dissatisfaction with a promptness depending upon involvement and the aggressiveness of offending males. A ratio $\frac{E}{M}$ may be defined as number of episodes at a certain level of erotic intimacy divided by the

TABLE 2. *Relationship Involvement and Erotic Intimacy Level at Which Offensiveness Occurs, by Episodes*

	Necking and Petting Above the Waist		Petting Below the Waist		Attempted Intercourse and Attempted Intercourse with Violence		
	N	Per Cent	N	Per Cent	N	Per Cent	Total
Ride home First date Occasional date	411	55.0	60	31.4	25	30.1	496 (48.5%)
Regular or Steady date	295	39.4	104	54.5	43	51.8	442 (43.3%)
Pinned Engaged	42	5.6	27	14.1	15	18.1	84 (8.2%)
Totals	748	100.0	191	100.0	83	100.0	1022 (100.0%)

$\chi^2 = 57.26$; d.f. $= 4$; P $< .001$; C $= .230$.

number of men offensively aggressive at that level. The tolerance ratios $\frac{E}{M}$ of Table 3 represent frequency of repeated offensiveness by the same man at a given level. A ratio of 2.00 would
mean that on the average each offending man was guilty of two
episodes at a given level. A ratio of 1.00 means that no man was
permitted a repetition of his offensive conduct at a particular
level. Presumably the ratios vary according to successful preven-
tion of aggression and with termination of relationships which
led to offensive behavior.

It is interesting to note that at the milder level of necking,
about half the men repeated their offensive behavior. For others
the situation was defined after the first offense or the relationship terminated. Since it has been shown in Table 2 that offensiveness at the necking level was associated with casual dating,
it is probable that dating relationships without emotional involvement were selectively broken, thus curtailing offensive
behavior. It is interesting to note a higher tolerance ratio at the
next two levels of erotic intimacy, meaning that on the average
offensive behavior was repeated about twice. The probable explanation is greater emotional involvement of the girls in more
meaningful relationships with corresponding exploitability. At
the fourth level the tolerance ratio drops to 1.52 suggesting that
in spite of emotional involvement the aggression went beyond
whatever tolerance was furthered by emotional involvement.
Given violence and threats of violence no repetition was per-

TABLE 3. *Number of Men, Episodes, and Tolerance Ratio for
Five Levels of Erotic Intimacy*

Levels of Aggression	Men	Episodes	$\frac{E}{M}$
Necking	231	367	1.58
Petting above the waist	177	381	2.15
Petting below the waist	92	191	2.07
Attempted intercourse	48	73	1.52
Attempted intercourse with violence	10	10	1.00
Man-level total	558*	1022	
Number of men	388		

* Multiple count due to some men active more than once at same or
different levels.

mitted, even though seven out of the ten such episodes involved girls in regular-dating, "pinned," or engaged relationships. Whether these seven episodes led to selective termination or redefinition of courtship relationships is unknown.

III   EMOTIONAL EFFECTS, REACTIONS AND HYPOTHETICAL REACTIONS

The offended respondents were asked to define their emotional reaction to offensive episodes by adjectives such as anger, guilt, and fear. While the terminology varied, it proved easy to group responses in the four categories of Table 4. Table 4 indicates that guilt feelings may vary with involvement and degree of aggression. The stress upon guilt is at a maximum at the intermediate level, probably associated with emotional involvement on the part of the girls and possibly provocation. Guilt feelings seem to be somewhat relieved by more extreme male aggressiveness for which girls could disclaim responsibility. It is probable that, within limits, involvement furthers guilt feelings, shared stigma, and corresponding exploitability.

The offended respondents were also asked with the aid of an 8-item checklist what they did about offensive episodes and had opportunity to make responses in their own words. The replies were readily grouped into the five categories of Table 5. Table 5 shows the limited reliance upon authority. The percentage of

TABLE 4. *Emotional Reactions of Offended Respondents by Level of Erotic Intimacy*

	Necking and Petting Above the Waist		Petting Below the Waist		Attempted Intercourse and Attempted Intercourse with Violence		Total	
	N	Per Cent	N	Per Cent	N	Per Cent		
Anger	138	48.4	45	42.0	27	35.0	210	(44.78%)
Guilt	53	18.6	28	26.2	16	20.8	97	(20.68%)
Fear	42	14.7	25	23.4	29	37.7	96	(20.47%)
Disgust, disillusionment or confusion	52	18.3	9	8.4	5	6.5	66	(14.07%)
Totals	285	100.0	107	100.0	77	100.0	469	(100.00%)

$\chi^2 = 30.03$; d.f.$=6$; P$<.001$

TABLE 5. *Answers of Respondents to the Question "What Did You Do?"*

	Necking and Petting Above the Waist		Petting Below the Waist		Attempted Intercourse and Attempted Intercourse with Violence			Critical Ratios— Columns 1 and 3
	N	Per Cent	N	Per Cent	N	Per Cent	Total	
Selective avoidance	126	36.95	21	25.30	21	30.88	168 (34.15%)	
Discussion and warning re age group	115	33.73	17	20.48	11	16.18	143 (29.06%)	3.4
Secrecy	66	19.35	38	45.78	33	48.53	137 (27.85%)	4.5
Discussion with aggressor	11	3.23	3	3.62	3	4.41	17 (3.46%)	
Report to authority	23	6.74	4	4.82	0		27 (5.48%)	
Totals	341	100.00	83	100.00	68	100.00	492 (100.00%)	

girls reporting offensive episodes to authorities was insignificant in spite of the claims of a counseling service. "Discussion and warnings" within the companion group, such as a sorority, was less common at the more extreme levels of erotic intimacy while secrecy became the more common policy.

Evidence is available from both offended and non-offended respondents concerning comparative hypothetical reactions. The offended were asked "What would you now do?" presumably after reflection upon offensive experience. In every case non-offended respondents volunteered answers to this hypothetical question in spite of their own lack of offensive experiences. The responses could be readily grouped within the eleven categories shown in Table 6, five of which could be grouped under the heading "Appeals to Authority." Especially striking is the greater emphasis of the offended upon personal interaction with the aggressor in terms of reason and rebuke.[2] While appeals to

[2] It may seem strange that in Table 6 "secrecy" and "discussion and warning re age group" are infrequently mentioned as adjustive reactions as compared with their prominence in the checkings of Table 5. The answer probably lies in the fact that the data of Table 5 were largely derived from a checklist rather than from volunteered statements as in the case of Table 6. Respondents given an open-ended question as to what they would *do* would naturally neglect the passive reaction of secrecy.

TABLE 6. *Comparative Hypothetical Adjustive Reactions of Offended and Non-Offended Respondents*

	Offended		Non-Offended		Critical Ratios— Offended vs. Non-Offended
	N	Per Cent	N	Per Cent	
Discussion with aggressor: reason and rebuke	157	37.92	109	16.42	8.1
Deterrence or avoidance: physical and verbal	135	32.61	187	28.16	
Selective avoidance	76	18.36	169	25.45	3.2
Vague or cynical	24	5.80	31	4.67	
Discussion and warning re age group	13	3.14	47	7.08	2.7
Secrecy	6	1.45	17	2.56	
APPEALS TO AUTHORITY					
Report to parents	2	.48	26	3.92	
Report to academic authority	1	.24	39	5.87	
Report to civic authority	0		18	2.71	
Report to clergy	0		2	.30	
"Report it" and "Report it to authorities"	0		19	2.86	
Total Appeals to Authority		.72			15.66
Totals	414	100.00	664	100.00	

authority were generally unfavored, girls reporting offensive experiences were especially disinclined to favor this type of adjustive reaction. There is some support for our ideal-typical formulation that exploitation and stigma lead to withdrawal from institutional protection with ultimate increased dependence upon the pair relationships.

In terms of possibly altered selective perception it might be expected that offended girls would give higher estimates of the prevalence of offensive behavior than would non-offended girls. The offended girls estimate that the average college girl experiences 4.2 offensive episodes in the course of a college year. The corresponding mean estimate made by non-offended respondents was only 2.7 (C.R.=4.9).

Summary. There is evidence on one campus suggesting that in courtship relationships there is a progressive pattern of exploitation, involvement, ambivalent resistance, awareness of shared stigma and reduced reliance upon institutional controls with corresponding stress on control within the dyadic relationship.

One possible educational implication of this study is that college girls should be trained in *informed* self-reliance. Extreme offensive experience associated with stigma seems to reduce reliance upon parents, peer groups and certainly upon formal agencies of control and guidance. However, to avoid cumulative personal exploitation and exploitation of other victims because of secrecy, parents, peer groups and formal agencies should operate so as to avoid stigmatization. The self-reliant girl, really in need of help and judiciously aware of that need, should not be made to fear a confusion of punitive and advisory functions.

IV

Early Stages of the Oedipus Conflict*

BY MELANIE KLEIN

In my analyses of children, especially of children between the
ages of three and six, I have come to a number of conclusions of
which I shall here present a summary.

I have repeatedly alluded to the conclusion that the Oedipus
complex comes into operation earlier than is usually supposed. In
my essay, "The Psychological Principles of Infant Analysis,"[1]
I discussed this subject in greater detail. The conclusion which I
reached there was that the Oedipus tendencies are released in
consequence of the frustration which the child experiences at
weaning, and that they make their appearance at the end of the
first and the beginning of the second year of life; they receive
reinforcement through the anal frustrations undergone during
training in cleanliness. The next determining influence upon the
mental processes is that of the anatomical difference between the
sexes.

The boy, when he finds himself impelled to abandon the oral
and anal positions, for the genital, passes on to the aim of
penetration associated with possession of the penis. Thus he
changes not only his libido-position, but its *aim,* and this enables him to retain his original love-object. In the girl, on the
other hand, the *receptive* aim is carried over from the oral to
the genital position: she changes her libido-position, but re-

* Read at the Tenth International Psycho-Analytical Congress, Innsbruck, September 3, 1927.
[1] *The International Journal of Psychoanalysis,* Vol. VIII, 1927.

tains its aim, which has already led to disappointment in relation to her mother. In this way receptivity for the penis is induced in the girl, who then turns to the father as her love-object.

The very onset of the Oedipus wishes, however, already becomes associated with incipient dread of castration and feelings
of guilt.

The analysis of adults, as well as of children, has familiarized
us with the fact that the pregenital instinctual impulses carry
with them a sense of guilt, and it was thought at first that the
feelings of guilt were of subsequent growth, displaced back on to
these tendencies, though not originally associated with them.
Ferenczi assumes that, connected with the urethral and anal
impulses, there is a "kind of physiological forerunner of the
super-ego," which he terms "sphincter-morality." According to
Abraham, anxiety makes its appearance on the cannibalistic
level, while the sense of guilt arises in the succeeding early anal-
sadistic phase.

My findings lead rather further. They show that the sense of
guilt associated with pregenital fixation is already the direct
effect of the Oedipus conflict. And this seems to account satisfactorily for the genesis of such feelings, for we know the sense
of guilt to be simply a result of the introjection (already accomplished or, as I would add, in process of being accomplished)
of the Oedipus love-objects: that is, a sense of guilt is a product
of the formation of the superego.

The analysis of little children reveals the structure of the
superego as built up of identifications dating from very different
periods and strata in the mental life. These identifications are
surprisingly contradictory in character, overindulgence and excessive severity existing side by side. We find in them, too, an
explanation of the severity of the superego, which comes out
especially plainly in these infant analyses. It does not seem clear
why a child of, say, four years old should set up in his mind an
unreal fantastic image of parents who devour, cut and bite. But
it is clear why in a child of about one year old the anxiety
caused by the beginning of the Oedipus conflict takes the form
of a dread of being devoured and destroyed. The child himself
desires to destroy the libidinal object by biting, devouring and
cutting it, which leads to anxiety, since awakening of the
Oedipus tendencies is followed by introjection of the object,
which then becomes one from which punishment is to be ex-

pected. The child then dreads a punishment corresponding to the offense: the superego becomes something which bites, devours and cuts.

The connection between the formation of the superego and the pregenital phases of development is very important from two points of view. On the one hand, the sense of guilt attaches itself to the oral and anal-sadistic phases, which as yet predominate; and, on the other, the superego comes into being while these phases are in the ascendant, which accounts for its sadistic severity.

These conclusions open up a new perspective. Only by strong repression can the still very feeble ego defend itself against a superego so menacing. Since the Oedipus tendencies are at first chiefly expressed in the form of oral and anal impulses, the question of which fixations will predominate in the Oedipus development will be mainly determined by the degree of the repression which takes place at this early stage.

Another reason why the direct connection between the pregenital phase of development and the sense of guilt is so important that the oral and anal frustrations, which are the prototypes of all later frustrations in life, at the same time signify *punishment* and give rise to anxiety. This circumstance makes the frustration more acutely felt, and this bitterness contributes largely to the hardship of all subsequent frustrations.

We find that important consequences ensue from the fact that the ego is still so little developed when it is assailed by the onset of the Oedipus tendencies and the incipient sexual curiosity associated with them. Still quite undeveloped intellectually, it is exposed to an onrush of problems and questions. One of the most bitter grievances which we come upon in the unconscious is that this tremendous questioning impulse, which is apparently only partly conscious and even so far as it is cannot yet be expressed in words, remains unanswered. Another reproach follows hard upon this, namely, that the child could not understand words and speech. Thus his first questions go back beyond the beginnings of his understandings of speech.

In analysis both these grievances give rise to an extraordinary amount of hate. Singly or in conjunction they are the cause of numerous inhibitions of the epistemophilic impulse: for instance, the incapacity to learn foreign languages, and, further, hatred of those who speak a different tongue. They are also responsible for direct disturbances in speech, etc. The curiosity which shows itself plainly later on, mostly in the fourth or fifth year of life, is not the beginning, but the climax and termination, of this phase of development, which I have also found to be true of the Oedipus conflict in general.

The early feeding of *not knowing* has manifold connections. It unites with the feeling of being incapable, impotent, which soon results from the Oedipus situation. The child also feels this frustration the more acutely because he *knows nothing* definite about sexual processes. In both sexes the castration complex is accentuated by this feeling of ignorance.

The early connection between the epistemophilic impulse and sadism is very important for the whole mental development. This instinct, roused by the striving of the Oedipus tendencies, at first mainly concerns itself with the mother's womb, which is assumed to be the scene of all sexual processes and developments. The child is still dominated by the anal-sadistic libido-position which impels him to wish to appropriate the contents of the womb. He thus begins to be curious about what it contains, what it is like, etc. So the epistemophilic instinct and the desire to take possession come quite early to be most intimately connected with one another and at the same time with the sense of guilt aroused by the incipient Oedipus conflict. This significant connection ushers in a phase of development in both sexes which is of vital importance, hitherto not sufficiently recognized. It consists of a very early identification with the mother.

The course run by this "femininity" phase must be examined separately in boys and in girls, but, before I proceed to this, I will show its connection with the previous phase, which is common to both sexes.

In the early anal-sadistic stage the child sustains his second severe trauma, which strengthens his tendency to turn away from the mother. She has frustrated his oral desires, and now she also interferes with his anal pleasures. It seems as though at this point the anal deprivations cause the anal tendencies to amalgamate with the sadistic tendencies. The child desires to get possession of the mother's feces, by penetrating into her body, cutting it to pieces, devouring and destroying it. Under the influence of his genital impulses, the boy is beginning to turn to his mother as love-object. But his sadistic impulses are in full activity, and the hate originating in earlier frustrations is powerfully opposed to his object-love on the genital level. A still greater obstacle to his love is his dread of castration by the father, which arises with the Oedipus impulses. The degree in which he attains to the genital position will partly depend on his capacity for tolerating this anxiety. Here the intensity of the oral-sadistic and anal-sadistic fixations is an important factor. It affects the degree of hatred which the boy feels toward the mother; and this, in its turn, hinders him to a greater or lesser extent in attaining a positive relation to her. The sadistic fixations exercise also a decisive influence upon the formation of the superego, which is coming into being whilst these phases are in the ascendant. The more cruel the superego the more terrifying will be the father as castrator, and the more tenaciously in the child's flight from his genital impulses will he cling to the sadistic levels, from which his Oedipus tendencies in the first instance then also take their color.

In these early stages all the positions in the Oedipus development are cathected in rapid succession. This, however, is not noticeable, because the picture is dominated by the pregenital impulses. Moreover, no rigid line can be drawn between the active heterosexual attitude which finds expression on the anal level and the further stage of identification with the mother.

We have now reached that phase of development of which I spoke before under the name of the "femininity-phase." It has its basis on the anal-sadistic level and imparts to that level a new content, for feces are now equated with the child that is longed for, and the desire to rob the mother now applies to the child as well as to feces. Here we can discern two aims which merge with one another. The one is directed by the desire for children, the intention being to appropriate them, while the other aim is motivated by jealousy of the future brothers and sisters whose appearance is expected and by the wish to destroy them in the womb. A third object of the boy's oral-sadistic tendencies in the mother's womb is the father's penis.

As in the castration-complex of girls, so in the femininity-complex of the male, there is at bottom the frustrated desire for a special organ. The tendencies to steal and destroy are concerned with the organs of conception, pregnancy and parturition, which the boy assumes to exist in the womb, and further with the vagina and the breasts, the fountain of milk, which are coveted as organs of receptivity and bounty from the time when the libidinal position is purely oral.

The boy fears punishment for his destruction of his mother's body, but, besides this, his fear is of a more general nature, and here we have an analogy to the anxiety associated with the castration-wishes of the girl. He fears that this body will be mutilated and dismembered, and, among other things, castrated. Here we have a direct contribution to the castration-complex. In this early period of development the mother who takes away the child's feces signifies also a mother who dismembers and castrates him. Not only by means of the anal frustrations which she inflicts does she pave the way for the castration-complex: in terms of psychic reality she *is* also already the *castrator*.

This dread of the mother is so overwhelming because there is combined with it an intense dread of castration by the father. The destructive tendencies whose object is the womb are also directed with their full oral- and anal-sadistic intensity against the father's penis, which is supposed to be located there. It is upon his penis that the dread of castration by the father is focused in this phase. Thus the femininity-phase is characterized by anxiety relating to the womb and the father's penis, and this anxiety subjects the boy to the tyranny of a superego which devours, dismembers and castrates and is formed from the image of father and mother alike.

The aims of the incipient genital libido-positions are thus crisscrossed by and intermingled with the manifold pregenital tendencies. The greater the preponderance of sadistic fixations the more does the boy's identification with his mother correspond to an attitude of rivalry toward the woman, with its blending of envy and hatred; for on account of his wish for a child he feels himself at a disadvantage and inferior to the mother.

Let us now consider why the femininity-complex of men seems so much more obscure than the castration-complex in women, with which it is equally important.

The amalgamation of the desire for a child with the epistemophilic impulse enables a boy to effect a displacement on to the intellectual plane; his sense of being at a disadvantage is then concealed and overcompensated by the superiority he deduces from his possession of a penis, which is also acknowledged by girls. This exaggeration of the masculine position results in excessive protestations of masculinity. In her paper entitled "Notes on Curiosity,"[2] Mary Chadwick, too, has traced the man's narcissistic overestimation of the penis and his attitude of intellectual rivalry toward women to the frustration of his wish for a child and the displacement of this desire on to the intellectual plane.

A tendency to excess in the direction of aggression, which very frequently occurs, has its source in the femininity-complex. It goes with an attitude of contempt and "knowing better," and is highly asocial and sadistic; it is partly conditioned as an attempt to mask the anxiety and ignorance which lie behind it. In part it coincides with the boy's protest (originating in his fear of castration) against the feminine role, but it is rooted also in his dread of his mother, whom he intended to rob of the father's penis, her children and her female sexual organs. This excessive aggression unites with the pleasure in attack which proceeds from the direct, genital Oedipus situation, but it represents that part of the situation which is by far the more asocial factor in character-formation. This is why a man's rivalry with women will be far more asocial than his rivalry with his fellow-men, which is largely prompted through the genital position. Of course the quantity of sadistic fixations will also determine the relationship of a man to other men when they are rivals. If, on the contrary, the identification with the mother is based on a more securely established genital position, on the one hand his relation to women will be positive in character, and on the other the desire for a child and the feminine component, which play so essential a part in men's work, will find more favorable opportunities for sublimation.

In both sexes one of the principal roots of inhibitions in work is the anxiety and sense of guilt associated with the femininity phase. Experience has taught me, however, that a thorough analysis of this phase is, for other reasons as well, important from a therapeutic point of view, and should be of help in some obsessional cases which seem to have reached a point where nothing more could be resolved.

In the boy's development the femininity-phase is succeeded by a prolonged struggle between the pregenital and the genital positions of the libido. When at its height, in the third to the fifth year of life, this struggle is plainly recognizable as the

[2] *Internationale Zeitschrift für Psychoanalyse*, Bd. XI, 1925.

Oedipus conflict. The anxiety associated with the femininity-phase drives the boy back to identification with the father; but this stimulus in itself does not provide a firm foundation for the genital position, since it leads mainly to repression and over-compensation of the anal-sadistic instincts, and not to overcoming them. The dread of castration by the father strengthens the fixation to the anal-sadistic levels. The degree of constitutional genitality also plays an important part as regards a favorable issue, i.e., the attainment of the genital level. Often the outcome of the struggle remains undecided, and this gives rise to neurotic troubles and disturbances of potency.[3] Thus the attainment of complete potency and reaching the genital position will in part depend upon the favorable issue of the femininity-phase.

I will now turn to the development of girls. As a result of the process of weaning, the girl has turned from the mother, being impelled more strongly to do so by the anal deprivations she has undergone. The genital now begins to influence her mental development.

I entirely agree with Helene Deutsch,[4] who holds that the genital development of the woman finds its completion in the successful displacement of oral libido on to the genital. Only, my results lead me to believe that this displacement begins with the first stirrings of the genital impulses and that the oral, receptive aim of the genital exercises a determining influence in the girl's turning to the father. Also I am led to conclude that not only an unconscious awareness of the vagina, but also sensations in that organ and the rest of the genital apparatus, are aroused as soon as the Oedipus impulses make their appearance. In girls, however, onanism does not afford anything like so adequate an outlet for these quantities of excitation as it does in boys. Hence the accumulated lack of satisfaction provides yet another reason for more complications and disturbances of female sexual development. The difficulty of obtaining complete gratification by onanism may be another cause, besides those indicated by Freud, for the girl's repudiation of the practice, and may partly explain why, during her struggle to give it up, manual masturbation is generally replaced by pressing the legs together.

[3] Compare here Reich: *Die Funktion des Orgasmus,* Internationaler Psychoanalytischer Verlag.
[4] H. Deutsch: *Psychoanalyse der weiblichen Sexualfunktion.*

Besides the receptive quality of the genital organ, which is brought into play by the intense desire for a new source of gratification, envy and hatred of the mother who possesses the father's penis seem, at the period when these first Oedipus impulses are stirring, to be a further motive for the little girl's turning to the father. His caresses have now the effect of a seduction and are felt as "the attraction of the opposite sex."[5]

In the girl identification with the mother results directly from the Oedipus impulses: the whole struggle caused in the boy by his castration-anxiety is absent in her. In girls as well as boys this identification coincides with the anal-sadistic tendencies to rob and destroy the mother. If identification with the mother takes place at a stage at which the oral- and anal-sadistic tendencies predominate, dread of a primitive maternal superego will lead to the repression and fixation of this phase and interfere with further genital development. Dread of the mother, too, impels the little girl to give up identification with her, and identification with the father begins.

The little girl's epistemophilic impulse is first roused by the Oedipus complex; the result is that she discovers her lack of a penis. She feels this lack to be a fresh cause of hatred of the mother, but at the same time her sense of guilt makes her regard it as a punishment. This embitters her frustration in this direction, and it, in its turn, exercises a profound influence on the whole castration-complex.

This early grievance about the lack of a penis is greatly magnified later on, when the phallic phase and the castration-complex are in full swing. Freud has stated that the discovery of the lack of a penis causes the turning from the mother to the father. My findings show, however, that this discovery operates only as a reinforcement in this direction, since it follows on a very early stage in the Oedipus conflict, and is succeeded by the wish for a child, by which it is actually replaced in later development. I regard the deprivation of the breast as the most fundamental cause of the turning to the father.

Identification with the father is less charged with anxiety than that with the mother; moreover, the sense of guilt toward her

[5] We regularly come across the unconscious reproach that the mother has seduced the child while tending it. The explanation is that at the period when she had to minister to its bodily needs the Oedipus tendencies were awaking.

impels to overcompensation through a fresh love-relation with her. Against this new love-relation with her there operates the castration-complex which makes a masculine attitude difficult, and also the hatred of her which sprang from the earlier situations. Hate and rivalry of the mother, however, again lead to abandoning the identification with the father and turning to him as the object to be secured and loved.

The little girl's relation with her mother causes the relation to her father to take both a positive and a negative direction. The frustration undergone at his hands has as its very deepest basis the disappointment already suffered in relation to the mother; a powerful motive in the desire to possess him springs from the hatred and envy against the mother. If the sadistic fixations remain predominant, this hatred and its overcompensation will also materially affect the woman's relation to men. On the other hand, if there is a more positive relation to the mother, built up on the genital position, not only will the woman be freer from a sense of guilt in her relation to her children, but her love for her husband will be strongly reinforced, since for the woman he always stands at one and the same time for the mother who gives what is desired and for the beloved child. On this very significant foundation is built up that part of the relation which is connected exclusively with the father. At first it is focused on the act of the penis in coitus. This act, which also promises gratification of the desires that are now displaced on to the genital, seems to the little girl a most consummate performance.

Her admiration is, indeed, shaken by the Oedipus frustration, but unless it is converted into hate, it constitutes one of the fundamental features of the woman's relation to the man. Later, when full satisfaction of the love-impulses is obtained, there is joined with this admiration the great gratitude ensuing from the long-pent-up deprivation. This gratitude finds expression in the greater feminine capacity for complete and lasting surrender to a love-object, especially to the "first love."

One way in which the little girl's development is greatly handicapped is the following. While the boy does in reality possess the penis, in respect of which he enters into rivalry with the father, the little girl has only the unsatisfied desire for motherhood, and of this, too, she has but a dim and uncertain, though a very intense, awareness.

It is not merely this uncertainty which disturbs her hope of future motherhood. It is weakened far more by anxiety and sense of guilt, and these may seriously and permanently damage the maternal capacity of a woman. Because of the destructive tendencies once directed by her against the mother's body (or certain organs in it) and against the children in the womb, the girl anticipates retribution in the form of destruction of her own capacity for motherhood or of the organs connected with this function and of her own children. Here we have also one root of the constant concern of women (often so excessive) for their personal beauty, for they dread that this too will be destroyed by the mother. At the bottom of the impulse to deck and beautify themselves there is always the motive of restoring damaged comeliness, and this has its origin in anxiety and sense of guilt.[6]

It is probable that this deep dread of the destruction of internal organs may be the psychic cause of the greater susceptibility of women, as compared with men, to conversion-hysteria and organic diseases.

It is this anxiety and sense of guilt which is the chief cause of the repression of feelings of pride and joy in the feminine role, which are originally very strong. This repression results in depreciation of the capacity for motherhood, at the outset so highly prized. Thus the girl lacks the powerful support which the boy derives from his possession of the penis, and which she herself might find in the anticipation of motherhood.

The girl's very intense anxiety about her womanhood can be shown to be analogous to the boy's dread of castration, for it certainly contributes to the checking of her Oedipus impulses. The course run by the boy's castration-anxiety concerning the penis which *visibly* exists is, however, different; it might be termed more acute than the more chronic anxiety of the girl concerning her internal organs, with which she is necessarily less familiar. Moreover, it is bound to make a difference that the boy's anxiety is determined by the paternal and the girl's by the maternal superego.

Freud has said that the girl's superego develops on different lines from that of the boy. We constantly find confirmation of the fact that jealousy plays a greater part in women's lives than in men's, because it is reinforced by deflected envy of the male

[6] Compare Hárnik's paper at the Innsbruck Psycho-Analytical Congress: "Die ökonomischen Beziehungen zwischen dem Schuldgefühl und dem weiblichen Narzissmus."

on account of the penis. On the other hand, however, women especially possess a great capacity, which is not based merely on an overcompensation, for disregarding their own wishes and devoting themselves with self-sacrifice to ethical and social tasks. We cannot account for this capacity by the blending of masculine and feminine traits which, because of the human being's bisexual disposition, does in individual cases influence the formation of character, for this capacity is so plainly maternal in nature. I think that, in order to explain how women can run so wide a gamut from the most petty jealousy to the most self-forgetful loving kindness, we have to take into consideration the peculiar conditions of the formation of the feminine superego. From the early identification with the mother in which the anal-sadistic level so largely preponderates, the little girl derives jealousy and hatred and forms a cruel superego after the maternal imago. The superego which develops at this stage from a father-identification can also be menacing and cause anxiety, but it seems never to reach the same proportions as that derived from the mother-identification. But the more the identification with the mother becomes stabilized on the genital basis, the more will it be characterized by the devoted kindness of an indulgent mother-ideal. Thus this positive affective attitude depends on the extent to which the maternal mother-ideal bears the characteristics of the pregenital or of the genital stage. But when it comes to the active conversion of the emotional attitude into social or other activities, it would seem that it is the paternal ego-ideal which is at work. The deep admiration felt by the little girl for the father's genital activity leads to the formation of a paternal superego which sets before her active aims to which she can never fully attain. If, owing to certain factors in her development, the incentive to accomplish these aims is strong enough, their very impossibility of attainment may lend an impetus to her efforts which, combined with the capacity for self-sacrifice which she derives from the maternal superego, gives a woman, in individual instances, the capacity for very exceptional achievements on the intuitive plane and in specific fields.

The boy, too, derives from the feminine phase a maternal superego which causes him, like the girl, to make both cruelly primitive and kindly identifications. But he passes through this phase to resume (it is true, in varying degrees) identification with the father. However much the maternal side makes itself felt in the formation of the superego, it is yet the paternal super-ego which from the beginning is the decisive influence for the man. He too sets before himself a figure of an exalted character upon which to model himself, but, because the boy is "made in the image of" his ideal, it is not unattainable. This circumstance contributes to the more sustained and objective creative work of the male.

The dread of injury to her womanhood exercises a profound influence on the castration-complex of the little girl, for it causes her to overestimate the penis which she herself lacks; this exaggeration is then much more obvious than is the underlying anxiety about her own womanhood. I would remind you here of the work of Karen Horney, who was the first to examine the sources of the castration-complex in women in so far as those sources lie in the Oedipus situation.

In this connection I must speak of the importance for sexual development of certain early experiences in childhood. In the paper which I read at the Salzburg Congress in 1924, I mentioned that when observations of coitus take place at a later stage of development they assume the character of traumata, but that if such experiences occur at an early age they become fixated and form part of the sexual development. I must now add that a fixation of this sort may hold in its grip not only that particular stage of development, but also the superego which is then in process of formation, and may thus injure its further development. For the more completely the superego reaches its zenith in the genital stage the less prominent will the sadistic identifications be in its structure and the more surely will an ethically fine personality be developed and greater possibilities of mental health be secured.

There is another kind of experience in early childhood which strikes me as typical and exceedingly important. These experiences often follow closely in time upon the observations of coitus and are induced or fostered by the excitations set up thereby. I refer to the sexual relations of little children with one another, between brothers and sisters or playmates, which consist in the most varied acts: looking, touching, performing excretion in common, fellatio, cunnilingus and often direct attempts at coitus. They are deeply repressed and have a cathexis of profound feelings of guilt. These feelings are mainly due to the fact that this love-object, chosen under the pressure of the excitation due to the Oedipus conflict, is felt by the child to be a substitute for the father or mother or both. Thus these relations, which seem so insignificant and which apparently no child under the stimulus of the Oedipus development escapes, take on the character of an Oedipus relation actually realized, and exercise a determining influence upon the formation of the Oedipus complex, the subject's detachment from that complex and upon his later sexual relations. Moreover, an experience of this sort forms an important fixation-point in the development of the superego. In consequence of the need for punishment and the repetition-compulsion, these experiences often cause the child to subject himself to sexual traumata. In this connection I would refer you to Abraham,[7] who showed that experiencing sexual traumata is one part of the sexual development of children. The analytic investigation of these experiences, during the analysis of adults as well as of children, to a great extent clears up the Oedipus situation in its connection with early fixations and is therefore important from the therapeutic point of view.

Summary. I wish above all to point out that they do not, in my opinion, contradict the statements of Professor Freud. I think that the essential point in the additional considerations which I have advanced is that I date these processes earlier and that the different phases (especially in the initial stages) merge more freely in one another than was hitherto supposed.

The early stages of the Oedipus conflict are so largely dominated by pregenital phases of development that the genital phase, when it begins to be active, is at first heavily shrouded and only later, between the third and fifth years of life, becomes clearly recognizable. At this age the Oedipus complex and the formation of the superego reach their climax. But the fact that the Oedipus tendencies begin so much earlier than we supposed, the pressure of the sense of guilt which therefore falls upon the pregenital levels, the determining influence thus exercised so early upon the Oedipus development on the one hand and that of the superego on the other, and accordingly upon character-

[7] Karl Abraham, *Selected Papers,* International Psycho-Analytical Library, No. 13.

formation, sexuality and all the rest of the subject's development —all these things seem to me of great and hitherto unrecognized importance. I found out the therapeutic value of this knowledge in the analyses of children, but it is not confined to these. I have been able to test the resulting conclusions in the analysis of adults and have found not only that their theoretical correctness was confirmed, but that their therapeutic importance was established.

V

The Dread of Woman

*Observations on a Specific Difference in the Dread Felt by
Men and by Women Respectively for the Opposite Sex*

By Karen Horney

In his ballad of *The Diver* Schiller tells how a squire leaps into a dangerous whirlpool in order to win a woman—at first
symbolized by a goblet. Horror-struck, he describes the perils
of the deep by which he is doomed to be engulfed:

Yet at length comes a lull o'er the mighty commotion,
As the whirlpool sucks into black smoothness the swell
Of the white-foaming breakers—and cleaves through the ocean
A path that seems winding in darkness to hell.
Round and round whirled the waves—deeper and deeper still driven,
Like a gorge through the mountainous main thunder-riven!

Happy they whom the rose-hues of daylight rejoice,
The air and the sky that to mortals are given!
May the horror below never more find a voice—
Nor man stretch too far the wide mercy of Heaven!
Never more—never more may he lift from the sight
The veil which is woven with Terror and Night!

Below at the foot of the precipice drear,
Spread the glowing, and purple, and pathless Obscure!
A silence of Horror that slept on the ear,
That the eye more appalled might the Horror endure!
Salamander—snake—dragon—vast reptiles that dwell
In the deep, coil'd about the grim jaws of their hell.

(Translation by Bulwer Lytton.)

The same idea is expressed, though far more pleasantly, in the "Song of the Fisherboy" in *Wilhelm Tell*:

> The clear smiling lake woo'd to bathe in its deep,
> A boy on its green shore had laid him to sleep;
> Then heard he a melody
> Flowing and soft,
> And sweet as when angels are singing aloft.
> And as thrilling with pleasure he wakes from his rest,
> The waters are murmuring over his breast;
> And a voice from the deep cries,
> "With me thou must go, I charm the young shepherd,
> I lure him below."
>
> (Translation by THEODORE MARTIN.)

Men have never tired of fashioning expressions for this experience: the violent force by which man feels himself drawn to the woman, and, side by side with his longing, the dread lest through her he might die and be undone. I will mention particularly the moving expression of this dread in Heine's poem of the legendary Lorelei, who sits high on the bank of the Rhine and ensnares the boatman with her beauty.

Here once more it is water (representing, like the other "elements," the primal element "woman") that swallows up the man who succumbs to a woman's enchantment. Ulysses had to bid his seamen bind him to the mast in order to escape the allurement and the danger of the sirens. The riddle of the Sphinx can be solved by few, and most of those who attempt it forfeit their lives. The royal palace in fairy tales is adorned with the heads of the suitors who have had the hardihood to try to solve the riddles of the king's beautiful daughter. The goddess Kali[1] dances on the corpses of slain men. Samson, whom no man could conquer, is robbed of his strength by Delilah. Judith beheads Holofernes after giving herself to him. Salome carries the head of John the Baptist on a charger. Witches are burnt because male priests fear the work of the devil in them. Wedekind's "Earth Spirit" destroys every man who succumbs to her charm, not because she is particularly evil, but simply because it is her nature to do so. The series of such instances is infinite: always, everywhere the man strives to rid himself of his dread of women

[1] See Daly's account in his article: "Hindumythologie und Kastrationskomplex," *Imago*, Bd. XIII, 1927.

by objectifying it: "It is not," he says, "that I dread her; it is
that she herself is malignant, capable of any crime, a beast of
prey, a vampire, a witch, insatiable in her desires. She is the very
personification of what is sinister." May not this be one of the
principal roots of the whole masculine impulse to creative work
—the never-ending conflict between the man's longing for the
woman and his dread of her?[2]

To primitive sensibilities the woman becomes doubly sinister
in the presence of the bloody manifestations of her womanhood.
Contact with her during menstruation is fatal[3]: men lose their
strength, the pastures wither away, the fisherman and the hunts-
man take nothing. Defloration involves the utmost danger to the
man. As Freud shows in "The Taboo of Virginity,"[4] it is the
husband in particular who dreads this act. In this work Freud
too objectifies this anxiety, contenting himself with a reference
to the castration-impulses which do actually occur in women.
There are two reasons why this is not an adequate explanation
of the phenomenon of the taboo itself. In the first place, women
do not so universally react to defloration with castration-impulses recognizable as such: these impulses are probably confined to women with a strongly developed masculine attitude.
And, secondly, even if defloration invariably aroused destructive impulses in the woman, we should still have to lay bare (as
we should do in every individual analysis) the urgent impulses
within the man himself which make him view the first—forcible
—penetration of the vagina as so perilous an undertaking; so
perilous, indeed, that it can be performed with impunity only
by a man of might or by a stranger who chooses to risk his life
or his manhood for a recompense.

Is it not really remarkable (we ask ourselves in amazement),
when one considers the overwhelming mass of this transparent
material, that so little recognition and attention are paid to the

[2] Sachs explains the impulse to artistic creation as the search for
companions in guilt. In this, I think, he is right, but he does not seem to
me to go deeply enough into the question, since his explanation is one-
sided and takes into account only part of the whole personality, namely,
the superego. (Sachs: *Gemeinsame Tagträume*, Internationaler Psychoanalytischer Verlag.)

[3] Compare Daly: "Der Menstruationscomplex," *Imago*, Bd. XIV, 1928;
and Winterstein: "Die Pubertätsriten der Mädchen und ihre Spuren im
Märchen," *Imago*, Bd. XIV, 1928.

[4] Freud: "The Taboo of Virginity" (1918), *Collected Papers*. Vol. IV.

fact of men's secret dread of women? It is almost more remarkable that women themselves have so long been able to overlook
it; I will discuss in detail elsewhere the reasons for their
attitude in this connection (i.e., their own anxiety and the im-
pairment of their self-respect). The man on his side has in the
first place very obvious strategic reasons for keeping his dread
quiet. But he also tries by every means to deny it even to himself. This is the purpose of the efforts to which we have alluded,
to "objectify" it in artistic and scientific creative work. We may
conjecture that even his glorification of women has its source
not only in the cravings of love, but also in his desire to give the
lie to his dread. A similar relief is, however, also sought and
found in the disparagement of women which men often display
ostentatiously in all their attitude. The attitude of love and
adoration signifies: "There is no need for me to dread a being
so wonderful, so beautiful, nay, so saintly"; that of disparagement implies: "It would be too ridiculous to dread a creature
who, if you take her all round, is such a poor thing."[5] This last
way of allaying his anxiety has a special advantage for the man:
it helps to support his masculine self-respect. The latter seems
to feel itself far worse threatened—far more threatened at its
very core—by the admission of a dread of women than by the
admission of dread of a man (the father). The reason why the
self-feeling of men is so peculiarly sensitive just in relation to
women can only be understood by reference to their early development, to which I shall return later.

In analysis this dread of women is revealed quite clearly. Male
homosexuality has for its basis, in common indeed with all the
other perversions, the desire to escape from the female genital,
or to deny its very existence. Freud has shown that this is a
fundamental trait in fetishism,[6] in particular; he believes it, however, to be based not on anxiety, but on a feeling of abhorrence
due to the absence of the penis in women. I think, however, that

[5] I well remember how surprised I was myself the first time I heard
the above ideas asserted—by a man—in the shape of a universal proposition. The speaker was Groddeck, who obviously felt that he was stating
something quite self-evident when he remarked in conversation: "Of
course men are afraid of women." In his writings Groddeck has repeatedly emphasized this fear.

[6] Freud: "Fetishism," *The International Journal of Psychoanalysis*, Vol.
IX, 1928.

even from his account we are absolutely forced to the conclusion that there is anxiety at work as well. What we actually see is dread of the vagina, thinly disguised under the abhorrence. Only *anxiety* is a strong motive to hold back from his goal a man whose libido is assuredly urging him on to union with the woman. But Freud's account fails to explain this anxiety. A boy's castration-anxiety in relation to his father is not an adequate reason for his dread of a being whom this punishment has already overtaken. Besides the dread of the father there must be further dread, the object of which is the woman or the female genital. Now this dread of the vagina itself appears unmistakably not only in homosexuals and perverts, but also in the dreams of every male analysand. All analysts are familiar with dreams of this sort and I need only give the merest outline of them: e.g., a motor-car is rushing along and suddenly falls into a pit and is dashed to pieces: or a boat is sailing in a narrow channel and is suddenly sucked into a whirlpool; there is a cellar with uncanny, blood-stained plants and animals, or one is climbing a chimney and is in danger of falling and being killed.

Dr. Baumeyer, of Dresden,[7] allows me to cite a series of experiments which rose out of a chance observation and which illustrates this dread of the vagina. The physician was playing ball with the children at a treatment center and, after a time, showed them that the ball had a slit in it. She pulled the edges of the slit apart and put her finger in, so that it was held fast by the ball. Of 28 boys whom she asked to do the same, only 6 did it without fear and 8 could not be induced to do it at all. Of 19 girls 9 put their fingers in without a trace of fear; the rest showed a slight uneasiness but none of them serious anxiety.

No doubt the dread of the vagina often conceals itself behind the dread of the father, which is also present; or, in the language of the unconscious, behind the dread of the penis in the woman's vagina.[8]

[7] The experiments were conducted by Frl. Dr. Hartung at a children's clinic in Dresden.

[8] Boehm, "Beiträge zur Psychologie der Homosexualität." *Internationale Zeitschrift für Psychoanalyse*, XI, 1925. Melanie Klein, "Early Stages of the Oedipus Conflict," *The International Journal of Psychoanalysis*, Vol. IX, 1928; "The Importance of Symbol-Formation in the Development of the Ego," *The International Journal of Psychoanalysis*, Vol. XI, 1930; "Infantile Anxiety-Situations Reflected in a Work of Art and in the Creative Impulse," *The International Journal of Psychoanalysis*, Vol. X, 1929, p. 436.

There are two reasons for this: in the first place, as I have already said, masculine self-regard suffers less in this way, and, secondly, the dread of the father is more actual and tangible, less uncanny in quality. We might compare the difference to that between the fear of a real enemy and of a ghost. The prominence given to the anxiety relating to the castrating father is therefore tendentious, as Groddeck has shown, for example, in the analysis of the thumb-sucker in *Struwwelpeter:* it is a man who cuts off the thumb, but it is the mother who utters the threat, and the instrument with which it is carried out—the scissors—is a female symbol.

From all this I think it probable that the masculine dread of the woman (the mother) or of the female genital is more deep-seated, weighs more heavily and is usually more energetically repressed than the dread of the man (father), and that the endeavor to find the penis in women represents first and foremost a convulsive attempt to deny the existence of the sinister female genital.

Is there any ontogenetic explanation of this anxiety? Or is it not rather (in human beings) an integral part of masculine existence and behavior? Is any light shed upon it by the state of lethargy—even the death—after mating which occurs frequently in male animals?[9] Are love and death more closely bound up with one another for the male than for the female, in whom sexual union potentially produces a new life? Does the man feel, side by side with his desire to conquer, a secret longing for extinction in the act of reunion with the woman (mother)? Is it perhaps this longing which underlies the "death-instinct"? And is it his will to live which reacts to it with anxiety?

If we endeavor to understand this anxiety in psychological and ontogenetic terms, we find ourselves rather at a loss if we take our stand on Freud's notion that what distinguishes infantile from adult sexuality is precisely that the vagina remains "undiscovered" for the child. According to that view, we cannot properly speak of genital primacy: we must rather term it a primacy of the phallus. Hence it would be better to describe the period of infantile genital organization as the "phallic phase."[10]

[9] Bergmann: *Muttergeist und Erkenntnisgeist.*

[10] Freud: "The Infantile Genital Organization of the Libido" (1923), *Collected Papers*, Vol. II.

The many recorded remarks of boys at that period of life leave no doubt of the correctness of the observations on which Freud's theory is based. But if we look more closely at the essential characteristics of this phase, we cannot help asking whether his description really sums up infantile genitality as such, in its specific manifestation, or applies only to a relatively later phase of it. Freud states that it is characteristic that the boy's interest is concentrated in a markedly narcissistic manner on his own penis: "The driving force which this male portion of his body will generate later at puberty expresses itself in childhood essentially as an impulsion to inquire into things—as sexual curiosity." A very important part is played by questions as to the existence and size of the phallus in other living beings.

But surely the essence of the phallic impulses proper, starting as they do from organ sensations, is a desire to *penetrate*. That these impulses do exist can hardly be doubted: they manifest themselves too plainly in children's games and in an analysis of little children. Again, it would be difficult to say what the boy's sexual wishes in relation to his mother really consisted in if not in these very impulses; or why the object of his masturbation-anxiety should be the father as the castrator, were it not that masturbation was largely the autoerotic expression of hetero-sexual phallic impulses.

In the "phallic phase" the boy's psychic orientation is predominantly narcissistic: hence the period in which his genital impulses are directed toward an object must be an earlier one. The possibility that they are not directed toward a female genital, of which he instinctively divines the existence, must certainly be considered. In dreams, both of earlier and later life, as well as in symptoms and particular modes of behavior, we find, it is true, representations of coitus which are oral, anal, or sadistic without specific localization. But we cannot take this as a proof of the primacy of corresponding impulses, for we are uncertain whether, or how far, these phenomena already express a displacement from the genital goal proper. At bottom all that they amount to is to show that a given individual is influenced by specific oral, anal or sadistic trends. Their evidential value is the less because these representations are always associated with certain effects directed against women, so that we cannot tell whether they may not be essentially the product or the expression of these effects. For instance, the tendency to debase women may express itself in anal representations of the female genital, while oral representations may express anxiety.

But, besides all this, there are various reasons why it seems to me improbable that the existence of a specific female opening should remain "undiscovered." On the one hand, of course, a boy will automatically conclude that everyone else is made like himself; but on the other hand his phallic impulses surely bid him instinctively to search for the appropriate opening in the female body—an opening, moreover, which he himself lacks, for the one sex always seeks in the other that which is complementary to it or of a nature different from its own. If we seriously accept Freud's dictum that the sexual theories formed by children are modeled on their own sexual constitution, it must surely mean in the present connection that the boy, urged on by his impulses to penetrate, pictures in fantasy a complementary female organ. And this is just what we should infer from all the material I quoted at the outset in connection with the masculine dread of the female genital.

It is not at all probable that this anxiety dates only from puberty. At the beginning of that period the anxiety manifests itself quite clearly, if we look behind the often very exiguous façade of boyish pride which conceals it. At puberty a boy's task is obviously not merely to free himself from his incestuous attachment to his mother, but, more generally, to master his dread of the whole female sex. His success is as a rule only gradual: first of all he turns his back on girls altogether, and only when his masculinity is fully awakened does it drive him over the threshold of anxiety. But we know that as a rule the conflicts of puberty do but revive, *mutatis mutandis,* conflicts belonging to the early ripening of infantile sexuality and that the course they take is often essentially a faithful copy of a series of earlier experiences. Moreover, the grotesque character of the anxiety, as we meet with it in the symbolism of dreams and literary productions, points unmistakably to the period of early infantile fantasy.

At puberty a normal boy has already acquired a conscious knowledge of the vagina, but what he fears in women is something uncanny, unfamiliar and mysterious. If the grown man continues to regard woman as the great mystery, in whom is a secret he cannot divine, this feeling of his can only relate ultimately to one thing in her: the mystery of motherhood. Everything else is merely the residue of his dread of this.

What is the origin of this anxiety? What are its characteristics? And what are the factors which cloud the boy's early relations with his mother?

In an article on female sexuality[11] Freud has pointed out the most obvious of these factors: it is the mother who first forbids instinctual activities, because it is she who tends the child in its babyhood. Secondly, the child evidently experiences sadistic impulses against its mother's body,[12] presumably connected with the rage evoked by her prohibitions, and according to the talion principle this anger has left behind a residue of anxiety. Finally —and this is perhaps the principal point—the specific fate of the genital impulses itself constitutes another such factor. The anatomical differences between the sexes lead to a totally different situation in girls and in boys, and really to understand both their anxiety and the diversity of their anxiety we must take into account first of all *the children's real situation* in the period of their early sexuality. The girl's nature as biologically conditioned gives her the desire to receive, to take into herself;[13] she feels or knows that her genital is too small for her father's penis and this makes her react to her own genital wishes with direct anxiety: she dreads that if her wishes were fulfilled, she herself or her genital would be destroyed.[14]

The boy, on the other hand, feels or instinctively judges that his penis is much too small for his mother's genital and reacts with the dread of his own inadequacy, of being rejected and derided. Thus he experiences anxiety which is located in quite a different quarter from the girl's: his original dread of women is not castration-anxiety at all, but a reaction to the menace to his self-respect.[15]

In order that there may be no misunderstanding let me emphasize that I believe these processes to take place purely

---

[11] *The International Journal of Psychoanalysis, ante,* p. 281.

[12] Compare the work of Melanie Klein, quoted above, to which I think insufficient attention has been paid.

[13] This is not to be equated with passivity.

[14] In another paper I will discuss the girl's situation more fully.

[15] I would refer here also to the points I raised in a paper entitled "Das Misstrauen zwischen den Geschlechtern," *Die psychoanalytische Bewegung,* 1930.

instinctively on a basis of organ sensations and the tensions of organic needs; in other words, I hold that these reactions would occur even if the girl had never seen her father's penis or the boy his mother's genital, and neither had any sort of intellectual knowledge of the existence of these genitalia.

Because of this reaction on the part of the boy, he is affected in another way and more severely by his frustration at the hands of his mother than is the girl by her experience with her father. A blow is struck at the libidinal impulses in either case. But the girl has a certain consolation in her frustration: she preserves her physical integrity; whereas the boy is hit in a second sensitive spot—his sense of genital inadequacy, which has presumably accompanied his libidinal desires from the beginning. If we assume that the most general reason for violent anger is the foiling of impulses which at the moment are of vital importance, it follows that the boy's frustration by his mother must arouse a twofold fury in him: first through the thrusting back of his libido upon itself and, secondly, through the wounding of his masculine self-regard. At the same time old resentment springing from pregenital frustrations is probably also made to flare up again. The result is that his phallic impulses to penetrate merge with his anger at frustration, and the impulses take on a sadistic tinge.

Here let me emphasize a point which is often insufficiently brought out in psychoanalytical literature, namely, that we have no reason to assume that these phallic impulses are naturally sadistic and that therefore it is inadmissible, in the absence of specific evidence in each case, to equate "male" with "sadistic," and on similar lines "female" with "masochistic." If the admixture of destructive impulses is really considerable, the mother's genital must, according to the talion principle, become an object of direct anxiety. Thus, if it is first made distasteful to him by its association with wounded self-regard, it will by a secondary process (by way of frustration-anger) become an object of castration-anxiety. And probably this is very generally reinforced when the boy observes traces of menstruation.

Very often this latter anxiety in its turn leaves a lasting mark on the man's attitude to women, as we learn from the examples already given at random from very different periods and races. But I do not think that it occurs regularly in all men in any considerable degree, and certainly it is not a *distinctive* characteristic of the man's relation to the other sex. Anxiety of this sort strongly resembles, *mutatis mutandis,* anxiety which we meet with in women. When in analysis we find it occurring in any noteworthy intensity, the subject is invariably a man whose whole attitude toward women has a markedly neurotic twist.

On the other hand I think that the anxiety connected with his self-respect leaves more or less distinct traces in every man and gives to his general attitude to women a particular stamp which either does not exist in women's attitude to men or, if it does, is acquired secondarily. In other words, it is no integral part of their feminine nature.

We can only grasp the general significance of this male attitude if we study more closely the development of the boy's infantile anxiety, his efforts to overcome it and the ways in which it manifests itself.

According to my experience the dread of being rejected and derided is a typical ingredient in the analysis of every man, no matter what his mentality or the structure of his neurosis. The analytic situation and the constant reserve of the woman analyst bring out this anxiety and sensitiveness more clearly than they appear in ordinary life, which gives men plenty of opportunity to escape from these feelings either by avoiding situations calculated to evoke them or by a process of overcompensation. The specific basis of this attitude is hard to detect because in analysis it is generally concealed by a feminine orientation, for the most part unconscious.[16]

To judge by my own experience, this latter orientation is no less common, though (for reasons which I will give) less blatant, than the masculine attitude in women. I do not propose to discuss its various sources here; I will only say that I conjecture that the early wound to his self-regard is probably one of the factors liable to disgust the boy with his male role.

His typical reaction to that wound and to the dread of his mother which follows from it is obviously to withdraw his libido from her and to concentrate it on himself and his genital. From the economic point of view this process is doubly advantageous: it enables him to escape from the distressing or anxiety-fraught situation which has developed between himself

---

[16] Compare Boehm, "The Femininity-Complex in Men," *The International Journal of Psychonanalysis,* Vol. XI, 1930.

and his mother, and it restores his masculine self-respect by reactively strengthening his phallic narcissism. The female genital no longer exists for him: the "undiscovered" vagina is a denied vagina. This stage of his development is fully identical with Freud's "phallic phase."

Accordingly, we must understand the enquiring attitude which dominates this phase and the specific nature of the boy's enquiries as expressing a retreat from the object and a narcissistically tinged anxiety which follows upon this.

His first reaction, then, is in the direction of a heightened phallic narcissism. The result is that to the wish to be a woman, which younger boys utter without embarrassment, he now reacts partly with renewed anxiety lest he should not be taken seriously and partly with castration-anxiety. Once we realize that masculine castration-anxiety is very largely the ego's response to the wish to be a woman, we shall not altogether share Freud's conviction that bisexuality manifests itself more clearly in the female than in the male.[17] We shall prefer to leave it an open question.

A feature of the phallic phase which Freud emphasizes shows up with special clearness the narcissistic scar left by the little boy's relation with his mother: "He behaves as if he had a dim idea that this member might be and should be larger."[18] We must amplify the observation by saying that this behavior begins, indeed, in the "phallic phase," but does not cease with it; on the contrary, it is displayed naïvely throughout boyhood and persists later as a deeply hidden anxiety about the size of the subject's penis or his potency, or else as a less concealed pride about them.

Now one of the exigencies of the biological differences between the sexes is this: that the man is actually obliged to go on proving his manhood to the woman. There is no analogous necessity for her: even if she is frigid, she can engage in sexual intercourse and conceive and bear a child. She performs her part by merely *being*, without any *doing*—a fact which has always filled men with admiration and resentment. The man on the other hand has to *do* something in order to fulfill himself. The ideal of "efficiency" is a typical masculine ideal.

[17] Freud, "Female Sexuality," *The International Journal of Psychoanalysis, ante,* p. 281.
[18] "The Infantile Genital Organization of the Libido," *Collected Papers,* Vol. II.

This is probably the fundamental reason why, when we analyze women who dread their masculine tendencies, we always find that they unconsciously regard ambition and achievement as attributes of the male, in spite of the great enlargement of women's sphere of activity in real life.

In sexual life itself we see how the simple craving of love which drives men to women is very often overshadowed by their overwhelming inner compulsion to prove their manhood again and again to themselves and others. A man of this type in its more extreme form has therefore one interest only: to conquer. His aim is to have "possessed" many women, and the most beautiful and most sought-after women. We find a remarkable mixture of this narcissistic overcompensation and of surviving anxiety in those men who, while wanting to make conquests, are very indignant with a woman who takes their intentions too seriously, or who cherish a lifelong gratitude to her if she spares them any further proof of their manhood.

Another way of averting the soreness of the narcissistic scar is by adopting the attitude described by Freud as the propensity to debase the love-object.[19] If a man does not desire any woman who is his equal or even his superior—may it not be that he is protecting his threatened self-regard in accordance with that most useful principle of "sour grapes"? From the prostitute or the woman of easy virtue one need fear no rejection, and no demands in the sexual, ethical or intellectual sphere: one can feel oneself the superior.[20]

This brings us to a third way, the most important and the most ominous in its cultural consequences: that of diminishing the self-respect of the woman. I think that I have shown that men's disparagement of women is based upon a definite psychic trend toward disparaging them—a tendency rooted in the man's psychic reactions to certain given biological facts, as might be expected of a mental attitude so widespread and so obstinately maintained. The view that women are infantile and emotional

[19] Freud. "Contributions to the Psychology of Love," *Collected Papers*, Vol. IV.

[20] This does not detract from the importance of the other forces which drive men to prostitutes and which have been described by Freud in his "Contributions to the Psychology of Love," *Collected Papers*, Vol. IV; and by Boehm in his "Beiträge zur Psychologie der Homosexualität," *Internationale Zeitschrift für Psychoanalyse*, Bd. VI, 1920 and Bd. VIII, 1922.

creatures and, as such, incapable of responsibility and independence is the work of the masculine tendency to lower their self-respect. When men justify such an attitude by pointing out that a very large number of women really do correspond to this description, we must consider whether this type of woman has not been cultivated by a systematic selection on the part of men. The important point is not that individual minds of greater or lesser caliber, from Aristotle to Moebius, have expended an astonishing amount of energy and intellectual capacity in proving the superiority of the masculine principle. What really counts is the fact that the ever precarious self-respect of the "average man" causes him over and over again to choose a feminine type which is infantile, non-maternal and hysterical, and by so doing to expose each new generation to the influence of such women.

VI

On Homosexuality and Gender Identity*

By Ralph R. Greenson

This contribution is based on the proposition that a study of gender identity will offer valuable insights into some of the special problems concerning the fate of the homosexuality in various types of patients. *Gender identity* refers to one's sense of being a member of a particular sex; it is expressed clinically in the awareness of being a man or a male in distinction to being a woman or a female. (The term was formulated in collaboration with Stoller, whose presentation deals with another aspect of this subject.) The starting point of this paper is the clinical finding that for most psychiatric patients in our society the appearance of homosexuality in their treatment stirs up a peculiar kind of dread (Freud, 1937, 1938). It is my contention that for these patients the awareness of homosexuality poses a threat to their gender identity. This seems to be true of neurotics, paranoid patients, and even some types of homosexuals, each of whom handle the problem differently. The only patients who seem to have no anxiety about their gender identity are the bisexuals and the typical overt homosexuals. I shall try to explain these differences.

The most obvious material comes from a curious finding in both male and female neurotics whenever homosexuality first

* Contribution to "Symposium on Homosexuality" presented at the International Psycho-Analytic Congress, Stockholm, July-August 1963.

enters the clinical picture. These patients react with a sense of dread and as a rule behave as though I had said: "You *are* a homosexual." Sometimes they actually misquote me as having said so, sometimes they express this statement as their own conclusion. At other times this is not verbally stated but can be reconstructed from their material. The notion "I am a homosexual" is perceived as an oppressive, earth-shaking revelation and leads to a sense of impending panic. If we pursue the analysis of the idea "I am a homosexual" the patient will describe his feeling of losing a component of his self, a cornerstone he had taken for granted, something central to his sense of "Who am I," his identity in terms of gender. One of my patients put it very succinctly when he said: "I feel as though you are going to say to me: 'I have news for you; you are neither a man nor a woman, you are a freak.'"

It is striking that the neurotic adult reacts as though the gender of his sexual object determines his own gender. He does not respond as do most overt homosexuals, who seem to proclaim: I am a man even though I have sexual relations with men or play the role of a woman.

At this point I want to present an unusual clinical example which will highlight some of these points and lead us even deeper into the problem.[1]

Clinical Example

A woman of feminine appearance in her late thirties presented herself in our research project, having been sent to us by the Department of Gynecology because a fistula developed between her rectum and an artificial vagina. Her story can be condensed as follows: The patient was born a boy and until puberty felt like a boy. Anatomically he had been a completely normal male. Then at age 19 he became sexually and romantically attracted to a man. This aroused such great anxiety that he could not yield to the instinctual temptation. Instead he was deter-

[1] This material was observed in a research project on "Gender Identity" now in progress at the University of California School of Medicine at Los Angeles. Dr. R. Stoller and Daniel Greenson provided many of the clinical data and N. Leites contributed some of the formulations. But it should be noted that the patients were not in analysis, and the material obtained was from a series of face-to-face interviews, psychological tests, social case-work, etc.

mined to find out whether he was a man or not—and volunteered in the paratroopers. He successfully endured the invasions of Sicily and Italy, was wounded in action, and received many decorations. All in all he completed four years of combat duty as a thoroughly competent paratrooper in World War II. After the war, the patient realized he had proved nothing—he had felt lonely and an outsider among the men. However, the prospect of sexual relations with a man was still abhorrent and frightening to him. This would be homosexuality, and the patient felt that this was both impossibly repulsive and also some vague kind of overwhelming threat. At this point he became possessed by the idea that he was "really" a woman. He then learned of operations being performed in one of the Scandinavian countries which would make for a surgical change in gender. He went to Scandinavia and he had his penis, testes, and scrotum removed. After he returned to the United States, he changed his name to a woman's name, dressed as a woman, regularly took estrogen injections, and in this state was able to embark on sexual relationships with men.

After the patient began a serious love affair with a man, he changed his gender on his birth certificate, married, adopted a baby girl, and then had the first of two operations for the purpose of building an artificial vagina in the perineal space. This was mainly for her husband's pleasure since the patient's sexuality was limited to cuddling and other aspects of skin eroticism. When the patient appeared at our research clinic, she looked remarkably feminine, the sparse facial hair barely visible under her makeup. She had been legally married some five years, had an adopted baby of four years, was in the process of adopting a second child, wore women's clothes apparently naturally, talked and moved as a typical woman, etc. We could not find any clearcut signs of psychosis, borderline state, or conspicuously severe neurosis in our investigations.

The "trans-sexual" paratrooper had a dread of homosexuality similar to that of neurotic adults. His attitude toward his sexual object was also comparable in that it became decisive for his gender identity. He seems to have reacted according to the formula: If I love a man then I must be a woman. Instead of repressing these ideas he surgically "suppressed" them; he changed his anatomical gender. For this man there was something more precious than genital organs, and even his gender.

He had to achieve that dissimilarity between gender of sex object and his own gender as it exists in heterosexuals. To do so he had to alter his body in order to support his belief concerning his gender. In a way the clinical picture can be understood as a circumscribed, well-organized delusional system which was successful in so far as it made it possible for the patient to lead an apparently happy life as a woman (Goldberg, A.; Wexler, M.; Leites, N.).

How different all this is from the situation in the usual overt homosexual. For the pervert, neither the gender of the sexual object nor the enactment of fantasies of being of a different sex influences his gender identity. He knows he is a man even though he may play different roles. It seems that for him his anatomy is the determining factor. The same is true for bisexuals.

In order to begin to understand these different outcomes, it is necessary to formulate some ideas about the development of identity and in particular the development of gender identity in the child. I believe we can speculate as follows:

At first the infant cannot distinguish between self and external world. As perception and thinking develop this step is made; the child can differentiate between me and not-me. This we may call the beginning of the core identity. But this has no sexual or gender connotation until the child becomes aware of the differences between the sexes. This seems to be brought about by three factors: (a) awareness of the anatomical and physiological structures in himself; this would include sexual sensations and awareness of objects with different genitals, (b) the parental and social figures which label him in accordance with his sexual structures and others in accordance with theirs, (c) a biological force which seems to be present from birth and which can be decisive in pushing a child in the direction of a particular gender. At any rate, the awareness of the existence of two sexes comes about. Thus, "me-ness" becomes connected with gender—I am a boy, etc. Gender has become attached to the core identity: I, John—"this person with this body, this penis, different from girls, I am a boy, etc." In the late phallic phase the gender identity becomes attached to and includes the impulse and fantasy: "I, John, a boy, like to do sexual things to those 'different' creatures, to girls."

I am distinguishing three different phases:

(i) I am me, John;
(ii) I am me, John, a boy; and
(iii) I am me, John, a boy, which means that I like to do sexual things with girls.

This is just a bare and primitive outline of what I imagine takes place in the development of gender identity.

It would seem that in each phase of development different elements are essential for the preservation of one's identity. Later pathological formations seem to indicate this. For example, the neurotic adult seems to need some awareness of sexual attraction to a person of the opposite sex in order to maintain his gender identity. He will attempt to ward off his hostility or loathing which might make him impotent and less masculine, but nevertheless he still feels he is a man. However, sexual excitement toward a man would throw him in a panic, his gender identity would be in jeopardy. This seems to be true of so-called normal people in our society.

This need to maintain a diversity of gender between love object and self (as a condition of maintaining one's own gender) seems to be true of the paranoid patient as well. He seems to project his homosexuality onto some other object, in order to deny that the homosexual impulses are his own. These patients seem to have reached phase three and in attempting to maintain the diversity of gender between self and object sacrifice a part of their self which is perceived as external voices, hallucinations, etc. Frank homosexual activity in paranoids is, I believe, extremely rare. Furthermore, confused and disoriented as such psychotic patients may be, they usually remain true to their gender identity. Even in their delusions, men may believe themselves to be Napoleon, or Caesar, or Hitler, but rarely, if ever, Cleopatra, etc. Schreber felt he would be cured *if* he were transformed into a woman; but he never felt he achieved this and in the acute stage of his illness he was plagued by projections of his homosexuality (Freud, 1911). The trans-sexual paratrooper seemed to accomplish what Schreber hoped for and failed. He did transform himself into a woman and he did seem to obtain some form of "cure."

The only adults who seem to be able to dispense with this diversity in gender between self and the love object are the homosexual perverts. I imagine some of them remain fixated to phase two and thus their sense of gender identity is independent of the sex of the love object. These would be the truly bisexual people who can enjoy sex with both genders. They rarely if ever come for treatment. The homosexual most often described in the psychoanalytic literature is usually strictly homosexual. He too is bound to a unit consisting of gender of object and gender identity, but differently. I would speculate that such persons did reach phase three but were severely traumatized at this level (cf. Gillespie, 1956; Socarides 1963; and Wiedeman 1962). As a consequence they became phobic about the heterosexual object and became antiheterosexual. Then they regressed to the level of phase two but could not become bisexual because of their phobia about heterosexuality. This results in a rigid homosexuality. This is the type of homosexual we see most frequently in psychoanalytic practice.

I am well aware that all these speculations leave many questions unanswered which I hope future investigations will clarify. In 1905, in the *Three Essays*, Freud demonstrated the relative separateness of the triad: instinctual zone, sexual activity, and sexual object. The present contribution adds another element for consideration in sexual activity. Not only do we ask what part of the body is doing what to whom, but who am I who is doing this.

REFERENCES

FENICHEL, H. Personal Communication.

FREUD, S. (1905). *Three Essays on the Theory of Sexuality*, S.E., Vol. 7.

——— (1911). "Psychoanalytic Notes on an Autobiographical Account of a Case of Paranoia." S.E., Vol. 12.

——— (1937). "Analysis Terminable and Interminable." S.E., Vol. 23.

——— (1940). "An Outline of Psychoanalysis." *Int. J. Psycho-Anal.*, Vol. 21.

GILLESPIE, W. (1956). "The General Theory of Sexual Perversions." *Int. J. Psycho-Anal.*, Vol. 37.

GOLDBERG, A. Personal Communication.

GREENSON, D. Personal Communication.

LEITES, N. Personal Communication.

SOCARIDES, C. (1963). "The Historical Development of Theoretical and Clinical Concepts of Overt Female Homosexuality." *J. Amer. Psychoanal. Assoc.* Vol. 2.

WEXLER, M. Personal Communication.

WIEDMAN, C. (1962). "Survey of Psychoanalytic Literature on Overt and Male Homosexuality." *J. Amer. Psychoanal. Assoc.*, Vol. 10.

VII

The Role of Narcissism in the Emergence and Maintenance of a Primary Identity*

By Heinz Lichtenstein

Few concepts are as pivotal in psychoanalytic theory as the concept of narcissism. It serves simultaneously as the conceptual support for a new departure in the libido theory, and for the study of the development of object relations, with far-reaching consequences for the clinical approach to the psychoneuroses and the psychoses. In addition, it is the anchor for the new ego psychology, and, last but not least, on it rests, as a basis, the structural reformulation of metapsychology. It is not surprising therefore that a concept which must support such a multitude of theoretical edifices is at once indispensable and yet exposed to an extraordinary degree of "conceptual stress." In this sense narcissism can still be spoken of, as Jones (1955) did, as a "disturbing" concept. As a consequence, there have been numerous attempts to redefine it, make it handier by eliminating some of its original, Freudian connotations, replace some of its uses with new, more specific terms, etc. (Balint, 1960; Bing et al., 1959; Jacobson, 1954; Kaywin, 1957).

This paper endeavors to contribute to these efforts at obtaining a clearer view of what is implied in the concept of narcissism. It hopes to accomplish this result, however, by a somewhat different approach to the problem. This approach consists of the

* Presented at Scientific Meeting of Boston Psychoanalytic Society and Institute, Inc., 21 April, 1962.

somewhat paradoxically sounding attempt to differentiate between a variety of psychological phenomena that are all condensed in the one concept of narcissism, and simultaneously to
pay close attention to the underlying truth which justifies
Freud's insistence on uniting all the phenomena under one
single concept. To make such an approach possible, I shall take
the liberty of dealing with narcissism not so much as an abstract
concept, but as a kind of ideogram, i.e., a pictorial symbol or a
"word in its visual, not in its auditory, form, the mere tracing of
which evokes the whole group of ideas or notions that it con-
notes" (Etiemble, 1954). It is, I believe, no coincidence that in
Freud's treatment of narcissism visual images abound. One of
these is, of course, the mirror; another, the amoeba and its
pseudopodia (Jones, 1955). I believe it is justifiable to add a
third visual image, although it does not occur in the context of
any discussion of the concept of narcissism. I am referring here
to Freud's (1911) use of the bird's egg as a model of a closed
psychological system. Freud says: "A neat example of a psychical
system shut off from the stimuli of the external world and able
to satisfy even its nutritional requirements autistically . . . is
afforded by a bird's egg with its food supply enclosed in its
shell; for it, the care provided by its mother is limited to the
provision of warmth." The closest approach to the shell-enclosed
bird's egg in human psychology would be the condition of the
embryo during the intra-uterine phase and that of the individual
during sleep. To both of these Freud refers specifically as
narcissistic states, as in the passage in the *Introductory Lectures*
where he says that "The likeness we see in the condition which
the sleeper conjures up again every night to the blissful isolation of the intra-uterine existence is thus confirmed and amplified
in its mental aspects. In the sleeper the primal state of the
libido-distribution is again reproduced, that of absolute narcissism, in which libido and ego-interests dwell together still, united
and indistinguishable in the self-sufficient self" (1917).

I believe that it is helpful to be aware of the analogy between
these models of narcissistic states and the reference to the bird's
egg. Not only does Freud's use of the bird's egg as a model of a
closed psychic system bring to our mind Freud's nearness to
embryological thinking, but it also illuminates one of the conceptual dilemmas surrounding narcissism. Defining this dilemma
as a psychological version of the old problem concerning the

priority of the chicken or the egg is intended as more than a mere manner of speaking. In this case the question takes the form: What is first, object-cathexis or ego-cathexis? These questions are usually formulated in terms of primary narcissism versus primary love. Primary narcissism implies that in the earliest stages of development no objects are cathected and all libidinal cathexis rests in the ego. This theory, as proposed by Freud, has been criticized because of certain logical contradictions. At this early stage, the argument goes, there is no ego that could be cathected, consequently we should relinquish the concept of primary narcissism. "Primary narcissism might be thought of as the primary state of energy distribution not truly narcissistic, since no sufficient ego structure exists for cathexis of a self-representation. The energy in this primary state seems much more of a physiological nature." (Bing *et al.*, 1959.) Jacobson's (1954) reasoning also implies that the concept of primary narcissism in the sense in which Freud applied it is not compatible with our present concepts of ego-development. In this view, the ego must first develop before there can be any object-cathexis.

In contrast to this position, Balint (1960) "makes the assumption that the cathexis of its environment by the foetus must be very intense." For Balint such a primary cathexis does not necessarily imply a true primary object-cathexis. "This environment . . . is probably undifferentiated; on the one hand, there are as yet no objects in it; on the other hand it has hardly any structure, in particular no sharp boundaries toward the individual." Thus Balint can postulate that the child has a primary love relation to the mother which then becomes the condition under which the ego can develop. For the ego psychologist this view is as self-contradictory as for Balint is the concept of primary narcissism. Kanzer (1961), obviously referring to Balint's conceptualizations, states that "in his later works Freud indicated with sufficient clarity the need for distinctions between objects and their psychic representatives, so that it should not be possible today to speak of any 'primary object love' that is not filtered through the perceiving apparatus of the ego." Behind this logical dilemma we can easily recognize the problems inherent in the concept of *development* that find their expression in that paradox about the chicken and the egg. Developmental theory demands that everything living originate from another living organism. Consequently if we know that the presence of a primordial cell is required to give rise to new life, it is logically necessary to assume the previous existence of this primordial cell. On the other hand, we also know that such primordial cells, like the egg, can develop only in the organism of a living system. Consequently both statements, that the chicken must be first or that the egg must be first, are equally the consequences of developmental logic.

The extent to which the genetic approach to psychic phenomena has been influenced by theories developed from embryological experiments has recently been re-emphasized by Spitz (1959). Spitz distinguishes between congenital equipment, maturation, psychological development, and biological development. While there are obvious differences between the concept of biological development as used by embryologists and the psychoanalytic concept of psychological development, all these concepts have one idea in common: that of a progressive process of change and growth which leads from a very simple, almost unstructured primary configuration to a very complex, highly individualized, and highly structured end-condition that we equate with the idea of maturity. The whole process is *irreversible* in the sense that any kind of backward development would be implying some form of disintegration of the organized structure which had been achieved by the developmental process. I believe that it is this concept of development, with some modifications, that is implied in the genetic approach of psychoanalysis.

With the introduction of the concept of narcissism, however, Freud introduced an altogether different concept of development: one which permits the notion of reversibility of the developmental process. This reversibility is from now on understood as an essential aspect of psychological development. It may *sometimes* be equivalent to regression in the sense of disintegration, but not always, as Freud's frequent reference to the phenomenon of sleep indicates. Ernst Kris (1936) recognized this implied developmental reversibility when he spoke of regression in the service of the ego. It is my belief that Freud's insistence on distinguishing between a primary and a secondary narcissism is due to his need of a concept that implied the dimension of developmental reversibility. The concept of narcissism introduced a developmental concept incompatible with earlier concepts borrowed from embryology, symbolized by the image of the bird's egg. This new concept of development required a new image, and Freud found this new image in his famous simile of the amoeba. As the amoeba can send forth pseudopodia to external objects and then retract them again, in a similar manner libido can be cathected to objects and be again withdrawn. Under certain conditions this may be a pathological process, but it has a normal aspect too. Thus Freud envisages a rhythm of libidinal object cathexes and ego cathexes: "All through the subject's life his ego remains the great reservoir of his libido, from which object-cathexes are sent out and into which the libido can stream back again from the objects. Thus narcissistic libido is constantly being transformed into object-libido, and *vice versa*" (1925). In the *New Introductory Lectures* Freud states: "We must understand that the ego is always the main reservoir of libido, from which libidinal cathexes of objects proceed, and into which they return again, while the greater part of this libido remains perpetually in the ego. There is therefore a constant transformation of ego-libido into object-libido."

I do not agree with those, such as Kanzer (1961), who look upon the simile of the amoeba essentially as an abstraction to describe libidinal forces in a strictly mechanistic and quantitative manner. While it is true that Freud repeatedly refers to the ego as a reservoir of narcissistic libido, I believe that the central concept illustrated by the amoeba is that of constant libido transformation throughout life. This assumption of a back-and-forth movement requires an entirely different concept of development as applied to psychic phenomena. I have suggested the analogy of thematic development, borrowed from musical theory. A musical theme is developed as it undergoes variations. But the variations may revert to the original, undeveloped theme without destroying the structure of the composition. We could refer to the musical theme as a primary configuration and consider its variations as secondary elaborations. If narcissism implies a thematic configuration, it would then be necessary to juxtapose a primary configuration to secondary transformations, or, as we are accustomed to say, developments. Since I am aware that this musical analogy has its limits, I shall later on try to replace it with a more abstract formulation of this different concept of development.

First, however, I want to raise the question whether there is any clinical evidence that the concept of narcissism implies the emergence, in Freud's thinking, of new phenomena demanding a new approach to the problem of psychic development. An indirect evidence for such an assumption I see in the fact that Freud gave the new concept that he was introducing into analytic theory the name narcissism. Freud (1914) claims that he simply adopted the terminology of P. Näcke, who had described under this name a perversion consisting of the use of the own body as the only sexual object. In the *New Introductory Lectures* Freud (1932) puts it somewhat differently, however, when he states: "We have borrowed the name of *narcissism* from the Greek legend." I believe that the implications of the Greek myth must have been significant enough to Freud to move him to choose this particular term. It appears to me striking that in many contributions to the theory of narcissism it is customary to speak of Narcissus as a youth who died after falling in love with himself. This, however, is not what the story of Narcissus claims. Narcissus, as we all know, fell in love with his mirror image in a pond. There is, of course, a considerable difference between being in love with oneself and being in love with one's mirror image, as has been noted by Greenacre, Elkisch, and others. The image in the mirror is not real in the same sense in which the ego or the self are real. Somebody who is in love with his mirror image loves a picture or a phantom which he can never possess and reach. This inability ever to reach the object of his love or even touch it was, according to the Greek myth, the cause of Narcissus' death. If the phenomenon of narcissism refers to the love of one's mirror image, it seems important to deal with the psychological meaning of the mirror and mirror images. The mirror introduces a *third* element between the lover and his object; What, or who, is symbolically represented by the mirror? Finally, he who looks into a mirror does not see only himself. A mirror reflects a great many more things than the person who looks into the mirror. The mirror includes the room, and possibly other persons—in short, a part of the world in which the individual exists. Someone who sees in the mirror nothing but himself has apparently a very special kind of looking that suppresses everything else except his own picture in the mirror.

These are only some of the implications that enter into a concept derived from the myth of Narcissus. I believe it is impossible

to rid narcissism of the mirror hidden in the concept. I derive
support for this belief from the fact that only five years after
Freud's paper on narcissism, in 1919, Géza Róheim published a
volume entitled *Spiegelzauber* (Mirror magic). In this work he
examines in great detail everything that has been reported about
customs and rituals involving the mirror. Róheim aims to show
that the concept of narcissism, as Freud has just introduced it,
could explain the immensely varied and complex mirror rituals,
mirror tabus, mirror superstitions that exist apparently all over
the world. It is, however, difficult to suppress the feeling that
Róheim was keenly aware that mirror magic also contributed
something to our understanding of narcissism. This seems implied in the motto given to the book, a quotation from one of
the Upanishads, which reads as follows: "The Self, indeed, one
must see, one must hear, one must understand, one must reflect
upon; indeed he who has seen the Self, has heard the Self, has
understood and recognized the Self, to him the whole universe
will be known." Does this motto not appear to contradict the
psychoanalytic notion that narcissism, the libidinal involvement
with the self, destroys the capacity to relate to the world?
Róheim does not see any contradiction, perhaps because he
paid so much attention to the meaning of the mirror and its
psychological implications. I must confine myself to listing the
contents of Róheim's book to give an approximate idea of the
richness and ramifications of mirror rituals and customs. Róheim
first discusses the relationship of child and mirror, in both negative and positive rituals. He goes on to describe the role of the
mirror as a means of predicting the future. Another chapter
discusses the magic powers given to kings and rulers by means
of the mirror. Róheim then gives an extensive description of the
many forms of love magic that involve the use of a mirror. To
give one example of such magic: in certain rituals the mirror
enables the girl to see her future husband. Róheim discusses,
furthermore, tabus concerning the use of the mirror; superstitions with regard to the broken mirror; the custom of covering
mirrors at certain occasions. And in the last chapter he deals
with the equating of the heavenly bodies, particularly the sun,
with the mirror. This mere listing of the themes of Róheim's
book on mirror magic confirms Elkisch's assertion that "whenever we deal with the mirror phenomenon we are dealing with
something enigmatic, uncanny, with a thing that has been made

the screen for man's projections of the mysterious and the uncanny" (Elkisch, 1957.)

Elkisch points out that, aside from the role of the mirror in
mystical religion, folklore, fairy tale, and myth, poets and writers
of all times "have used the mirror symbolically or allegorically
in various meaningful ways." She sees the reason for this wide
use of the mirror as a symbol of the mysterious and the uncanny
in the fact that it appears to reflect man's soul or inner self,
making thus exactly the same point as is implied by Róheim's
motto to his book. According to Elkisch, the mirror may either
refer to the possibility of man's losing his self or his soul, and
thus become a symbol of death, or it may become a means of
retrieving the lost self. For this latter reason, Elkisch believes the
mirror is "so fascinating to psychotic patients." "The very activity
of mirroring whereby, according to animistic thinking, one loses
his soul, (appeared) in . . . psychotic patients as an intriguing
attempt to rescue the lost. . . . Each of (my) patients was gaz-
ing at his image as if through such mirroring he might restore
his self-identity." Similar conclusions have been reached by
M. L. Miller (1948) through the analysis of mirror dreams,
which have also been investigated by Kaywin (1957) and
Eisnitz (1961).

Greenacre (1958), discussing the early physical determinants
in the development of the sense of identity, devotes a lengthy
discussion to the relationship between confusion of sexual
identity in twins or pseudotwins of the opposite sex and the
Narcissus myth. For Greenacre the various versions of the myth,
and the role in it of the nymph Echo, refer to the bisexual
identification and the confusion of identity in the development
of twins. "Such is the beautiful condensation of the myth that it
emphasizes also the two-facedness of identity—not only the contrast with the opposite, but also the need to look at the self-
image as though from the outside, apparent in the repetition of
Echo and the reflection of Narcissus."

I believe that these examples from psychoanalytic literature
suffice to support the conclusion that the concept of narcissism
has suggested to many authors problems transcending the issues
of ego-cathexis versus object-cathexis. The mirror and the act of
mirroring introduce problems of the emergence of a primary
identity, of identity confusion, of loss of identity, and of identity
maintenance as well. I believe that the concept of narcissism

compels us to investigate the relationship between the experience of mirroring and the emergence of a primary identity on the one hand, and the relationship of such a primary identity to the development of the ego on the other hand.

Rollman-Branch (1960), in an interesting study, examines the question of primary object need. Her extensive studies of the ethological and animal-experimental literature lead her to the conclusion that there may be some human need which could be compared to what in animals is described as the need for companionship, a need apparently independent of feeding. "If the critical period of form attachment to an object passes unused, a fear and flight reaction sets in (in animals)." Rollman-Branch compares this animal "attachment behavior" to certain observations of infants. "Infants need a certain . . . amount of human contact aside from the satisfaction of their physical needs. Deficiency in this contact with mother or mother substitute around the age of six months may lead to marasmus and death."

In my paper "Identity and Sexuality" (1961) the existence of something akin to primary object need as described by Rollman-Branch was proposed. I spoke of the phenomenon as a mirroring experience. I was referring to the libidinal cathexis of the mother with regard to the child which I saw as necessary for the infant's survival and further development. I followed the terminology of Elkisch (1957), Greenacre (1958), Mahler (1958) and others in emphasizing the mirroring quality of the sensory responsiveness on the part of the infant to the mother's libidinal attachment. This mirroring cannot, of course, be understood in terms of any visual perception, but a reflection through touch, smell, and other primitive sensations. What is dimly emerging in this mirror is, at least in the beginning, not a primary love object, but the outlines of the child's own image as reflected by the mother's unconscious needs with regard to the child. Since man has no innate *behavioral* adaptedness to his environment, he can be human in infinite ways. It is, according to this theory, the specific unconscious need of the mother that actualizes out of these infinite potentialities one way of being, in the child, namely being the child for this particular mother, responding to her unique and individual needs. Thus, I suggested that in this first, archaic mirroring experience of the child a primary identity emerges which may be called narcissistic. This primary identity is not as yet a sense of identity, for that presupposes consciousness. It is thought of rather as a primary organizational principle without which the process of developmental differentiation could not begin.

Perhaps this first basic orientation may be described as a psychological version of the tropism of primitive biological systems. Insofar as it is understood as an organizational principle making possible the process of psychological development proper, the primary identity of the child is comparable to the concept of organizers of the psyche in the terminology of Spitz (1959). Spitz assumes that in the earliest stage of non-differentiation the infant is not capable of differentiating between incoming stimuli. This is certainly true if compared to the stage where the child is capable of responding with the smiling response, which is an indicator, as Spitz has shown, of a perception of a gestalt. But in order to arrive at the smiling response, must we not postulate that the libidinal stimuli emanating from the mother have a specific, different effect from other stimuli on the child? I am inclined to assume such a specific effect in view of the lack of instinctual direction in the human infant. In the human organism this turning toward the source of libidinal stimuli provides the only direction, a direction which must exert an organizing effect on all later development.

I have found some confirmation and support for this view in the work of Spiegel, particularly in his recent paper "The Self, the Sense of Self and Perception" (1959). From this very rich study I shall select a few propositions which seem to me to have an important bearing on the question of the emergence of a primary identity and ego development on the one hand, and the relationship of narcissism and primary identity on the other. Spiegel investigates patients who suffer from disturbances in the feeling of personal identity and of reality of one's own person. He re-examines psychoanalytic concepts of the self. He states that "it may be advisable to stress the basic distinction between the self just described and self-feeling. Self-feeling is an ultimate, not further describable clinical fact, but the self is *not a clinical* fact in the same sense that self-feeling is. It is a conceptualization or a construct which we invoke to clarify clinical phenomena, just as we use the constructs of the ego, superego, id, and defense mechanisms for the same purpose. But while the distinction between clinical fact and construct is usually maintained in these examples, in the area we are now interested in self and self-feeling are treated as one." Spiegel attributes to the self a biological function similar to that of the frame of reference for visual perception. Quoting the gestalt psychologist Koffka (1935), Spiegel gives the following example of the relationship of the frame of reference to perception: "If a train goes up a steep mountain, the trees and telephone poles will appear as oblique—not vertical. . . . But after we put our head out of the window the trees will soon appear vertical. In the first instance we accepted the car window as the source of our cues for horizontality and verticality. Therefore the tree had to appear as if it were oblique against the assumedly vertical car window frame. Once we put our head out of the window the tree appears vertical against the true verticality of the external world." Spiegel continues: "I would extend this concept of the frame of reference . . . to include what Freud calls 'innere Wahrnehmung' (internal perception). The orderly perception of these internal states requires a frame of reference that possesses a continuity in time. I believe it may prove profitable to consider the self . . . as a frame of reference or zero point to which representation of specific mental and physical states are referred, against which they are perceived and judged." Summarizing, Spiegel: "The operational significance of the concept 'self' is its function as framework." He proposes that "perceptions having to do with self-feeling result from the ego's relating of a single or small number of self-representations to the self considered as framework." Disturbances in the development of the self as a framework have, in Spiegel's view, a special relevance for those patients with a chronically shaky sense of personal identity. Alterations in the sense of personal identity can be explained, he thinks, by a rapid oscillation between self-representation and object-feeling: "For example, the genital is an aspect of the self that frequently receives the greatest cathexis. Its representation in states of sexual excitement is consequently more vulnerable to the oscillation just described and therefore tends to become a source of alterations in self-feeling, as . . . in orgasm, an extreme example of altered self-feeling."

It is very difficult to condense the very closely reasoned arguments of Spiegel without making them appear obscure. I have been trying to bring into focus two important points made by him: First, before there can be any kind of *sense* of self there has to be a framework, a zero point which must precede all other mental developments. This framework of zero point Spiegel calls the self. For reasons which I cannot here enumerate, I prefer to call it a primary identity. Secondly, according to Spiegel, there exists a close connection between the constancy of this frame of reference and sexuality. He sees sexuality as simultaneously contributing to intense self-feeling and also threatening it by what he calls oscillation. I believe that his work supports the view, that the emergence of an organizing principle has to precede psychological development. This framework or organizing principle has a close and demonstrable relationship to the development of the sense of personal identity.

Spiegel's postulate of a close correlation between sexuality and the constancy of self-representation lends support to my proposition that the outlines of a primary identity become delineated through the processes stimulated by the maternal libidinal cathexis to the child. The child, while not capable of perceiving the maternal object or of possessing a sense of self or of identity, experiences its existence as reflected by the libidinal cathexis of the mother. The mother, in contrast to the non-human environment, reflects back to the child a configuration of its own presence. I have suggested (1961) that this primary identity has the form of an identity theme, i.e., the specific reflection received from the mother conveys to the child a primary identity defined as instrumentality in relation to the mother. This thematic identity will be "developed" in the course of life as an infinite variety of identity transformations, as a simple musical theme is developed into a symphony. This development is reversible, so that we are entitled to speak of a primary and a secondary method of identity maintenance. The primary identity is always based on a mirroring experience. It does not enable the individual truly to cathect an object. Instead, it uses the object as a mirror in which to reflect the outlines of his primary identity. Since this primary method of identity maintenance originated during a phase when there was no differentiation between the subject and the object, this narcissistic libidinous mirroring reinforces the identity delineation through magnification and reduplication (echo). Seeing the reflection of one's own figure on a cloudbank under certain conditions of lighting while climbing a mountain makes one's person seem like a giant shadowy configuration which mirrors every move. This type of mirroring is a well-known form of a narcissistic object relation in which the object serves as a mirror for a faltering or undeveloped identity. As Erikson (1959) has said "For where an assured sense of identity is missing, even friendship and affairs become desperate attempts at delineating the fuzzy outline of identity by mutual narcissistic mirroring." We can see here the narcissistic omnipotence as a result of the pattern of identity maintenance through mirroring in the object.

But a different form of identity maintenance develops when the pure reflective mirroring experience is replaced by an increasing significance of eliciting a corresponding *action*, thus replacing mirroring by a pattern of *acting* and *reacting* to one another. Only now can we speak of a *sense* of identity maintained by the capacity to select types of actions which will bring a corresponding reaction from the other. This form of identity maintenance implies an ever-extending capacity to elicit reactions to one's own *action* in an ever-widening social group. But as we leave the early group of love objects, people no longer react to our individuality, but to the particular function we may represent for them. Thus the danger arises that instead of *maintaining* a sense of identity the reaction to a *depersonalized* social role may empty the sense of identity and create the danger of alienation. Under such circumstances a return to the earlier, mirroring experiences will again become necessary. Such mirroring experiences will most likely be intensely libidinal and narcissistic, leading even to a temporary object loss. But in such experiences the identity theme of the individual will be reinforced, so that in the normal person he can again return to the more adult pattern of acting and expecting supporting reaction from the others. Such fluctuation from narcissistic mirroring of one's own identity in the object to rediscovery of the other as a partner in a configuration of mutual interaction is the phenomenon to which Freud refers when he speaks of the fact that there is a constant transformation of ego libido into object libido and *vice versa*. It may be more precise today to speak of rhythmic changes in the pattern of identity maintenance. In the adult such return to the primary identity maintenance by mirroring may sometimes indicate regressive phenomena, at other times it may indicate a second birth in the sense in which Erikson (1958), following William James, has used this term.

Here we return to the problems implied in the concept of psychological development. At the beginning of this paper I suggested that the imagery of narcissism, such as the amoeba and the mirror, imply a new concept of development, different from the developmental processes which we usually conceptualize as progressive and irreversible. I shall now attempt to define this concept of development by borrowing from mathematics (Keyser, 1922) the concept of transformation and invariant. I would then describe the concept of a primary identity as an invariant the transformations of which we could call development. Not being a mathematician, I cannot be sure whether this application of the concept of transformation and invariant is appropriate for problems of psychological development. What I want to emphasize is the fact that psychological development seems to require the postulation of an invariant, to which all transformations must be related. Here I find myself before problems whose appropriate conceptualization must be left to future investigation.

Let me then summarize the propositions of this paper. The introduction of the concept of narcissism was an attempt on the part of Freud to follow the analogy of embryological thinking consistently, leading to the concept of a closed psychic system comparable to a bird's egg. But the concept of narcissism became a kind of catalyst that opened up entirely new theoretical horizons. These are implicit in the imagery of the amoeba as well as in the mirror of Narcissus. They introduce problems of human identity and indicate their relationship to the development of psychic structure. These identity problems, though never explicitly stated, exerted their influence in that they gave rise to a completely different concept of development. Freud's insistence on retaining the distinction between primary and secondary, when speaking of narcissism, does not constitute just a flaw in Freud's thinking. I believe that in some of his seemingly self-contradictory formulations, in which the theory of narcissism abounds, we must see the breakthrough of new insights. These new insights, hidden behind the imagery of narcissism, are problems of identity emergence and identity maintenance. They foreshadow the necessity for a new concept of development which may be tentatively described in terms of an invariant and its transformations. If these propositions prove tenable, the concept of narcissism contains as radical a revolution of Freud's thinking as does his reformulation of early dynamic psychoanalytic theory in terms of the structural concepts.

REFERENCES

BALINT, M. (1960). "Primary Narcissism and Primary Love." *Psychoanal. Quart.*, Vol. 29.

BING, J. F., McLAUGHLIN, F., and MARBURG, R. (1959). "The Metapsychology of Narcissism." *Psychoanal. Study Child*, Vol. 14.

EISNITZ, A. J. (1961). "Mirror Dreams." *J. Amer. Psychoanal, Assoc.*, Vol. 9.

ELKISCH, P. (1957). "The Psychological Significance of the Mirror." *J. Amer. Psychoanal. Assoc.*, Vol. 5.

ERIKSON, E. H. (1958). *Young Man Luther* (New York: Norton.)
——— (1959). "The Problem of Ego Identity." In: *Identity and the Life Cycle* (New York: Int. Univ. Press.)

ETIEMBLE (1954). "New China and the Chinese Language." *Diogenes*, Vol. 8 (London: Curwen.)

FREUD, S. (1911). "Formulations on the Two Principles of Mental Functioning." *S.E.*, Vol. 12.
——— (1914). "On Narcissism: An Introduction." *S.E.*, Vol. 14.
——— (1917). *Introductory Lectures on Psycho-Analysis. S.E.*, Vols. 15, 16.
——— (1925). *An Autobiographical Study. S.E.*, Vol. 20.
——— (1932). *New Introductory Lectures on Psychoanalysis* (London: Hogarth, 1933.)

GREENACRE, P. (1958). "Early Physical Determinants in the Development of the Sense of Identity." *J. Amer. Psychoanal. Assoc.*, Vol. 6.

JACOBSON, E. (1954). "The Self and the Object World." *Psychoanal. Study Child*, Vol. 9.

JONES, E. (1955). *The Life and Work of Sigmund Freud*, Vol. II, p. 302 (New York: Basic Books.)

KANZER, M. (1961). "Ego Interest, Egoism, Narcissism." Presented at the Panel on Narcissism at the Fall Meeting of the Amer. Psychoanal. Assoc. (*in press*).

KAYWIN, L. (1957). "The Concept of Self-Representation." *J. Amer. Psychoanal. Assoc.*, Vol. 5.

KEYSER, C. J. (1922). "The Group Concept." In: *The World of Mathematics*, ed. J. R. Newman, Vol. III (New York: Simon & Schuster, 1956.)

KOFFKA, K. (1935). *Principles of Gestalt Psychology.* (New York: Harcourt, Brace.)

Kris, E. (1936). "The Psychology of Caricature." In: *Explorations in Art* (New York: Int. Univ. Press, 1952.)

Lichtenstein, H. (1961). "Identity and Sexuality. A Study of their Interrelationship in Man." *J. Amer. Psychoanal. Assoc.*, Vol. 9.

Mahler, M. S. (1958). "Problems of Identity." Abstr. *J. Amer. Psychoanal. Assoc.*, Vol. 6.

Miller, M. L. (1948). "Ego Functioning in Two Types of Dreams." *Psychoanal. Quart.*, Vol. 17.

Róheim, Géza (1919). *Spiegelzauber* (Leipzig and Vienna: Int. Psychoanal. Vlg.)

Rollman-Branch, H. S. (1960). "On the Question of Primary Object Need." *J. Amer. Psychoanal. Assoc.*, Vol. 8.

Spiegel, L. A. (1959). "The Self, the Sense of Self and Perception." *Psychoanal. Study Child*, Vol. 14.

Spitz, R. A. (1959). "A Genetic Field Theory of Ego Formation" (New York: Int. Univ. Press.)

VIII

The Femininity Complex in Men[*]

BY FELIX BOEHM

As early as 1915, when the third edition of the *Drei Abhandlungen zur Sexualtheorie* appeared, Freud remarked in a footnote: "This [observation] shows that in human beings there is no such thing as pure masculinity or pure femininity, either in the *psychological*[1] or the biological sense. On the contrary, we find in every individual a combination of the characteristics of his or her sex, as biologically determined, with biological traits belonging to the other sex and a blending of activity and passivity, not only in so far as these *psychic* characteristics depend on the biological but also where they are not so dependent" (italics mine).

In the *Ego and the Id* Freud says: "This is one of the ways in which bisexuality takes a hand in the subsequent vicissitudes of the Oedipus complex. The other way is even more important. For one gets the impression that the simple Oedipus complex is by no means its commonest form, but rather represents a simplification or schematization which, to be sure, is often enough adequate for practical purposes. Closer study usually discloses the more complete Oedipus complex which is twofold, positive and negative, and is due to the bisexuality originally present in children: that is to say, a boy has not merely an ambivalent attitude toward his father and an affectionate object relation

[*] Read before the German Psycho-Analytical Society, November 12, 1929.
[1] P. 42.

toward his mother, but at the same time he also behaves like a girl and displays an affectionate feminine attitude to his father and a corresponding hostility and jealousy toward his mother. It is this complicating element introduced by bisexuality that makes it so difficult to obtain a clear view of the facts in connection with the earliest object-choices and identifications, and still more difficult to describe them intelligibly. It may even be that the ambivalence displayed in the relations to the parents should be attributed entirely to bisexuality."[2]

In my opinion not sufficient justice has been done in analytical literature to the great significance of these hypotheses of Freud's. I intend therefore to direct your attention to various facts, knowledge of which is important in the analysis of men. My own experience, too, has repeatedly taught me that in the negative Oedipus attitude boys do not simply hate the mother, but envy her and are jealous of the part she plays with the father. Many boys and youths are conscious of envying girls and women because of the many points in life and in family-relations in which they are favored, especially by the father. The young male is conscious of a wish to avenge himself, and many boys in their younger days have experienced a feeling of hatred for a long, thick "pigtail." Similarly, in every case in which latent or manifest homosexual impulses have made themselves felt, the man has been jealous of some female rival; he has felt hatred, envy and jealousy of any woman who was on intimate terms with the male object of his desire. These jealous impulses can be very clearly observed in a man whose close friend has just been married, and we may be certain of coming across them in the analysis of every male patient.

Let me quote an example which I met with in my own practice: A patient who had become conscious of some latent homosexuality and had reacted to the discovery with very marked feelings of guilt and inferiority, told me of a homosexual period

[2] In another place ("Some Psychological Consequences of the Anatomical Distinction between the Sexes," *The International Journal of Psychoanalysis*, Vol. VIII, p. 135), Freud says: "The matter is made more difficult to grasp by the complicating circumstances that even in the boys the Oedipus complex has a double orientation, active and passive, in accordance with their bisexual constitution; the boy also wants to take his mother's place as the love-object of his father—a fact which we describe as the feminine attitude."

in his life, roughly between the ages of nine and eleven. He said: "It happened that some battleships came into harbor at the place where I lived and I conceived a sentimental attraction to the sailors, especially for one man, with whom I corresponded for quite a long time. They used to invite women from our town to festivities on board. I was jealous of these women because of their association with the sailors. I can quite well recall my feelings of envy and jealousy of these girls."

Here are some further particulars from this man's analysis: In his education and in his professional career as a physician he had been perfectly equal to the demands made upon him but, on occasion, he suffered from impaired potency. He said of himself: "My achievements show a great fluctuation: slackness and passivity alternate with a capacity for pulling myself together and accomplishing a great deal, considerably more than anyone would expect of men. Often I give an impression of affectation and then suddenly I surprise people by a display of unexpected virility. It amuses me to make my fellow-physicians believe for quite a long time that I am lacking in intelligence and then to astonish them by some wholly unexpected intellectual feat." I commented: "Like a woman who carries an invisible fetus for a long period and then surprises those about her by suddenly producing a loudly wailing infant."

The patient displayed great resistance to the uncovering of a desire in him to beget a mighty hero or the savior of the world. Instead, feminine tendencies made their appearance: "A colleague of mine in hospital gave a little party just after an operation in which I had assisted. I was still wearing my white gown with wide, loose sleeves and I wondered whether I ought to fasten these with elastic bands. I thought: 'No, I won't do that. My arms are like a woman's and the effect will be piquant. Any girl might be glad to have arms like mine.' So I went to the party with my sleeves loose. Smoking in this get-up seemed like mixing masculine and feminine traits, and I immediately thought that I must seem like a Pasha. I thought that I combined the characteristics of a woman and a Pasha. . . . I have small, feminine hands and am proud of them. . . .

"Yesterday I had a pain in the upper part of my thigh and the gluteal region. I have not been able to make up my mind to stop wearing my thin, short underclothes and probably I have caught a chill. They looked so coquettish and reminded me of a woman's fine undergarment. . . . Last night I had the following dream: I was in my room and I saw in a looking-glass the reflection of my head only. I had on some feminine head-dress, a hat or rather a kerchief such as old women wear at home. My face was round and pretty and pleased me. I had dark hair, but my face had not such an animated expression as that of my grandmother. The reflection in the glass was smiling. . . . My associations to this dream are as follows: I am said to be very like my mother. The reflection in the mirror was like the daughter and the wife of one of my father's employers. . . . Once, when I was nine years old, my stepsister, aged twenty, was sitting opposite me and I rubbed my penis against her knees. Later when I read something about onanism and recollected this scene, I had an overwhelming sense of guilt."

I pointed out to the patient the connection between the sense of guilt, which he must assuredly have had at the time of this episode, and his feminine attitude at the same age toward the sailors. He thereupon recalled a "quite new" memory: "The very first time my stepsister visited my home, a year earlier, I fell head over ears in love with her, she being nineteen years old at the time. I had already noticed that my father was enamored of her, and I thought I had caught sight of him kissing her. It would therefore have worried me terribly if a year later he had found out that I had rubbed myself against her knees. The first time she paid us a visit, my father gave her a pair of fine, new snowshoes, quite up-to-date, whereas I had only a shabby old pair. I felt very jealous of her and could not understand why my father should make a favorite of her."

His stepsister's visits stirred up feminine as well as masculine tendencies in him. The next dream he had was as follows: "I saw a shaven patch, where generally there is hair, and I saw part of a female genital organ." His associations to this dream were as follows: "When a man has just shaved, people say he is as smooth as a sucking-pig or a child's buttocks; when a woman is going to have an abdominal operation, the genital region is shaved. During the first months of my analysis I consciously took the greatest pains to make progress in it; now, for a long time, I have behaved in analysis like a woman who feels the child growing within her. . . . I have another association to that dream: I think I had a vague feeling that the shaven patch was part of my own body."

The patient complained of a new symptom—a spasmodic contraction of the walls of the stomach and intestines. Giving his associations to this he said: "In the summer of my ninth year an older boy told me the facts of sex. I was staying at the seaside, and there were pools in which were little fish, about two centimeters long. Yesterday you compared my behavior with that of a pregnant woman. Today my mistress was complaining of a headache, and I asked if she also felt sick. She said: 'No, that comes later on.' I have got a slight headache myself to-day. . . . It is true that the shape of the little fishes which I told you about reminds me of spermatozoa." In other words, the patient's spasmodic contractions of the stomach represented symptoms of pregnancy (or labor pain). I interpreted his dreams and associations by telling him that his ostensible masculinity was a mask for marked feminine tendencies.

Another patient, about thirty years old, who had come to me for treatment because of defective potency and the frequent occurrence of *ejaculatio praecox*, had been consistently successful in life and gave no one the impression that he was ill. There could be no question of any particular passivity, only he had never so far succeeded in wooing a woman for himself. He gave the following association of his own accord: "When I was a boy and, I think, still when I was adolescent, I used when in the bath to squeeze my genitals in between my legs and press the upper part of my arms together so that they looked like a woman's bosom. I used to think to myself: 'If anyone comes in now, he won't know whether I am a man or a woman.' . . . As a child I often used to try to press my testicles up into my body till they disappeared; that was a very common game. . . . And I used to try in different ways to draw my penis up to my navel" [i.e., he tried to have coitus with himself]. . . . I used to envy acrobats because they could reach their own genitals with their faces. . . . When I can't get an erection, I feel as if I must bend backwards from the loins [here he made the motion of coitus in a woman]; but that is a feminine movement. . . . In an earlier dream my grandmother stabbed me in the heart with a dagger. Blood flowed in streams and I screamed so loudly that I awoke. . . . You once told me that this was a typical dream amongst women. . . . The first time I tried to have coitus I was unsuccessful because I stretched my legs apart, that is to say, I acted like a woman during coitus."

Here there are two points I wish to note: attempts to conceal the testicles between the thighs or to press them up into the abdomen, to contract the muscles of the thorax so as to counterfeit a woman's breasts, or to insert the penis into the mouth or the navel (i.e., to have coitus with oneself) are so common amongst boys that I have never yet analysed a man without his telling me that he practiced these or similar tricks as a boy. Moreover it is by no means unusual for adult men to try them.[3] One man, who certainly was a manifest homosexual, told me that on the various occasions when he attempted coitus he had the very greatest difficulty in finding the opening of the vagina, because he always felt compelled to open his legs wide. He said the reason was that this position stimulated great sensation on the inner side of the thighs.

I will now give some details from the analysis of a young man whose most prominent symptom—apart from a complete inability to approach a woman whom he desired (till he began treatment he had only had intercourse with prostitutes)—was a very pronounced indecision. Nevertheless he had been outwardly so far successful in life that the laity would not have regarded him as ill. We had once been discussing the equation gold= feces, and the next day he brought the following dream: "One of my left front teeth had come out and a gold tip had come off the next tooth. I had swallowed both these objects." His associations were as follows: "My stepfather's miserliness towards me— my own miserliness—I am too miserly to put capital into the business—I will not allow myself or my principal to lay out money on the most necessary things. Think of my 'twilight state' before we began analysis. I was supposed to be doing business and, instead, I would wander about the town all night looking for a watercloset. That is to say, I did not want to defecate. I prefer masturbation to coitus."

I said to the patient: "When you masturbate, you are at once the man and the woman. In your dream you swallowed semen (the white tooth) and feces (the gold filling), and in this way you impregnated yourself."

He immediately produced the following associations: "When I was from five to seven years old, I used constantly to exchange my own (boy's) toys for dolls, with which I played a great deal.

[3] Compare P. Näcke's work on "Narcissism," published in 1899.

When I was between four and six years of age, I saw a very beautiful silk dress in an aunt's house and wanted to try to cut off a piece of it for myself. At the age of eight or nine I tried to knit like my mother and at ten years old I watched an aunt crocheting and imitated her with some success. When I was about ten, I used to devour books for schoolgirls. I liked to wear knickerbockers opening with a flap, like the old-fashioned shape for women, so that I had to crouch down to urinate, which pleased me. At a spa where I stayed I used at first to bathe on the women's side; when I was older, I had to bathe with my father in the men's baths. I had a great longing to go back to the women's baths and regretted that I was too big. . . .

"On the telephone people often address me as 'Fräulein' because I suddenly assume a high voice. . . . I should like you to support me, that is to say, I should like to be fed by you, as my mother fed me. . . . In a book called *Frau als Hausärztin* I read that there are many men who constantly torment their wives with sexual desires. I mentally cursed these men and sympathized with the woman. I also regretted that I was a boy and would have to grow up into a man. If I had been a girl, my father would never have beaten me for wanting to possess my mother. When I was a child I read of a rising amongst Indians, in which they stabbed all the boys but let the girls live. I should like to have been a girl.

"Because I masturbated, my mother threatened that my penis would rot away. Girls have a slit instead, so that there is nothing there to rot away. When I was excited, people could see that my penis was erect, but excitation was not noticeable in girls. When I masturbated, I lost semen, whereas girls could not lose semen."

At this point I will interpolate something that another patient told me. He said, "If I cried, when I was a boy, people said to me that boys must not cry, that later on I should have to be a soldier like my uncles and that a soldier does not cry even when his head is cut off. I thought to myself: Then I would rather not be a boy and not become a soldier. Why must I be a boy, anyhow?" Another patient discussed a question which often occurred to him and disquieted him: "How could I conceal an erection in certain situations, for instance, in fancy-dress?"

Although in the three cases here outlined analysis revealed without difficulty a number of feminine traits, the patients were by no means of the type called by Ferenczi[4] "subject-homo-erotic." On the contrary they were men who all alike suffered from defective potency. And perhaps this is no mere coincidence.

Let me now pass on to describe certain mental processes which may be frequently observed both in analysis and in life in general.

It happened that, a death having occurred in a certain family, a letter was addressed to the eldest sister, condoling with her and the other members, but there was no separate letter for the youngest brother. All the others thought this quite right, for there were good reasons for not writing directly to him, but the brother felt that an unjustifiable preference had been shown to his sisters, and he was furious. He was a man who all his life had tried to assert his masculinity and to tyrannize over women.

I had a patient who had never in her life experienced complete sexual gratification and who recognized only the clitoris as a sexual organ. In her analysis she displayed marked penis-envy and was never weary of railing at men, especially those of a pronounced masculine type. Analysis showed that this was because her own wish to be a man was frustrated. Conversely, I believe that, when men are always finding fault with women, it is because they are angry that they cannot themselves be women as well. The patient I mentioned earlier, who could never find the opening to the vagina because, during coitus, he always felt compelled to stretch his legs apart, was incapable in analysis of uttering the words "woman" or "girl." He used instead, with every sign of hatred, to employ a coarse term for the vagina.

When boys are still too young for sexual intercourse, it is a common thing for them, obviously impelled by sexual impulses, to depict coitus in obscene drawings. Frequently they draw the female genital organ, evidently because they wish they themselves could have it,[5] or (more narcissistically) possess it in their own bodies. This idea seems strange because we are much too inclined to regard the vagina simply as a woman's genital organ. The similar representation of a cloaca almost presupposes this.

[4] "The Nosology of Male Homosexuality (Homo-erotism)." *Contributions to Psycho-Analysis* (1916) p. 303.

[5] We have a parallel to this in the cave-drawings recently discovered in the South of France: the so-called "tectiform" objects depicted on the bodies of wild animals are said to represent snares and to express the wish, "would that these beasts were in our snares."

The two antithetical ideas—that a man falls into a cloaca and that he has one on his own person, by means of which he can get rid of large masses, do not seem extraordinary to us. (Compare, in this connection, the figures vomiting water on the Minster at Freiburg and other cathedrals.)

Many men have a trick of putting their fingers between their toes when undressing: a habit they speak of in analysis with a profound sense of guilt. I think it is a form of masturbation, like sucking the thumb and inserting the fingers into the nose and ears. To boys the spaces between the toes, like the mouth, nose, ears and navel, represent the female genital. Many boys scratch the mucous membrane of the nose till it bleeds; that is to say, they are manufacturing a wound on their own bodies. (We must remember that the unconscious conceives of the vagina as a bleeding wound.) A patient of about thirty years old once said to me: "It vexes me that women have two openings in the lower part of their bodies, while men have only one. I envy them that."

We know that in men the rectum often plays the part of the vagina. In his "Contributions to the Masculinity Complex in Women,"[6] van Ophuijsen says: "Fantasies of auto-erotic coitus also occur, in which the rectum takes the place of the vagina and the feces that of the penis." The same is true of men, but with them it is not merely a matter of fantasy but of behavior. We all know how men who suffer from constipation employ the feces as a penis and the rectum as a vagina in anal masturbation. In many such men a discharge of semen (not simply of prostate secretion) occurs during defecation.

We regard the smoking of a large, heavy cigar as a sign of a specially virile nature and we are accustomed to think of the cigar as a penis-symbol. But we forget that there is another side to this: the smoker keeps on putting the cigar into his mouth, which he is using as a receptive, erotogenic organ. Freud traces a strong craving to smoke to the pleasurably-toned act of smoking at the mother's breast.

It is very common for men to indulge in an outburst of temper when they are vainly tormenting themselves in the attempt to force a stud through the stud-holes in shirt and collar. Possibly the passive role played by the stud-holes is not without significance.

[6] *The International Journal of Psychoanalysis,* Vol. V, 1924, p. 47.

One of my patients told me the following facts: "When my father was a young man, he used to clean his ears daily with a little horn-spoon. As he grew older and my mother did not wish to have any more children, he took to drinking, like many men whose sexual intercourse with their wives encounters obstacles. In his old age he formed the habit of syringing his ears daily" (i.e., he had made his ears an erotogenic zone). In the fantasies of drunkards the mouth often plays the part of the vagina; drinking is frequently a substitute for being suckled, i.e., for a mainly passive act. Again, some drunkards identify themselves in fantasy with a woman into whose mouth a man urinates. In this connection the fact seems to me of peculiar significance that men whose sexual enjoyment is frustrated so often become drunkards; that is, they begin to behave in a "feminine" (passive) manner. One recalls the impressive description in Freud's *Drei Abhandlungen* of pleasure-sucking in infants. He speaks of a kind of orgasm occurring after the child has been suckled.[7] We shall not be far wrong in saying that a baby boy, thus fed, lies in a state of bliss like that of a woman after coitus. His behavior while he is being suckled is passive and feminine, in that he is *receptive,* and the penis-like nipple is introduced into his mouth, which is a receptive organ. We know that boy babies often chew the breast hard with their jaws, sometimes actually wounding the nipple. That is to say, the oral-cannibalistic phase of development comes into play when they are sucking. On the other hand there is a great resemblance to coitus performed by the mouth.

An exhaustive analysis of a dipsomaniac convinced me that, for him, drinking was a feminine activity, which was bound to recur whenever he had had unsatisfactory intercourse with his mistress—a married woman. I think it is no mere coincidence that this particular patient (who, be it remarked in passing, had commanded a company calmly, with assurance, throughout the war) gave evidence of an unusual number of feminine feelings. I quote some of them, taken at random: "I am a woman. An employer whom I respect is lying on the top of me; how would he behave in that situation?" "Yesterday, when I was in the bath, I made a movement exactly like that of a woman during coitus."

[7] Compare Radó's remarks on "alimentary orgasm," in "The Psychical Effects of Intoxication." *The International Journal of Psychoanalysis,* Vol. IX, 1928, p. 313.

"Recently, when I was in bed, I tried to imagine the sensations of my mistress during intercourse, and I made pretty turns and twists." (He referred to sexual movements.) "Sometimes I have an unpleasant sensation in my abdomen; I can produce the feeling at will." "Today someone told me about an operation for hemorrhoids. I had a feeling of anxiety, a sensation as if someone had hurt *me* in the rectum, and I felt a contraction there." "Yesterday I heard a woman telling about a case of very difficult childbirth. I immediately felt in my own abdomen all the sensations she was describing." "I suddenly have a feeling that, if I kicked up my legs very high, a female genital might be visible." "Last night I had a distinct physical sensation, as if I were a woman having intercourse. The feeling was between the rectum and the genitals." During the first eighteen months of his analysis, this patient nearly always lay with his legs wide apart, although I repeatedly drew his attention to this symptom. I would note here that many male patients can describe in fantasy how pleasant it would be to be a woman and have intercourse as a woman—this is so even when feminine tendencies do not play any special part in their life.

That patient of whom I have just spoken told me that he was very sensitive to excitation in the region of the perineum, but that the glans penis was quite insensitive. In the course of his analysis the sensibility gradually transferred itself forwards to the scrotum and finally to the glans penis.[8] This phenomenon is familiar to women who are skilled in erotic experiences; when they want to produce erection in a man of feeble potency, they do not stimulate the penis, but the region of the perineum, the scrotum or the inside of the thighs. I think that in all little boys the perineum is an erotogenic zone. Many men recollect feeling a pleasurable stimulus there when playing "Ride-a-cock-horse," an excitation which may extend to the scrotum but only rarely leads to erection.[9] The situation is very similar in women; in girl-children and neurotic women it is only the clitoris (the

[8] Compare Abraham's remarks on this subject, in his "Ejaculatio Praecox," *Selected Papers on Psycho-Analysis*, 1927, p. 284.

[9] We know that even infants at the breast can have erections. In a paper entitled: "Beitrag zur Psychologie des Liebeslebens" (*Internationale Zeitschrift*, Bd. IX, 1923, S. 215), I reported the case of a baby boy of thirteen months, who regularly, when he was undressed, tried to put his mother's hand against his penis.

rudimentary penis) which is sensitive to excitation; they have not yet discovered the vagina as a sexual organ. In boys and neurotic men the most sensitive region is that which, in biological evolution, corresponds to the vaginal aperture and the parts immediately around it in women. The sensitiveness of the penis, and especially of the glans, develops only gradually. One neurotic patient told me that in coitus he had a feeling of tension, a convulsive contraction, all along the perineum, from the scrotum to the rectum, and he thought that this prevented ejaculation.

The distaste felt by many men for everything feminine arises out of the repression of the wish to be a woman. Thus some men detest a broad pelvis, large buttocks or hanging breasts, because these are feminine attributes. Behind the hatred of the peculiarly feminine characteristics of women there lies the wish to possess these characteristics oneself and this, in turn, conceals envy of the larger penis which women are imagined to possess.[10] To the unconscious of men a woman's pendulous breasts represent a larger female penis. Thus a disparaging attitude toward women also originates in envy. For instance, one patient said: "I have revenged myself on women and especially on my mother by turning my back on them." Another patient, who suffered from *ejaculatio praecox* said: "Anyhow, it prevents the woman getting a child."

Children often show hatred of their mother in quite unmistakable fashion, especially if she is pregnant. I knew a boy, nearly three years old, whose mother was far advanced in pregnancy and who, when playing with a chain which she wore round her neck, tried to strangle her with it by sliding the clasp to and fro. This shows that he had death or castration wishes toward his mother in her pregnancy. Analysis showed that his motive was not simple rage against the coming rival but envy of his mother's condition.

We learn from our analyses that all boys are much preoccupied with the fact that only women can give birth to children. The boy has great difficulty in acquiescing in this inexorable decree of nature. One patient said to me: "It must be some comfort to a girl, even if not a very great one, to be able to say to herself:

[10] "You have such a big widdler because you are so big." Freud. "Analysis of the Phobia of a Five-year Old Boy." *Collected Papers*, Vol. III.

'Later, though not now, I shall have proper breasts and bear children,' whereas a boy has to realize that he never will have such breasts or bear children." Many little boys play with little girls the same game of having children; they put a cushion or some other object under their clothes and presently let it fall down and pretend that they have had a baby.[11] A little boy of nearly three years old used to imagine that he had given birth to a child, and whenever he had been on the chamber he would say: "Mother, come quick. I've born a beautiful baby." In all analyses of men we meet with fantasies of anal birth, and we know how common it is for men to treat their feces as a child.

Here are some examples of other unconscious fantasies about conception and parturition. One patient, who had been brusquely dismissed by his employer, for whom he had a sentimental adoration, fell into a state of deep depression. While in this condition he mentioned a fantasy of shooting himself in the mouth with a revolver or killing himself by thrusting a finger down his throat. He then recalled an earlier fantasy of deflowering a girl and then drinking his own semen and her blood: "Ejaculation is like a shot; a shot destroys blood-vessels and the blood mixes with the gunpowder and gas which come out of the pistol's mouth. In other words, blood mixes with semen. Semen produces conception and conception birth. Birth may cause death." (Probably these words contain an unconscious comparison between birth and an explosion, on the one hand, and procreation and an explosion, on the other.) Thus, underlying the suicide-fantasies is plainly the wish to conceive a child by his employer. Boys (like girls) imagine that in the act of procreation the man (or boy) loses his penis, has to let it be incorporated in the woman, who hides it away and turns it into a child. But the boy either does not suspect or will not admit the fact that she has no penis; he believes that she receives the child in addition to her own penis. He thinks she swallows up the penis (possibly the testicles too; these then form the breasts or the penis of the child). Or else the mother receives the father's penis through a hollow penis of her own and gives birth to the child through a kind of special tube. The thought of the act of procreation increases the boy's castration-anxiety, for he imagines that it involves the loss of

[11] Compare Reik's remarks on the *couvade* in his *Probleme der Religionspsychologie,* Internationale Psycho-analytische Bibliothek, Bd. V, S. 1.

his penis. And further it accentuates his envy of the woman, who receives the penis. A patient of twenty told me that he thought of the act of procreation as follows: A surgeon removes the testicles and grafts them into the woman's abdomen, through the navel. The man then has to wait a year for the testicles to grow again. This patient was much astonished to hear that he was mistaken. Hatred of women originates in this castration-anxiety.

Because boys imagine that conception and parturition are so complicated and uncanny, and because these processes are so mysterious to them, they have a passionate wish to share in them or else an intense envy of this capacity in women. In "The Economic Problem of Masochism"[12] Freud says, "from the final genital stage are derived of course the situations characteristic of womanhood, namely, the passive part in coitus and the act of giving birth." I think that the impression conveyed by parturition is one of *activity*—the expulsion of the child from the body seems a stronger evidence of potency than the process of erection. All men find it overwhelming when they see for the first time the baby's head appearing from the vagina. Envy of the woman's capacity to bear children (which I will call, for short, "parturition-envy") is a considerable incentive to the capacity for production in men.[13]

There is yet another form which men's envy of feminine attributes may assume, namely, envy of the woman's breasts. I think that when we are children we envy others if they have anything *more* than we ourselves have. It is inevitable that the female breasts should rouse envy in boys and call forth the wish to possess these organs, especially since the breasts, as I mentioned above, represent in the boy's unconscious a tremendous penis. Apart from this, however, they have a function different from any possessed by boys. A patient who had had a very deep analysis said to me: "I have gradually reconciled myself to the fact that other men and boys have larger penes than mine and can make their urine go farther and higher. But I can never get rid of a tormenting memory when I think of the following

[12] *Collected Papers*, Vol. II, p. 261.

[13] M. Chadwick writes very clearly and convincingly on this subject in a paper entitled: Über die Wurzel der Wissbegierde," *Internationale Zeitschrift*, Bd. XI, 1925, S. 54.

incident. I had a brother nearly eight years younger than myself, and one day his nurse took him on her knee to feed him. In order to remove the drops of milk which had dried on her breast, she took it in her hand and squeezed it so that a fine but forcible spurt of milk came out of the nipple and sprayed my face. This unexpected happening filled me with amazement and terror, and the thought took root in my mind: You will never be able to do that; women have the advantage of you there."

I said just now that it excites our envy when others have something *more* than we have ourselves. We may say, further, that when they have something *different*, something which we can never have, we experience a sense of inferiority. The quality of the "different" thing does not matter very much. We have so often been told, and every analysis of a woman confirms the fact, that little girls envy boys their power of passing urine in a continuous stream, further and higher than they themselves can manage it. But many men can recall an experience of their nursery days: how their little sisters could pass a broader stream of urine than they could and how it made a quite different, duller sound in the chamber. One of my patients remembered distinctly how it vexed and shamed him that he could not produce the same noise when urinating. In later life his great hobby was a garden-hose from which he could send out either a full stream or a fine spray of water.

All the phenomena which I have briefly described so far may be summed up in the term: the femininity-complex in men. The relations between this complex and masochism are obvious. I will not enter into them now, or my subject-matter will become too unwieldly.

I will now cite the cases of two male patients, both suffering from severe neuroses, to show the great importance in the structure of their illness of the "femininity-complex," which I had great difficulty in bringing to light.

Both the personal character and the symptom-complex of the first patient were very difficult to place in any category. He suffered from every imaginable pain and inconvenience, but no one symptom-complex was sufficiently marked to be made the basis of an exact diagnosis. His life was as indeterminate as was the clinical picture he presented; one would have said he had not the courage to be either bad or good. His pronounced masochism was always bringing him into difficulties, yet he had done well in his profession and had won a position of esteem. Nevertheless he took a gloomy view of the future and was always afraid of misfortune coming on him from without, partly as a punishment for trivial wrongdoing, and he was ceaselessly tormented by hypochondriacal ideas about his health. Constant examinations by specialists did not do much to reassure him.

When his youngest daughter died, his hypochondria became so acute that life was a torture to him. At first he used to think that morbid changes, swellings, etc., were taking place in his neck and throat; now he began to look out for similar changes and growths in his stomach, caecum and kidneys and to dread that he would have to undergo a dangerous surgical operation. At the same time defecation became more and more troublesome. When describing this, he had the following associations: "Recently it has occurred to me that possibly these difficulties are connected with an unconscious idea of anal birth. Perhaps my attitude to my other symptoms is like that of a woman during gestation." "I behave like an hysterical woman who wants to be told that she is ill, and I am exaggeratedly pleased when I am told the opposite." "During puberty I had a noticeable development of the breasts and I used to feel an itching in the nipples[14]; even at the age of twenty I looked like a girl." I reminded him that his idea that he had carcinoma of the abdomen first occurred to him when he heard of a case of carcinoma of the uterus. Many of his associations, when analyzed, gave plain evidence of the wish to be pregnant.[15]

The next day the patient reported the following dream: "A friend of my boyhood, Wilhelm, had fallen in the War. He had committed suicide for military and altruistic reasons. At the same time he was alive and engaged in all sorts of activities." The following were the associations to the dream: "In the last few days I have been reading a novel, the scene of which is laid in the tropics. One of the characters is a lieutenant who was taken prisoner in the War. He had an abdominal wound, which had healed badly, and he had lost all the badges of his officer's

[14] Other patients have told me of this irritation at the period of puberty, and in their analyses the discovery of repressed feminine tendencies occupied a prominent place.

[15] Compare Eisler, "A Man's Unconscious Phantasy of Pregnancy in the Guise of Traumatic Hysteria." *The International Journal of Psychoanalysis*, Vol. II, 1921, p. 255.

rank. He wore a uniform made up of all sorts of odd pieces, and one of the men in charge of the camp treated him badly and struck him. When it transpired that he really was a lieutenant, an apology was made to him. Wilhelm (a lieutenant) was actually killed in the War, but it is not known where. In many things he was very like me. In our childhood we shared many experiences and our parents brought us up on the same principles.

"In association with the idea of my parents it occurs to me that I recently told them a dream I had at the age of four. [He had long ago told his dream in analysis.] I wanted to go with my mother into the Zoological Gardens. At the gate there leapt out on us a raging tiger which tried to bite my mother. I held out my leg to it, so that it should not bite her. It bit me hard in the leg and then left the way clear into the Zoo." The patient then added a new detail: "I felt the burning pain quite distinctly." I pointed out to him that many of his associations showed that he identified himself to a great extent with the lieutenant in the novel and with his friend Wilhelm, and I asked what were his associations to the latter's falling in action. He replied with a joke about a fallen girl. I then pointed out that he was identifying himself with a girl. The patient said: "That makes me think of a funny story: A mother took her daughter to the doctor and said to her, 'Riekchen, stand straight, so that the doctor may see how crooked you are.'"

I explained that his latent wish in the dream was to turn into a girl (compare the badly abdominal wound of the lieutenant in the story), to behave as a girl and to fall, that is, to allow a man to have intercourse with him, and that the man was to be his father, who would then not injure his mother. I added that the patient must have had this wish in his fourth year and, since it was not fulfilled, had never been able to decide between the masculine and the feminine role. I said that he must have had a sense of guilt ever since this dream, for not having translated into action the wish it contained. Possibly one might even speak of a task (if not actually of a "life-task") which as yet he had not performed.

I reminded him that he had passionately loved the daughter who died and had identified himself deeply with her. And, further, that in his early childhood (at about the age of four to six) he had eagerly desired to have a little sister and perhaps had wished to be a girl himself. Now, since his youngest daughter's death, the impulse to assume the part of a woman was specially urgent.[16] On the other hand, from his identification with the lieutenant in the novel we should draw the conclusion that he wished his masculinity to receive some recognition.

I used the phrase "life-task" in this case because of certain analogies to that of another patient who directly employed that term. With him again it was impossible to arrive at a definite diagnosis, for he had symptoms of every neurotic disease known to us. Here is the history of his case: He had a pronounced masochistic disposition and, up to his thirtieth year, had been almost entirely impotent. From his childhood on, till he began analytic treatment, which extended over several years, he could enjoy sexual gratification only to the accompaniment of sadistic fantasies in which men were tortured. His moral masochism was carried to such a pitch that he was compelled to do himself some injury to pay for even the most trivial success in his public or private life. If, in order to get on in life, he made efforts to advance in his profession, he then felt impelled to obstruct the course of his analysis. If, on the other hand, he had done good work in this for one day or more, he would inevitably make some careless mistake in his employment, so that he either made a fool of himself or ran the risk of dismissal.

For years he had fruitlessly endeavored to complete his studies; now, at a certain stage in the analysis, he would repeat with increasing urgency the question whether he had any mental ability and whether analysis would bring his intellectual powers into evidence. One day he produced the following associations: "Masturbation is a mental discovery; it has enabled me to take lasting possession of my mother. She knows this, but my father does not." "At home, instead of saying 'my wife,' we say in fun 'my rib'; if children eat too much, people say to them: 'That will sprout out at your elbow.'"

He then described some vivid fantasies of the last few days. His mistress was going away, and he had had the desire to tear her to pieces with his teeth either during coitus or on a walk with her or else, when they were at a dance, to bite off one of her fingers. Here he made a slip of the tongue and said "to finger her," explaining it by saying that it meant to touch or

---

[16] Compare Freud's remarks in *The Ego and the Id* on the substitution of an identification for an object-cathexis and on the introjection of a lost object.

fondle the female genitals with one's fingers. "When I masturbate, I am really having intercourse with my mother, whom I have incorporated in myself, so that no one else can have coitus with her or 'finger' her. I was forcibly implanted by my father in my mother's body; my own omnipotence has enabled me to incorporate her in myself.

"From my earliest childhood I have never been able to drink milk, and especially the skin on it I can't bear to pass my lips. The last few days I have sucked my mistress' breasts, and the excitation I noted in them proved to me that a woman's breasts are sexual organs. If I incorporate my mother in myself, she cannot ever again suckle anyone as she did my brothers and sisters. Yesterday I asked my mistress to kiss my hand, and, when she refused, I kissed it myself again and again. My mother and I are one; either she kisses me or I kiss her."

I reminded him that of late he had had numerous associations, which he felt much resistance in producing, about the existence of a penis in women, and I interpreted a dream, dating from his fifth year, which he had told me at the beginning of his analysis: "I was walking with my mother across the highest bridge in the world." I told him that this meant that in his fantasies there was no difference between his mother and himself—she, as well as he, had a penis, or the two together had one. When he incorporated her (with her penis) in himself, through the mouth, she became his penis—the largest penis in the world. When he masturbated, he was "fingering" her penis. At the same time he had incorporated in himself her intellectual gifts (he had always regarded her as full of wisdom), and since then he had been inhibited from displaying these intellectual powers to the world.

After a time we noticed that it was only in the months just before my summer holidays that he made much progress and gained real insight in analysis and only in the holidays themselves that there was evidence of good therapeutic results. His associations showed that his behavior in analysis was exactly like that of a pregnant woman who tries as long as possible to conceal from the outside world the fact that she is with child, so as suddenly to give birth to a baby whom all can see.

In connection with this part of his analysis he had the following associations: "Yesterday morning, as I entered the office of the Ministry where I was employed, I had the following fantasy: If it turned out that I was a girl, what effect would it have on the women secretaries and on my colleagues? I could look at the girls naked, without feeling ashamed, and I could observe the men's penes without feeling envious." He had often said: "It hurts me that I am no longer a favorite with my chief," and I pointed out to him that he wanted to be the chief's "favorite" in the sense of mistress. One of his dreams showed that he had a markedly feminine attitude toward this man. His associations to the dream were as follows: "My father was the first in our town to engage a young girl as an employee and she had a privileged position in the business. After some consideration it was decided to let her use a lavatory at the office which was reserved for my father and which the male employees might not use." Further associations revealed the patient's envy of this girl's position in relation to his father.

A few days later the patient remembered that he had had a dream about some "religious idea." He then proceeded enthusiastically (and it was the first time in the course of his long analysis that he had become animated and forgotten himself) to develop an "ethical" or "religious" system, a "new creed," an "idea for conferring happiness on the whole world." The idea was that sons should renounce their active Oedipus and castration desires in relation to their fathers and should adopt a feminine attitude toward them, thus protecting their mothers from their fathers. He felt that he was the founder of this new universal religion—this was at the heart of many ideas he had that, once in his life, he would succeed in some quite extraordinary achievement in some field or other, and that this would bring him instant and boundless fame. In the next few days these associations were followed up by fantasies in which he protected his mother from acts of sexual aggression by his father. These he pictured to himself in various fantasies about his parents' intercourse, the fantasies taking shape from infantile sexual theories. As a child he had felt it incumbent on him to place himself protectively in front of his mother or to take her place, when there seemed any possibility that his father might assault or defile her.

The question now arises: Why could not my patient perform this task of his? A simple answer would be: because the constitutional masculine components in his nature rebelled against playing his feminine part. But I do not think this explanation is adequate. The process is certainly more complicated. Let me try to make it clear by describing a typical detail in the process of regression. We know that, in regression, pregenital phases of development become genitalized. A very common example of this is the attitude of misers or of patients suffering from morbid depression. They are afflicted with a constant dread of poverty and, however they are obliged to spend money, they have sensations similar to those experienced by men whose characters are on the genital level when in danger of losing a sexual object or threatened with castration. Every analyst has observed this process of genitalization so often that there is no need to give further examples of it.

Speaking of perversion Freud says: "It is brought into relation with the child's incestuous object-love, with its Oedipus complex. It first comes into prominence in the sphere of this complex, and after the complex has broken down it remains over, often quite by itself, the inheritor of its charge of libido, and weighed down by the sense of guilt that was attached to it."[17]

A similar process may be observed where there is regression to pregenital phases of development. Activity on these levels is accompanied by the same sense of guilt as genital activity. The metaphor we commonly use is that the sense of guilt is "shunted" along with the regression, just as railway-carriages are shunted from one set of rails to another.

There are other parallels, however, which can be drawn between perversion and the process of regression. In a "short communication" which I made on the subject of the perversions in 1920, I showed that in their development from the Oedipus complex the original goals of the Oedipus wishes are by no means renounced but merely disguised. Let me quote an instance from my paper. A patient who came to me for treatment on account of conscious passive homosexuality produced in his analysis fantasies of a man having coitus with him *per anum* and of his nipping off the other's penis. Or, again, he fantasied himself as a woman having sexual intercourse and injuring the man's genitals in various ways. In numerous associations he had described the female genital as a dangerous organ of castration

[17] "A Child is being Beaten," *Collected Papers,* Vol. II, p. 187.

and was very envious of women for possessing it.[18] I have dealt with this subject in greater detail in a paper I read at Würzburg, entitled "Homosexualität und Kastrationskomplex."[19] Here is an example which I quoted there: "A young homosexual had a strong fixation to his sister and used to masturbate her lover, to make him impotent when he was going to her. Here a homosexual act, which is universally construed by men as a token of friendship, was merely a disguise for an active attempt at castration."

I will now give another illustration to show that, in regression, not only does genitalization of the pregenital phases of development take place, broadly speaking, while the sense of guilt is "shunted" on to these, but also that none of the original Oedipus goals are abandoned. I know a certain lady whose father founded several important industrial concerns. He fell into debt and died prematurely. His daughter married and had a number of children and grandchildren, but after her father's death she had only one real interest, namely, the desire to see his business undertakings in a flourishing condition. Among several suitors she selected the one who seemed most able to re-establish these in a position of honor and esteem. She developed pronounced anal-sadistic traits, at the same time being exceedingly benevolent. All her thoughts and actions sprang from a single motive: the desire to increase the esteem in which her father was held, to add to his original property and to prevent its ever suffering loss (which she dreaded in a morbid fashion) or being ruined. Although her husband succeeded in establishing her father's business very satisfactorily, there was one action of his which she never forgave. Among the factory buildings there was an old chimney, which could be seen a long way off. Without consulting her, her husband had this pulled down to make room for a large building. My impression is that this woman's behavior on the anal-sadistic level corresponds to unconscious fantasies, on the genital level, connected with the incorporation within herself of her father's penis. She was constantly inspired by the wish to make the incorporated organ grow within her and someday to display

[18] All men know about the process of contraction in the sphincter-muscle of the rectum, and hence we constantly discover in male patients the fantasy that the vagina acts as an organ of castration and, as such, it arouses envy and fear.

[19] *Internationale Zeitschrift für Psychoanalyse*, Bd. XII, 1926.

it for the world to pay it respect, and she was incessantly tormented by the fear that she must lose this treasure which she had wrongfully appropriated.

I believe that this important detail in the process of repression can be demonstrated in every case. It is as though the young Oedipus assumed a mask, to escape the recognition of his wishes. He wants to produce the most harmless impression possible in his disguise. It is as if he said to himself and others: "Look, I have no genital wishes in relation to my mother, for I am still on the pregenital level." But the wishes have not really been renounced; the sense of guilt has been shifted, and activities on the earlier level of development are doomed to failure. This, I think, is a reason why the two patients whom I have described could not consistently carry their feminine wishes into action.

To explain what I have said about these two cases, I must tell you that the first patient originally told the dream about the tiger in the following form: "I wanted to go into the Zoological Gardens with my mother; at the gate a raging tiger leapt out on us and tried to bite her. I stretched out my leg to the tiger, so that he should not bite her. The tiger bit my leg hard." The words "and left the way clear into the Zoo" were a much later addition, and there is no doubt that they are the important ones. They show the reason why he wanted his father to treat him like a woman; it was so that the way to the mother might be left clear.

This, too, was the meaning of all the wishes of which the second patient told me, that the father should subject him to the perverse acts to which the mother had to submit; the idea was that the father should be diverted from the mother, so that the way to her should be clear for the son. It is as if he said: "In regressing to a feminine phase of development I will make use of pregenital mechanisms in order to achieve my genital aims. That is, my father will leave my mother in peace and I shall possess her." This was why these feminine wishes, which were most painful to the patients themselves, were weighted with a sense of guilt and could be brought into consciousness only by means of long and laborious analysis and could never be translated into action.

Both patients showed particularly strong resistance to conscious recognition of their castration-anxiety. But the fact that they did not carry out their feminine wishes produced, in its turn, feelings of guilt, for they were allowing the father to go on tormenting the mother. The life of these two men was a battle between masculine and feminine tendencies, and this had brought their personalities to the verge of dissociation. Their unusually strong feminine tendencies, to which their unconscious clung with peculiar obstinacy, made any real success in life impossible for them as men, and, if these tendencies had not gradually come to light, their analyses would have ended in failure.

In many cases the feminine wishes of male patients can be inferred from their reaction-formations and dreams quite early in analysis, in spite of great resistance. For instance, one man flew into a passion at the mere thought that his mistress might tickle him inside his ear or some other cavity of his body, while another was tormented with anxiety lest he should grow bald. (Compare the dream I quoted, in which the patient saw a shaven patch on his own body.)

The following conclusions may be drawn from what I have said. There is an early, feminine, phase of development, in which the boy's feelings are very much like those of a girl. One patient said to me: "In the first years of my life, when I was learning to walk, I had a doll from which I refused to be separated until it became a mere rag, with straw sticking out." In this phase the oral zone and the region of the perineum play a larger part as erotogenic zones than the penis. If analysis is carried far enough we find that boys go through a phase in which their attitude to the father is passive; they have a tender, girlish dependence on him and look to him for protection. In this phase the hate tendencies against him have not yet developed.

This phase of development, which belongs to a boy's very earliest years, sometimes receives further stimulus through regression taking place when the subject is attempting unsuccessfully to solve the Oedipus situation. The feelings of guilt will then attach themselves to it. It never entirely ceases to play a part in the lives of men. We may roughly indicate the course of development by saying that the male is first of all a little girl, then, when little by little he has mastered his castration-anxiety, he becomes a man and late in life becomes once more a woman.[20] In this scheme I am conforming to popular modes of speech; a

[20] It strikes me that we have here a parallel to the battle between the life and the death instincts.

boy is said still to have "girlish" characteristics, or a "girlish" nature; we say too (and I do not think the expression is confined to the German language) that a youth loses his "virginity" when he first has sexual intercourse, as if, before that, he had been a maiden and had become a man only through his first coitus. People say of an old man: "He is a regular old woman." But even in the prime of life a man's unconscious wishes to be a woman never quite cease; we all know men who hasten from one success to another and seem to have attained to full male genitality and yet are as difficult to deal with as any prima donna.

Fixation or regression to the feminine phase of development may bring out various phenomena, such as envy of the woman's functions—her capacity to bear and suckle children and to urinate in a way different from that of a man—or perhaps envy of her physical characteristics, the fact that she has breasts or, above all, a vagina. In neurotics it often gives rise to misogyny. Purely from the descriptive standpoint the man's vagina-envy seems very much like the woman's penis-envy. But I do not think the material I have quoted in this paper enables us to decide with any certainty whether the man's envy is as closely related to narcissism as the woman's or (leaving aside the constitutional bisexuality) whether it is substantially influenced by a passive-homosexual attitude toward the father.

In his paper "Some Psychological Consequences of the Anatomical Distinction between the Sexes"[21] Freud says: "but we shall, of course, willingly agree that the majority of men are also far behind the masculine ideal and that all human individuals, as a result of their bisexual disposition and of cross-inheritance, combine in themselves both masculine and feminine characteristics, so that pure masculinity and femininity remain theoretical contructions of uncertain content."

When analyzing a woman, our aim is to transform a neurotic being, in whom masculine and feminine traits are combined, into a wholly feminine personality. She will then abandon her penis-envy, so that the clitoris will no longer be the principal erotogenic zone but sexual feeling will attach itself to the mucous membrane of the vagina, which will develop its full sensibility. She will then be proud and glad of her femininty and will attain to complete womanhood. Conversely, in analyzing a man, it

[21] *The International Journal of Psychoanalysis,* Vol. VIII, p. 142.

will be our business to bring to light all his feminine traits, to free him from his wish to be a woman and thus to help him to the untroubled and uninterrupted exercise of complete masculine genitality.

In order to explain to my patients the alteration of the unconscious wishes to lead the life of a man or that of a woman, I use the illustration of the surface of a liquid in the two arms of a U-shaped tube. If pressure is applied to the surface on the one side, the liquid rises in the other, and vice versa. In support of my view let me quote the short analysis of a dream. The patient suffered from inhibitions but was by no means a manifest homosexual. The dream and the associations to it were as follows. "In the presence of another man I passed a large quantity of urine into a pail. . . . On dreaming this I woke up, with a sharp pain in my rectum. I thought of spasm of the sphincter-muscle. This pain often recurs in the night and is so severe that it makes me cry out. Sometimes it comes on me suddenly in the day as well, but my mind can be diverted from it, for instance, if I meet a man I know. It is true that, afterwards, the pain gets even worse. Some time ago, I was about to speak to a girl in the street, when the pain came on violently and prevented me. It came on once before, in an earlier dream, in which my father was performing coitus with me *per anum*. This pain in the rectum occurs if I have a strong erection in the night—or else it is that, when the pain occurs, there is an erection which persists for some time. At any rate the two things affect one another. I have a feeling of ease when a very large mass of feces passes through the anus. When I think of the passive homosexuality which analysis has brought to light in me, I don't know whether the pain indicates an inclination to experience coitus *per anum* or a defense against it." I told the patient that there was an analogy to his feelings in the spasm of the vagina from which some women suffer.

"Some days ago, a friend of mine—a singer—used the pail in my room (the pail of the dream) for passing urine. I had vigorously opposed his wish to spend the night with me, because I feared my landlady would think I was a homosexual. The singer is a great favorite with women and has had innumerable love-adventures. Probably I wanted to impress him in my dream; for coitus is like passing urine into a woman's body. My mistress has missed her last monthly period, a fact of which I am very proud. Although she is quite independent and her parents have long ceased to support her, I have a very bad conscience in regard to them." Here we see clearly the part played by the latent sense of guilt in bringing about a *reactive femininity*, if I may so express myself; the latent dream-thoughts contain the wish to go one better than a man whose love-life the dreamer envies. We detect also feelings of guilt on account of a pregnancy and the desire to experience coitus *per anum*, that is, to assume the functions of a woman.

If one tells a woman who is familiar with the results of psychoanalytical investigation that men envy women the vagina just as much as women envy men the penis, she will sometimes reply that she cannot picture how this can be so. The penis, she will say, is surely an organ of such great importance and value that it is natural for women to covet it, but she cannot understand a corresponding feeling in men for the vagina. In this connection I recall Freud's[22] words: "After a woman has become aware of the wound to her narcissism, she develops, like a scar, a sense of inferiority. When she has passed beyond her first attempt at explaining her lack of a penis as being a punishment personal to herself and has realized that that sex character is a universal one, she begins to share the contempt felt by men for a sex which is the lesser in so important a respect, and, so far at least as maintaining this judgment is concerned, she clings obstinately to being like a man." But men, who do not bear the mark of this wound to their narcissism, ought, one would think, to have no difficulty in admitting that the vagina represents to them an organ productive of pleasure and therefore worth coveting, even though the fact that they themselves lack this organ is something of a blow to their narcissism.[23]

[22] "Some Psychological Consequences of the Anatomical Distinction between the Sexes." *The International Journal of Psychoanalysis*. Vol. VIII, p. 138.

[23] In the discussion on this paper Dr. Fromm remarked that, in the early stages of the evolution of the race, there seems to be a parallel to the ontogenetic tendencies I have just described. So long as human beings subsisted entirely on the free gifts of nature, that is, without employing any skilled means for their support—the basis of life being exclusively natural production—the position of woman was bound to be superior to that of man, because she alone had the natural power of giving birth. She must, therefore, have been held in higher esteem. Only when man developed technical skill did the picture change and he himself come to occupy the foreground.

IX

The Castration Complex in the Formation of Character

By Franz Alexander

I PRELIMINARY REMARKS ON THE DYNAMICS OF SYMPTOM-FORMATION

A particularly favorable opportunity to gain some comprehension of the dynamics of symptom-formation presents itself in the study of those so-called "transitory symptoms" which arise under our eyes in the course of analytic work—a sort of product of the laboratory. Ferenczi, who first described these manifestations, pointed out their theoretic importance in that they enable experimental observations to be made of the dynamics of falling ill. Ferenczi[1] explains these symptom-formations arising during analytic work as manifestations of resistance against the process of making conscious certain unconscious tendencies which are displeasing to the ego and which have been brought near to the level of consciousness by analysis. Driven out of their old neurotic "positions" these tendencies are seeking an outlet in new symptoms and struggling to reach equilibrium afresh by this means. Truly a unique opportunity to study symptom-formation!

These transitory artificial products of the neurosis make their appearance in an unusually pronounced form during the analysis of what are called "neurotic characters." These are types well known to the analyst, people who suffer from no very definite symptoms of illness but whose behavior in life is in the highest

[1] Ferenczi: *Contributions to Psycho-Analysis*, 1916, p. 164. Chap. vii, "Transitory Symptom-Constructions during the Analysis."

degree impulsive and frequently even compulsive; they are unusually subject to the domination of their unconscious instinctual tendencies. The lives of such people display some remarkably irrational feature and their apparently senseless behavior—like the symptoms of neurotics—is comprehensible only to the trained eye of the analyst, able to perceive the unconscious motives behind it. This irrational behavior is obviously equivalent to neurotic symptoms in others; these people form a transition-type between the neurotic and the healthy. Their neurotic way of living has also some resemblance to the blunders of everyday life, which also owe their origin to unconscious motives; only, these impulse-ridden characters gratify their repressed tendencies, not in trivial everyday blunders, but in irrational compulsive actions literally at the most important and decisive moments of their lives. Whereas in the neuroses the unconscious makes use of special mechanisms, such as hysterical conversion, symbolic obsessive acts, delusional ideas, all characteristically isolated as far as possible from the rest of the person's life, the neurotic character interweaves his life with his neurosis—his life constitutes his neurosis. Teleologically considered, the symptoms of illness serve the purpose of satisfying, in a relatively harmless manner, those wishes that are in conflict with the conscious ego, of *localizing* them to the symptoms, and thereby preventing them from injuring the rest of life. The best illustration of the self-healing function of symptoms is provided by the final state of the paranoiac, which corresponds to a recovery with disablement. His behavior in and capacity for the common activities of life is often perfectly normal, his delusional system alone excepted; it has absorbed the whole of the pathologic matter into itself, as it were. All feeling of illness is lacking, too, and with some justification; the analyst will certainly reflect carefully before disturbing this equilibrium. Naturally in most types of neuroses the outcome is not so favorable, the tendencies that are incompatible with the ego cannot always be isolated in this way. As a contrast to this recovery with disablement we have many phobias, in which the anxiety encroaches ever further and further into life, making it at last intolerable; or certain obsessional neuroses, inhibiting every activity. With neurotic characters, however, the morbid process has not yet reached the stage of symptom-formation; the unconscious tendencies that would otherwise form symptoms can still find an outlet in certain irrational actions which are hardly influenced by consciousness, and make no use of any particular mechanisms.

It is difficult to find an answer to the dynamic problem: whether the pressure of the factor leading to illness—the damming-up of the libido—is not great enough to open up new paths and form symptoms as an outlet, or whether the defense-reaction of the organism—the repression—is not powerful enough altogether to exclude satisfaction in reality. In any case, the irrational neurotic behavior of the abnormal character entails more real satisfaction than a neurotic symptom does, and in its blind impulse-ridden way often creates more misery than a neurosis. Indeed, we know from Freud, especially from his recent work, that the repressing faculty (*Instanz*) is the conscience, that is, a social faculty, one that guards the individual from the satisfaction in reality of his asocial wishes and even punishes him for the satisfaction of them in fantasy. A section of the neurotic characters, certain impulse-ridden criminal types, plainly suffer from a deficiency of these defense-reactions. And it is just as unquestionable that another section of these people, driven by their instinctual tendencies perpetually to injure themselves in life do not fall ill of a neurosis simply *because*, by means of their apparently senseless self-injuries, they replace the symbolic overcompensations (self-punishments) of the obsessional neurotic by real ones, and in this way keep their oversensitive consciences clear. Should they be at any time deprived of the possibility of this real satisfaction, then, if these dynamic considerations are scientifically sound, we should expect them to fall ill of a neurosis. In actual fact, when such people come into the hands of an analyst, it is found that they already suffer from various neurotic symptoms. Yet as long as it is possible for the tendencies that are incompatible with the ego to be realized in behavior which eludes the vigilance of the censorship, all consciousness of illness is lacking; and this is the reason why, when such people are induced by those around them to undergo analysis, they are so particularly difficult. Even when this impulse-ridden behavior leads to the greatest hardships it is still consistently maintained, while its calamitous consequences are ascribed to the cruelty of fate or to chance. The unconscious is always victorious and seizes its satisfaction at the expense of the most elementary interests of the ego, as is plainly shown by the not at all uncommon final fate of such people—death by suicide.

The conclusion to which we are led by these reflections is that every "neurotic character" contains in it the germ of a particular form of neurosis, which must then break out if any deprivation ensues of the satisfaction in reality of the neurotic tendency. Curtailment of the real satisfaction may occur in two ways: by external circumstances, or by internal ones—the interference of the conscious ego. This second way occurs in the course of the analytic work, when the meaning of the irrational impulse-ridden conduct is made conscious on the occasion of its repetition in transference; so that under the control of consciousness the previous satisfactions are renounced. According to the considerations adduced above, it would be in this stage of the analysis that the transitory symptoms would arise—more, that a transitory and hitherto latent neurosis would develop. The analytic work removes the previous possibilities of satisfaction, by bringing the tendencies incompatible with the ego more and more under the control of the conscious faculties; under the pressure of this artificially-induced damming of the libido these tendencies escape into those neurotic symptoms which have hitherto been replaced by the actual neurotic satisfactions in life, and in which the tendencies find a fresh subterranean outlet. Neurosis is here also the obverse of neurotic behavior, just as it is of the perversions, with this difference, that the perverse satisfaction is accepted by the ego, whereas the neurotic behavior with its illogicality is unrecognized as a satisfaction.

The conditions under which "transitory symptoms" appear are in these cases unusually pronounced; the lines on which the interchangeable occurrence of neurosis or neurotic behavior may proceed are laid down by the patient's previous life. The circumstances are thus peculiarly favorable to comprehension of the origin and mechanism of development of a neurosis, because the disease is then a product of the laboratory and actually develops before our eyes out of apparent health. We can thus observe the universal mechanism by which the neuroses develop ordinarily, since it is even probable that an attempt at actual satisfaction *always* precedes the symbolic satisfaction of the incompatible tendencies in symptoms, and that symptoms only arise as substitutive satisfaction after this attempt is found to be impracticable or in consequence of an inner prohibition.[2]

[2] I would point to the development of children in this respect.

It must not be forgotten that these transitory illnesses during the treatment are actually nothing but transference-manifestations in the Freudian sense and consequently produced by resistance; they are the last attempts of the repressed tendencies to find a discharge in the form of action. Freud describes the transference as a "new edition" of an old disease.[3] The analysis of neurotic characters, in which the transitory symptoms and other transference-manifestations arise, not as substitutes for previous neurotic symptoms, but as an apparently quite new neurosis, show the transference in this character of a neurosis in a peculiarly convincing, perhaps even at first in a startling manner. The predilection shown by such cases for forming transitory symptoms may also be explained by the fact that with them it is not a *symptom* that is being discharged into the transference, but a much more real sort of satisfaction; consequently more is expected in the transference. Dynamically considered, every "transitory symptom" is merely an expression of the fact that a neurotic attachment has been loosened so quickly that it is not possible for the cathexis which has been set free to work itself out in transference-manifestations; that is, by resolving the symptoms one takes from the patient more satisfaction than can at the moment be made good to him in the transference or still less in reality. The block leads to new symptoms which nevertheless still retain a relation to the transference. In treating abnormal characters we destroy, not symptoms, but real or almost real satisfactions; the tension caused by the difference between the real satisfaction and the transference-satisfaction is too great, and so there arise transitory symptoms, or even a transitory neurosis, as by-products or also as transition-stages.

After these dynamic considerations I will add some observations.

II THE CASTRATION COMPLEX IN THE FORMATION OF CHARACTER

In his essay "Some Character Types Met with in Psycho-Analytic Work"[4] Freud gives us the prototype of an analytic understanding of neurotic characters. Our knowledge of certain more definite character-traits begins with his treatment of the

[3] Freud: *Introductory Lectures on Psycho-Analysis*, 1922, p. 371.
[4] Freud: "Einige Charaktertypen aus der Psychoanalytischen Arbeit," *Sammlung kleiner Schriften*, Vierte Folge, S. 521.

subject of anal erotism. A sharp line of demarcation between certain exaggerated character-traits and neurotic characters could hardly be drawn. By a character-trait we mean a certain stereotyped attitude in life; those people whom we call neurotic characters show this stereotyped attitude in the whole rhythm of their lives, at the most decisive moments and most important turning-points. Whereas the hysteric makes his body and the obsessional neurotic makes the everyday performances of life the medium in which he expresses his neurotic wishes, for the neurotic character, ridden by his instinctual tendencies, this medium consists of the whole course of his life, his actual *destiny*.

Freud gives us in *Beyond the Pleasure Principle*[5] a profound insight into the essential unity of neurotic symptoms, transference, and human destiny, by his view of them as the expression of a compulsion toward the repetition of an attempt to solve an unresolved conflict, to master subsequently a real experience that had been insuperable.

In the analytic re-adjustment of a neurotic character, therefore, we pursue the same object as with the neurosis, namely, that of discovering the real experience which is forever being repeated in the impulse-ridden behavior, and in which the irrational actions would for once have been justified.

During the analysis of such a neurotic character I was able to observe with unusual clearness the impulse-ridden actions being successively replaced by conversion-hysterical and paranoid symptoms. The dynamic processes described above came out with particular clearness in the course of the analysis. After the almost complete amnesia covering the first six to seven years of his life had been gradually dispersed, the patient's whole life lay before us as a series of situations and actions repeated again and again since his earliest childhood, under the weight of a truly demonic compulsion in the sense of an ever-recurring attempt to solve a primal conflict. His neurotic behavior in life took the place of the symptoms of this latent neurosis, so that, as the meaning of the actions replacing these symptoms was revealed and they were brought under the control of the judging, inhibiting faculty of consciousness and given up, this latent neurosis was bound to come to the fore. The dynamic process involved

[5] International Psycho-Analytical Press, 1922.

was similar to that in "active therapy," by which the patient is required to refrain from certain symptomatic acts, only that here the analyst's prohibition was replaced by the patient's conscious renunciation actuated by his new knowledge.[6] The life of this heavily impulse-ridden character contained nothing worthy of special mention; and yet the transparent way in which his life had formed itself under the pressure of the castration complex, and still more the paranoid symptoms which transiently appeared during the analysis—I might call it a paranoia in a nutshell, developing and dispersing before my eyes—offered an unusual opportunity for discovering much about the mechanism of this disease. The circumstances were also favorable in that the patient, though an intelligent man, was not a complicated type; his youth had been spent in rough, uncivilized surroundings and his later life in a large metropolis, so that he had been forced to go through ontogenetically in a double manner the phylogenetic adaptation of humanity to the requirements of a civilized community. This adaptation he accomplished externally quite well; he rose high in the business world and acquired a large fortune.

He came for advice on account of difficuties in his married life. He was beginning to doubt his wife's love and yet he somehow felt as if he himself were also responsible for the unhappiness of his marriage. After many years of married life he was just beginning to realize that his wife had married him for his money. He treated his wife—unconsciously, it is true—like a prostitute, overwhelmed her with luxury and demanded nothing from her but intercourse. Their married life consisted of nothing but the man's struggles to be allowed intercourse, which was always paid for in the same material way. These payments were often grotesque; the wife wanted a hat, perhaps, and he would give her six hats at once. The woman, who was sexually frigid in any case, began to perceive in her unconscious the meaning of this strongly anal-erotic tendency and reacted to it with a corresponding craving for presents. They were bound to each other, like the nut and the screw. His experience with women had always been the same; his first marriage and his earlier love-

[6] In another analysis of a neurotic character, the meaning of an attitude in life which was continually reproduced under compulsion was not discoverable until, after a prohibition in regard to it, it had taken the form of repetition in dreams and transitory symptoms.

affairs were merely unfinished versions of the same drama. His type of love-object was always the cold, calculating woman, who if she possessed a remnant of capacity for love was always forced back into anal-erotic regression by deliberate measures. One unconscious tendency in this was the well-known one described by Freud—the tendency to debase the love-object— which played an important part.[7] The woman is paid and thereby becomes a prostitute, being thus detached from the mother-*imago;* instead of tenderness she receives money. The repressed idea came back in another form, however. His wife was far superior to him in refinement, she corrects his speech, writes his letters, represents him in society; he feels inferior to her and thus reproduces the mother-son relationship. In his marriage therefore he made use of the well-known mechanism of a partial repression. The wife is made into a prostitute and the love regresses to an anal-erotic form of satisfaction, but along with this the superiority of the woman in the mother-*imago* is retained as an important factor.

The libido which was not attached anal-erotically sought an outlet by many and devious paths in his social[8] activities, his relations with friends and other business men, in the form of disguised (sublimated) homosexuality. Affectionate love for any woman was completely unknown to him; the remnant of love which had not regressed and become fixed on the anal-erotic level was fixed homosexually and sublimated. In the analysis the fate of this remnant came to be investigated first, and from it arose during the treatment the paranoid symptoms which will principally interest us.

The dissatisfactions and difficulties in his marriage first arose when his social activities began to be destroyed by external catastrophes. Social upheaval made it necessary for him to leave his home and to give up his occupation. In a few months all that he had achieved was reduced to nothing; he saved a small part of his fortune, it is true, but was condemned to almost complete inactivity by the outer circumstances. The outlet that the libido had hitherto found in his work, which on account of

---

[7] Freud, "Über die allgemeinste Erniedrigung des Liebeslebens," *Sammlung kleiner Schriften,* Vierte Folge, S. 213.

[8] *Sozial.* This Latin word is confined to scientific usage in German and has not the wide and often tendentious implications that it has in English. It simply means "in the world," "among people."—Tr.

its neurotic element must be discussed in more detail, was thus cut off, and the dammed-up libido led to dissatisfaction in his married life. It appeared as a dim longing for love, which was unrealizable in the married life that had been formed on the anal-erotic level and had satisfied the previous needs of the libido. Efforts to take up his former activities again also came to nothing, on account of both internal and external difficulties. And yet, since it seemed that the capacity to absorb libido anal-erotically had reached its height and no more libido could be dealt with in this manner, it was essential that the previous social activities, which as we shall see were already highly neurotic, should be replaced by new ones, in order to re-establish an equilibrium of the mental forces. There remained two possible alternatives: either the neurosis which was already latent in the neurotically tinged sublimations must be replaced by a manifest neurosis, or the marriage must be dissolved and an attempt made to find an outlet for the libido dammed-up by the overthrow of the sublimations in a new love-relationship on the genital level. At the beginning of the treatment the second alternative was much in the patient's mind; but the several attempts he had already made to leave his wife had come to nothing, which made him hesitate now. We know of course that this path was impassable and that every attempt to find a genital outlet would have come to grief. The Oedipus complex which had never been overcome stood in the way; even without a neurotic disposition, indeed, it stands as a formidable barrier against unlimited genital satisfaction and necessitates the formation of sublimations, that is, it forces a part of the sexual energy into social paths. In a neurotic character such as this the capacity for love on the genital plane which is so narrowly restricted by the Oedipus complex must first be enlarged by analysis, in order to make satisfaction of a normal kind in the relation to the love-object possible.

The external changes in his life were not of course alone responsible for the overthrow of the sublimations. The analysis showed that the social upheaval merely provided an occasion for the demonic feature in the neurosis of his life to appear in a more pronounced form and bring it about that the life's work of this man, who was in any case continually injuring himself in life from a neurotic sense of guilt, should be finally destroyed. He was forty years of age and it was indeed in reality no light matter for him to begin again; but the difficulty was materially increased by the neurotic tendency to self-injury which throughout his whole life had hindered the healthy tendencies toward sublimation and had rendered a great part of his energy sterile. The situation was similar to that of a professional violinist suffering from a neurotic cramp in his fingers, who then by chance or by some blunder injures his hand as well.

Attempts to take up his activities again under difficult external circumstances failed on account of neurotic behavior in the course of his work, which now evinced itself more and more. As a young man in favorable external conditions he had tolerated these neurotic inhibitions without serious disadvantage; but in the difficult conditions after the collapse of his business, they made it impossible for him to succeed in obtaining a position in the world even approximating to what he had had before, and thus to obtain a similar field for his activities.

This was the situation when the analysis began. Without following the course of the analysis chronologically, I shall endeavor to describe the course taken by that part of the libido which had hitherto been attached to social activities (homosexual), and which by being blocked had led to the dissatisfactions in married life and to the slight hypochondriacal symptoms which brought him to the analyst.

As has been said, the patient had never in his best years succeeded in sublimating his homosexual libido without neurotic signs, especially as it was strongly reinforced from the heterosexual libido, which was driven into a narrow channel by the Oedipus complex and found no adequate outlet. Analysis soon revealed a remarkable attitude which had been repeated in a stereotyped manner throughout his whole business career, the first occurrence of which was traced back to early childhood. He showed an impulsion to injure himself and, as it turned out, in a particular way—by being exploited or defrauded in some way. I should like to describe this impulsion as *passive kleptomania*, kleptomania become narcissistic and turned against the self. With an instinctive knowledge of men he knew how to choose his friends in such a way and how to combine with friendship some material transaction or other, usually of a financial nature, that in the end he was invariably simply cheated and defrauded. He did business only with friends and made his friends his business clients. Friendship and business were intimately connected, and always so that in the end he came off badly. Or else he lent money, pressed it on the borrower, especially when he knew that he would never get it back. He applied the proverbial saying, "Opportunity makes the thief," with an amazing ingenuity so that he might be stolen from. It was astonishing to find, as the story of his friendships unrolled itself in the analysis, that he had not had a single friend with whom there had not been some monetary transaction and by whom he had not in the end been more or less seriously injured. It had not been difficult to gratify his peculiar need; he could reckon upon one of the strongest impulses in man, his avarice, and had been able to select the right objects for his purpose with sure intuition. Nor was it difficult for him to ascribe his misfortunes among his friends to the cruelty of fate; in any case he learned nothing from his experiences and would learn nothing, but always repeated the same trick.

His peculiarity also showed itself in a well-known and less pathological form, in meticulous overconscientiousness and honorableness, to which quality he owed in part his considerable success in his career. It would have been tempting to regard his peculiar passive kleptomania as an exaggerated, caricatured conscientiousness and thus as an anal-erotic overcompensation; but the almost complete removal of the infantile amnesia showed that it represented first and foremost a persistent attempt to realize a castration wish, and that the equivalence of "money" and "penis," with a slighter emphasis on the connecting-link "feces," formed the unconscious basis of his impulse-ridden behavior. Through his whole career his attitude to those in authority and to representatives of the father had been highly characteristic. His great conscientiousness and trustworthiness always won him their good opinion and he had often been entrusted with very responsible offices. He always formed his relation with those in authority more and more into that of a father and son; and then, urged on by a dim sense of guilt, he worked with tense energy and utter self-sacrifice for their business interests. Through these qualities he acquired great wealth and a high position in a trade syndicate in his own country. Yet every acquisition of money made him feel guilty, and he relieved his conscience partly by devotion to work and partly by losing a part of it again in the passive kleptomaniac manner described above.[9] This attitude is well known to us as an anal-erotic overcompensation, but in this case its origin in the Oedipus complex was clearly betrayed by transference-factors involved, and was only fully comprehensible after elucidation of his castration complex. By transference-factors I mean that it was not a matter of indifference to him who caused him these material losses; but that he always selected as the objects of his passive kleptomania friends who were socially or intellectually superior to him, that is, who represented the father. He was inexorable against dishonesty in his subordinates; the unconscious basis of this attitude will be discussed later.

We know from Freud[10] that the loss of feces is felt as one of the earliest narcissistic wounds, in that it constitutes the loss of a pleasure-giving part of the body, and that it can suitably represent castration. I should like here to emphasize that the principal factor in the equivalence of feces and penis seems to consist in their *affective association,* to which the similarity in shape of the two objects is merely secondary. The *tertium comparationis* of this affective association may be expressed more or less as follows: The loss of a pleasure-giving part of the body *as a result* of a previous pleasurable sensation produced by it (stimulation of the mucous membrane). As he grows, every human being learns that every pleasure ends in "pain"; he learns it through the primal castration experiences—the loss of the pleasure-giving nipple after the pleasure of sucking (*oral* primal castration according to Stärcke[11]) and later the loss of the pleasure-giving stool after the anal pleasure of retention (*anal* primal castration according to Freud). An affective basis is therefore well prepared on which the fear or expectation of

---

[9] In this light his behavior looked like a caricature of charitableness and betrays the unconscious motives of this social expression of a sense of guilt. I found the anal-erotic basis of this attitude in an unsublimated form in another patient; as a child he used to retain the feces as long as he could, then evacuate a small portion of them and let it dry on the orifice, then take it off with his hand and throw it away, retaining the remainder for a while longer.

[10] Freud, "Über Triebumsetzungen, insbesondere der Analerotik," *Sammlung kleiner Schriften,* Vierte Folge, S. 139, and "Aus der Geschichte einer infantilen Neurose," *ibid.,* S. 579.

[11] Stärcke, "The Castration Complex," *International Journal of Psycho-Analysis,* 1921, Vol. II, p. 179.

castration may arise. As the earliest affective basis of all for the expectation of castration we may regard the act of birth, which entails the loss of the mother's body, actually a part of the child's own body, and also the loss of the fetal membranes.[12] At the moment of birth a pleasurable condition (the pleasure of absence of stimuli) and a pleasure-giving organ (the uterus) are lost for the first time in life, and are replaced by a painful condition.

The growing human being learns that every pleasure is closely followed by the loss of the pleasure-giving bodily organ (uterus, nipple, stool); so that on reaching the pleasure of onanism he is already prepared affectively to lose the corresponding pleasure-giving organ, the penis, and easily accepts the threat of castration as an obvious conclusion. The temporal sequence of the unconscious affective impressions is elaborated into a causal one (rationalized) and castration is to follow as a result of onanism. This affective basis also explains how the castration complex can play such as important part without any threat having been given—and that without drawing upon any phylogenetic explanation.

Whereas the loss of the nipple is felt as an impersonal cosmic necessity, the first transference-factors come into play during the training in cleanliness; and these the instinctive comprehension of the child's attendants recognizes, by endeavoring to soothe its narcissistic wound with praise and other signs of love. A sense of guilt, the conscience as an inhibitory faculty, plays no part so far. Feces are given up in return for a narcissistic equivalent, praise and tokens of love from those around. The Oedipus complex, the first social factor, first introduces an inhibitory faculty into the ego-system in the shape of the conscience, and the first dim consciousness of guilt bears upon the incest committed in the fantasy accompanying onanism. The ideal set up within the ego (the conscience) coincides with the person of the father[13] (introjection of the father); the castra-

[12] One is reminded of the penis-significance of garments, cloaks, etc. in dreams!

[13] Freud, "Zur Einführung des Narzissmus," *Sammlung kleiner Schriften.* Vierte Folge, S. 104. "The institution of the conscience was originally an embodiment of parental criticisms, later that of social criticisms, a process which repeats itself—the origin of a repression-tendency was originally an external prohibition or hindrance."

tion-punishment is usually expected at the hands of the father. This ideal, as Freud has shown in his *Group Psychology*, is later identified with the leader and finally with the community itself.[14] The incest wishes are renounced first of all for love of an ideal which is identical with the father, and then later for love of an ideal which becomes woven more and more into the ego itself.

With these considerations I hoped to make it clear that money as a narcissistically valuable substance is particularly well adapted, by the affective basis already established, to replace the penis in castration wishes. The same circumstance naturally brings about the other unconscious connection—money and feces —which is even earlier in time; and it is in accordance with the temporal sequence of things that the equivalence of money and penis should develop by way of anal erotism.

With his passive kleptomania our patient was first continually being castrated by those of his friends who were in some way superior to him; and then, when the social revolution brought in a new standard and private property was condemned, he rendered up his fortune to the community itself by a series of quite transparent blunders, and thus transferred to the community the role of the castrator. In order to make comprehensible the paranoid symptoms which appeared during the treatment I must trace back to his youth the history of his castration wishes —which so far have only been mentioned as an impulse-ridden tendency to self-injury.

At the time of the revolution he rescued the fortunes of certain of his friends and got them transferred abroad—and literally forgot to do the same for his own! It is true that he concealed a few articles of value, but later he allowed them to get into the hands of a friend who absconded with them. Before this he once performed a very great service for a business friend, for which he took nothing in return, and was later suspected of high treason for it. His whole life was a series of such incidents, which most frequently ended simply in money being stolen from him. In his youth he reacted with a quite special affectivity to detecting anyone, particularly a subordinate, in an attempt to defraud his chief. At the age of twenty he one day discovered a fellow-employee in the act of embezzling a large sum; the man

[14] Freud, *Group Psychology and the Analysis of the Ego.* International Psycho-Analytical Press, 1922.

offered him a big price for his silence, but he denounced him nevertheless. After this affair, which agitated him exceedingly, he suffered for a year from a gastric neurosis. He could take no food but fluids, and had a strong aversion to almost anything solid. After this recollection came up in the analysis there followed a transitory symptom in the form of an attack of diarrhea, which took the place of his habitual constipation. Hypochondriacal sensations of a globular nature in the larynx—he felt a stick in his throat—were repetitions of similar sensations which he had first had in youth at the same time as the gastric symptoms, after the affair of the embezzlement.

The analysis of these transitory bodily symptoms brought a mass of material into consciousness, of which one little kleptomanic incident in his childhood deserves special attention. It first gave me the assurance that I could justly regard his later tendency to self-injury, which I have called passive kleptomania, as a reversal of a primarily active tendency into a passive one. The mechanism of this reversal is that of a "turning of sadism upon the self," and here too the prominent part played by a sense of guilt in this reversal is evident.

As a schoolboy of nine or ten he stole obsessively from two of his school-fellows—chiefly pencils, pens, money, etc. Pocket-knives he would have liked to take, but did not "because they were too expensive." He most particularly wanted the school-bag of one of these boys, but he could not take it; it would have been too noticeable. They were both unusually clever boys, much cleverer than he, the best in the class; and on this account he envied them, but at the same time he liked them very much. After he had stolen anything he had an intense feeling of guilt, and very often put back the stolen article. He struggled with this compulsion and begged God to free him from this vice. It is to be noted that he stole only from these two friends.

Although the unconscious determination of this "relative kleptomania"—by which I would describe its restriction to particular persons—is transparent enough, I asked him to associate to the stolen articles, but without success. Nothing came to his mind. Only in regard to the school-bag which he so much wanted to steal did the censorship permit a gleam of light to fall on to the unconscious; probably because the chain of associations connecting this object to the repressed idea was longer than that connecting pens, pencils, etc. to it.

Associations to school-bag: "The school-bag had fur; it was made of hide . . . of an undressed deer-skin . . . deer . . . antlers . . . I am very fond of deer, they are so gay and lively." Deer represented manliness to him, as he remarked next.

I would call attention here to the idea of a "hide," which will play an important part in a later dream-interpretation. Behind this kleptomania was clearly the castration wish, which, as the analysis revealed in other ways, was directed first and foremost against the father's genital organ. The clever boys were well suited by their industry and mental superiority to reactivate at the beginning of the second puberty-period the first and earliest feelings of jealousy.

I will make use of this material to point out a surprising difference between the attitude of my patient and that of women with the classical type of kleptomania, who steal obsessively, regardless of whom they are stealing from. They steal on the principle of stealing for stealing's sake, without any affective impulse to injure someone else; I should say they steal without any object-transference. By their thefts they are trying to make good the cosmic injustice of their bodily configuration; their thefts have more of a narcissistic tone. Since there is no intention to injure there is also no sense of guilt; their actions are directed against an impersonal injustice. In my patient's obsessive thieving, however, it is just the transference-factor, the choice of those who were to be stolen from, which is characteristic. He stole only from superior school-fellows; he envied only a bigger penis, and not, like women, the penis in itself.

I do not suppose that this single observation suffices for us to draw any contrast in principle between male and female kleptomania in regard to the presence or absence of transference-factors (absolute and relative kleptomania) and of the sense of guilt.[15] I know that hardly a single analysis goes through with-

[15] In a conversation I had with Dr. Abraham, he informed me that he had often found in analysis other determinants of obsessive stealing, beside the envy of the penis mentioned by me, such as the impulsion to take by force the parent's love which was not forthcoming or any unobtainable pleasure of any kind. This last motive is obviously the ruling one in the habit very common among children of stealing good things to eat. The longing to take the mother from the father also unconsciously plays an important part. In the course of this conversation we came to the conclusion that in all these cases the ultimate impulse to obsessive stealing comes, at the deepest unconscious level, from the

out revealing minor kleptomaniac tendencies in childhood and that in women too the person stolen from often plays an important part. It seems to me, however, that the above considerations explain why the classical objectless kleptomania is met with *only in women.*

In the development of the patient's castration complex this kleptomanic episode marks an important period; for it shows in its active form the same impulse that, by a reversal into a passive form, later on expressed itself in the peculiarity of his neurotic character. The intense sense of guilt shows the struggle for repression which the conscience was waging against the envious attitude toward the father or his representatives—an attitude which in earliest childhood (the first puberty-period) had been overcome, but was revived again shortly before the second puberty-period. And in the course of further analysis an even earlier kleptomaniac episode was actually recalled. As a boy of five or six he often stole money from his father's pockets, and also other things like those he stole at school; even at that time, however, he did not keep the stolen property, but gave it away to his playmates.

Repression of this asocial impulse was not successful, and so an attempt at defense was sought by means of other mental mechanisms—first of all by *projection.* We see this method of defensive warfare in his behavior under temptation to steal, and in his impulsion generally to put himself into situations where the temptation to dishonesty is strong. As early as his fourteenth year he obtained by his honesty a position of great personal responsibility in a shop. After severe resistances in the analysis a series of recollections with a strong affective tone in regard to this period of his life came out; they were memories of the attempts of the customers to bribe him and of his strongly ambivalent feelings toward the head of the firm. He fought the temptations, remained honest, and projected the struggle be-

---

longing for the first source of pleasure; it is the unwillingness to be parted from the mother's breast. The nipple is the first love-token, the first source of pleasure to the child; this oral origin is evident in thefts of sweetmeats. Stealing because love or pleasure is not forthcoming merely shows that the first refusal of the mother's love, the withdrawal of the nipple, has not been overcome. Obsessive stealing would thus always arise out of an active castration-wish, if we take the castration-wish in Stärcke's extended meaning.

tween his conscience and his own aggressive tendencies out-
wards, despatched the enemy within him in his struggle with
the dishonest customers. His better nature, his ego-ideal, played
the part of the head of the firm by identification; the repressed
(or better, to-be-repressed) part of his personality was identified
with the customers. He dealt with his ambivalence by dividing
his ego into two by means of projection and identification, and
thus satisfied both the repressed and the repressing tendencies.
For this solution (the paranoid mechanism) of his conflict he
required situations in which he met with temptation. He kept
up this defense-mechanism until his twenty-second year, when
the affair of the embezzlement occurred; then for the first time
this form of defense against his asocial tendencies failed him.
He delivered up the thief and withstood the temptation, but yet
he fell ill with hypochondriacal and conversion symptoms in the
whole alimentary canal. Eating solid food was given up, as an
oral representation of the castration-wishes; the formation of a
hard stool, affectively overcharged on account of its penis-
significance and so rendered suspicious to the repressing tendency, was prevented by diarrhea. While in these symptoms the
fluid contents of the bowel served the purpose of the higher
repressing ego-system, the repressed active castration-wish obtained expression in the form of a hypochondriacal sensation of
a stick in the throat—he had swallowed a penis. These symptoms
strengthen the surmise that the patient was suffering from a
latent narcissistic neurosis, which was replaced by neurotic behavior in life and thereby prevented from breaking out. These
symptoms did in fact re-appear during the analysis at a time
when his impulse-ridden behavior came to light, and when he
was coming to believe that the unhappy end of all his friendships and the stereotyped repetition of material losses was not
due to the cruelty of fate, but to his own impulses to self-injury,
by which he relieved the burden on his conscience and from
which at the same time he extracted a passive masochistic
pleasure.

His recognition of this had a far-reaching effect. He suddenly
began to review all the relationships with friends that he had at
the moment, which were very numerous, and discovered that he
had invested the remnant of his fortune again systematically in
his friends' business undertakings, in such a way that all control
over it and insight into the inner conduct of affairs was out of

his hands. Examination into things showed him that he had again suffered serious losses in several directions. His attitude now underwent a very sudden and unnatural change. He who had never been capable of exercising any control over his own financial affairs, who regarded it as an insult to ask a friend for an account, now became suspicious and demanded balance-sheets; he changed completely, to the utter astonishment of all his friends and their circle. It was at this time, after the passive satisfaction that he had previously obtained in life had been brought under the control of the censorship and become impossible, that the hypochondriacal and conversion symptoms appeared as a substitute. The analysis and interpretation of these symptoms brought, as has been said, a mass of forgotten memories back into consciousness, and led to the rapid disappearance of these symptoms; only to be followed very shortly, however, by the paranoid symptoms, which had already been heralded by the sudden change of character shown in his suspicious attitude (character-regression, as Ferenczi has called it).

Among the memories unearthed at this time one was accompanied by especially strong feeling; as a child of six he had flung himself sobbing upon the body of his dead father, kissing his face, and had cried out: "I will do everything I can to make up for all that I have done against you!" The revival of this memory gave the impression of a cathartic abreaction; the repressed displaced affect broke out during the analytic session in all its original intensity. Sobbing and crying he saw before him with hallucinatory clearness the completely forgotten face of his dead father.

We may pause for a moment over this memory and consider that in it we have found the actual experience which was forever being reproduced again by the repetition-compulsion, and which brings sense and meaning into the patient's senseless behavior in life. His whole life literally consisted in "making up" for a dark mysterious sin, in perpetually discharging an oppressive unpayable debt. The oath that he swore by his father's dead body he literally carried into action in life; driven by a truly demonic compulsion, he paid back the pennies he had taken from his father's waistcoat pocket to any and every father-substitute who crossed his path in life.

These memories and the recognition they brought sufficed to effect the astonishing change of character described. But these analytic discoveries merely exposed the reaction of the conscience that, under the pressure of the sense of guilt, had turned the impulse to its passive form; behind it there lay, for the present still concealed, the necessary reconstruction of the aggressive active impulse—surmised and theoretically inferred, except for the transitory kleptomaniac episodes in school. Corresponding to this was the too sudden appearance of the change of character and the way in which it grew more and more marked: it replaced (with a character-regression) the memory of the repressed aggressive attitude. He became more and more suspicious, quarreled with all his friends, and could no longer endure their superiority which before he had sought so eagerly. He scented fraud in everything; was at one moment furious, at the next depressed; he went so far as to make a scene with one friend in a public place. His condition approached continually nearer to paranoia.

One day he told me he had been put on the Bolshevists' black list and was living in fear of the world-revolution that was soon going to take place; he would be one of the first victims, for he was already being watched. Now that he could no longer pay the world by damaging himself, by being deceived and stolen from, anxiety had developed. His neurotic behavior, like every neurotic symptom, had served as a protection against anxiety, forming as it did the passive discharge of an originally active libido. He felt guilty and paid, let himself be stolen from, in order to avoid a worse fate; he paid *in order to be able to keep his penis*. And then analytic recognition took away this defense against his neurotic fear of the community and the anxiety broke out in ideas of persecution. Indeed he had not been persecuted before because he had paid out money to prevent it.

One day, during the analysis of a dream, quite unmistakable paranoid symptoms appeared; they bore, however, a strong transference-character.

Dream: He was in a stable and saw hidden in a corner (perhaps behind a wall) a bear; it stood on two legs like a human being. The bear went up to a dark heap which he could not see clearly and *very carefully* picked up a furry hide off the heap; then went slowly along, and *very carefully* put the skin down in another place on the stable floor. In the background he saw two horses, one of which moved (perhaps it kicked out its hind leg) while the bear was carrying out this performance.

The first associations came without difficulty. The bear made him think that as a child he was called "Bear," and that his baptismal name meant "bear" in his own language. Then he remembered an incident of his childhood. He was perhaps five or six years old when a bear came into his father's stable-yard and tried to get into one of the stalls; it disappeared again, however, without taking anything. Then followed memories about being overtaken and robbed by gypsies. When I asked him for associations to a "hide," he became irritable. Nothing came to his mind . . . then a hesitating mutter . . . "Perhaps it was a wild boar's skin." The next association was . . . "Fur collar." Then he was silent a long time; suddenly he said:

"I feel something cold streaming on to me from you. You're sending out electricity on to me!"

Intense anxiety came over him; he was quite convinced of the reality of his delusional ideas. ("The man has electricity in his body!")

To complete the account in full of the course of this transitory paranoid condition I will interpolate here that interpretation of these delusional ideas led during this very session to relief of the anxiety and to understanding on the part of the patient. The way had been well prepared by the foregoing analysis. The dream was interpreted in the following sessions, and in a relatively short time we arrived, through a series of memories with a strong affective tone (among which was that already mentioned of stealing money from the father), at a practically complete mastery of his castration complex. The paranoid attitude also gave way and the exaggerated change to suspiciousness relaxed, but without any return of the impulsion to self-injury. The character change showed itself also externally; his expression, his manner, his handwriting, and above all his gait, altered conspicuously. He started a new business undertaking, and for the first time since his breakdown he again achieved success in it.

The meaning of the dream, however, was only revealed fully when the significance of the "very careful" operations of the bear came to light.

The bear steals the hide and goes about it very carefully like a thief (please refer to the memory of the bear, followed by that of being attacked by robbers). The hide obviously serves as a penis-symbol, as it did it in the former chain of associations: school-bag—hide—deer—maleness, and as is indicated too by the first associations to it: wild boar—fur collar. His next associations explain the intense anxiety that supervened together with the paranoid ideas of reference (the physician was sending out electricity on to him) when I first asked him for associations to "hide." As a child he was once terrified by a wild boar and another time by an otter. The next association to otter was: "Men often wear fur collars of otter skin" . . . "It was a big powerful otter" (otters are smooth, long, and cylindrical in shape). He had once as a child of five seen a stableman having intercourse with a peasant girl in the stable which he saw in his dream; it frightened him intensely because the girl screamed horribly. This brought memories of observing parental intercourse.

In the dream the hide stands for the greatly feared penis of the grown-up man (stableman, father); it is strongly endowed with affect, as is the chain of associations throughout: penis—fright—wild boar—otter, and it is to be noted that the exaggerated impression made by these animals is due to association by similarity of shape (otter and penis). In the dream, however, these terrifying animals are condensed into a *hide,* that is, are *dead;* and in the appearance of the bear as a body-snatcher (hide = corpse) the repressed wish is gratified—the wish that threatened to break forth from the unconscious at the moment when he stood by the dead body of the father he had feared and envied and who was now so harmless—*the wish to rob the dead father of his penis.* Instead of this wish there appeared in consciousness the sense of intense guilt: "I will do everything I can to make up for all that I have done against you!"

At the sight of his father lying dead, the conflict in the ambivalence surged up, if not for the first time, yet certainly with greatest intensity, when the death-wishes of fantasy were suddenly realized.

In the dream the hide is also a symbol of feces; the bear picks it up from a "heap." The first association to heap was "dung-heap"; a heap in a stable is obviously a heap of horse-dung. The word hide (*Fell*) also made him think of refuse (*Abfall*). At the moment that the bear picks up the hide the horse makes a threatening movement. The connection is clear: the bear steals horse-dung (money) from the horse (father). Directly after relating the dream the patient himself interpreted the two horses as the two parents. I should also like to emphasize that in the dream the bear behaves in the same way as the patient had behaved in life as a child when, because of his sense of guilt, he did not keep the things he had stolen from his father, but gave them away to his playmates. The bear puts the hide carefully back on the floor. As we have seen, he too in later life cannot keep the money he has earned and is impelled to give up some of it again.[16]

We saw that by the dream-work of condensation the hide has acquired a central significance. Besides this, the dream makes use of the (paranoid) projection mechanism. The division of the ego into two is clear: conscience (ego-ideal) is hidden behind a wall (endopsychic perception of repression) and looks on at the bear's operations; the latter at the same time stands for himself, the repressed part of himself which he projects into the outer world. The complete interpretation of this dream amounted to an explanation of the neurotic trait in the patient's character. The envy of the father's penis was displaced on to money, and then under the weight of the conscience was turned against himself in the form of an impulse to self-injury. Behind this last line of defense, by displacement, projection and reversal of the instinct, against the primitive aggressive castration wish, there lies as an intermediate stage the passive homosexuality, which comes to expression during the interpretation of the dream in the transitory paranoid delusion: the physician is sending out electricity on to him. A complete account of this transformation of the libido would be as follows:

1. *Primary attitude of envy directed against the father: the positive castration wish* (stealing money from the father).

2. Institution of an ego-ideal identified with the father (introjection of the father as the ego-ideal). As a result of this ambivalence a conflict of the conscience ensues (scene by the father's dead body). Under the pressure of the sense of guilt a transformation of the active castration wish into a passive one takes place by "turning upon the self" (talion punishment). Together with the passive castration wish appears the passive-

[16] His unconscious, which was in this respect so unusually sensitive, perceived only too plainly the structure of present-day commercial organization—that the money a man earns is taken away from someone else.

homosexual attitude to the father as a punishment, by identification with the suffering partner (sadistic-masochistic conception of coitus: the sexual act witnessed in the stable). This passive-homosexual current of feeling undoubtedly proceeds mainly from heterosexual libido dammed up by prohibitions against incest and parricide. It cannot remain in this crude homosexual form, however, because of fear of castration and fear of homosexual assault; it is therefore sublimated as:

3. *Passive submissive attitude to superiors and friends* (passive homosexuality) and *passive kleptomania* (castration wish). This last phase serves as an outlet for the libido at the same time sanctioned by conscience, and serves also as a defense against anxiety. The object of this anxiety was originally the paternal penis; later the anxiety takes the form of a dread of the community.

The defense-formula against the aggressive impulses runs therefore: It is not I who wishes to castrate my father and possess my mother, but *he* who wishes to castrate me and do to me what I should like to do to her. This defense-formula leads to anxiety, nevertheless; only after displacement from the penis to money and only after social sublimation of the passive homosexuality does it become adapted to keep the anxiety in check. At the moment when the analysis was undoing this whole process backward, when the wish-tendency behind the apparently accidental money-losses was exposed and had been renounced, the anxiety which lay concealed behind this defense-mechanism broke out as dread of the Bolshevists. The analysis went deeper, however, and in the interpretation of the "bear" dream substituted castration for the money losses, by bringing up the equivalence of money and penis. The anxiety which by displacement and sublimation had been disguised as dread of the community regressed to the naked dread of the homosexual assault that was now expected as a consequence of castration: "You are sending out electricity on to me!"

This quite unambiguous analysis of the mechanism by which a transitory paranoid anxiety developed will perhaps enable us to add a small contribution to the theory of paranoia or, rather, of delusions of persecution. This contribution becomes possible when we regard the result of this analysis in the light of Freud's recent more extended investigations into the ego-system.

The homosexual genesis of the paranoid ideas is quite clear in the case described, but we also obtain an insight into the original evolution of homosexuality—namely, projection of the aggressive castration wish and thereby division of the ego into two. The ego-ideal which arose out of introjection of the father is saved by a projection of the aggressive tendency incompatible with it; this latter then directs itself against the ideal. This aggressive side of the ego-system, which remains at this primitive level, after projection gratifies its castration wish against the higher side which is identified with the father, against the ideal. So that, by being deceived and stolen from by his friends, he was not merely punished for his aggressive covetous tendencies, but was also—as the man in possession who could be defrauded and robbed—their superior; and thus he acquired a father's position toward his friends. This contradiction made the passive attitude to his friends more tolerable. The whole mechanism, therefore, is similar to that described by Freud for melancholia; it is only less narcissistic, because the aggressive side remains projected. The incest wish is also at the same time guarded against by a similar process which, however, appears to be independent of the first process described; the active wishes in regard to the mother are resolved into an identification with her, through the passive homosexual attitude to the father. Both the active impulses which have been turned upon the self pass over together into passive homosexuality: the aggression against the father and the heterosexual impulse toward the mother turn into a passive female attitude in regard to the father (this entails at the same time self-punishment).[17] To sum up, in the libido-development under investigation three great stages are distinguishable:

1. The primary, sadistic, active, heterosexual. (Primal crime of incest and castration wishes.)

2. Following this, a defense against these asocial impulses by transformation of them into masochistic, passive-homosexual, and finally into

[17] My speaking of the incest wish in connection with the castration wish is only apparently an arbitrary digression; for the latter already includes the former. The envy of the father's penis is only intelligible when the incest wish is already in existence to give cause for this envy. With regard to the patient's tendency to identify himself with his mother, I may mention that he had since childhood had a habit of pinching his right nipple, which had grown considerably larger in the course of years as a result.

3. A defense by displacement and sublimation against the passive-homosexual outlet for the libido.

I should wish not to go further without pointing out that Freud has already described these three great stages as occurring in the evolution of civilization and particularly in the evolution of religion. The primal crime is the *first* stage. The passive submissive attitude to the totem-animal and later to the god is the *third* stage. The *second* stage of unsublimated homosexuality is not manifest; it is repressed, as also in the character-development I have been describing, only to appear after displacement from the father to the totem-animal or after sublimation from the father to the god. Freud has shown the supreme importance of repressed homosexual tendencies for the origin of religion in his paper, "The History of an Infantile Neurosis,"[18] which constitutes a confirmation out of individual psychology of the theory developed in *Totem and Tabu*. The part played by the unconscious passive homosexuality, which provokes anxiety and is guarded against, is the same in his case as in mine. In his case, so far as it is not worked off in hysterical bowel-symptoms, it leads to a caricature of religion, in my case to a caricature of the morals of capitalism.

The neurosis which expressed itself in the patient's whole career in life did not, however, constitute the entire solution of the father-conflict. He further made use of a more narcissistic mechanism: of the sense of inferiority, which also had its root in the castration complex.

Exaggerated feelings of inferiority strike the analytic eye at once as an intermediate stage on the way to delusions of inferiority, and it is not difficult to recognize in them the wish-tendency: that is, the tendency to self-punishment for a primary attitude of envy. The feeling of inferiority has indeed always an envious attitude inherent in it, and behaves reciprocally with it; envy is sadistically toned and inferiority masochistically. "I am too weak" means also "Another is stronger than I." The craving to create situations in which inferiority is felt is the same process that Freud has described as the repetition-compulsion to conjure up again and again a traumatic situation that had not been overcome. In feeling himself weaker than someone else, whether justifiably or not, a person with feelings of inferiority is re-

[18] Freud, *Sammlung kleiner Schriften*, Vierte Folge, S. 703.

creating the father-son situation which he has never overcome. The later course of this conflict is known: identification with the father and introjection of the father as ideal. The solution of the conflict is now attempted within the ego-system and the feeling of inferiority represents a feeling of tension between the ideal and the ego, as Freud remarks in his latest work.[19] Solution of the conflict is attempted narcissistically, as in melancholia. One part of the ego is raging against the other; to the ego-ideal this is a sadistic solution and to the ego it is a masochistic one. The ego envies the ideal and is punished for it by torturing feelings of inferiority, but it obtains masochistic pleasure from the punishment. This is the well-known sadistic-masochistic game of such characters; it takes place within the ego-system and absorbs the primary aggressive impulses which would otherwise be sublimated and applied in useful occupations. Delusions of grandeur are an extreme form of the outcome of this conflict; in them ego and ideal have combined; the ideal is cannibalistically incorporated into the ego, in the way that Freud has described in maniacal insanity.[20] Thus the tension is relieved and therefore this condition is so frequently a final one. These two ways of solving the conflict are well known to us in a milder form as character-traits; they are the "inferiority"-character, with his shy, anxious manner (melancholic type), and the exuberant character, with his self-confident, unrestrained manner (hypomanic type).

In my patient this origin of the feelings of inferiority in rivalry with older persons, in penis envy, was clearly visible. His first recollection of strong feelings of inferiority dated from his school-days, when he envied the cleverer boys and stole from them. Later the feeling of inferiority took a particularly torment-

[19] Freud, *Group Psychology and the Analysis of the Ego*, p. 106. International Psycho-Analytical Press, 1922.

[20] *Loc. cit.* I should only be following Freud's train of thought if I described the coincidence of the ego and the ideal as a cannibalistic form of identification, for he compares fits of mania with the festivals originating in the totem-feast, which is a cannibalistic act with an identification-tendency. Mania would then be a further step on the way to the narcissism which is entered upon in melancholia. In the latter the love-object is absorbed into the ego-system; in mania the splitting within the ego-system itself disappears, the cannibalistic identification of the ego with the object is then completed within the ego-system and an even more complete narcissism is thus achieved.

ing form: "I've learnt nothing; I don't know anything." Since he
tried to soothe this envy by stealing penis-symbols, it is clear
that the mechanism was one of displacement and sublimation
(of the envy on to the cleverness of the boys).

The other manifestation of his feeling of inferiority was his
shame about his Jewish birth. This shame was so pronounced
that he concealed the fact from his greatest friends and even
from his wife (he had been baptized). The connection between
this form of inferiority-feeling and the castration complex is well-
known. The two circumstances, that he had had little education
and was a Jew, were his most painful conscious conflicts, and
they expressed nothing else but the envious attitude of his early
years which had never been overcome. When we reflect that
the source of the ego-ideal is the identification with and introjection of the father, it is easily comprehensible that the inferiority-feeling, the conflict between ego and ego-ideal, should
assume the form of the primal conflict between father and son.
The way in which he relieved this tension, at times by an
arrogant hypomanic manner and fantastic pseudologia, at times
by depressive self-torturing, is a good illustration of the ap-
plicability of the Freudian melancholia mechanism as an explanation of feelings of inferiority. Perhaps one might venture
the assumption that the difference between delusions of
grandeur and delusions of inferiority, on the one hand, and
mania and melancholia, on the other, consists simply in this:
that in the first pair of neuroses it is *homosexual* libido that is
narcissistically introverted and sadistic-cannibalistically gratified
within the ego-system (between ego and ego-ideal), whereas in
the second pair of neuroses the *heterosexual* libido undergoes
the same fate.

III A PRIMAL FORM OF CASTRATION

In the course of my discussion of this case the patient's castration complex has been found to represent the castration wish
against the father turned upon himself, as a self-punishment in
order to relieve the sense of guilt. We know that this is only one
root of the complex, the one proceeding from the father-conflict.
We cannot forget, though, that the father-conflict is only one
side of the Oedipus complex; that is, it is the consequence of an

incest wish. Castration is not merely the talion punishment expected for the penis envy directed against the father; it is also
the punishment for the incest wish. In fact, the latter source of
it is the best known and the best recognized.

The part played by the incest wish in the formation of this
patient's castration complex was followed back very far. Analytic
recognition was again linked up with the solution of transitory
symptoms; understanding of them did not advance our knowledge of his social character-traits, which were, as we have seen,
fully explicable from the father-conflict, but they explained his
behavior in his marriage.

The transitory symptoms which replaced memories in this connection were again hypochondriacal—feelings of strangulation in
the throat, quite different from that of the stick in the throat
already mentioned, and feelings of pressure on the chest and
back. All these sensations felt as though the pressure was an
external one. These symptoms lasted for some days and were
peculiarly trying during the analytic session. Analysis of them
brought to light a mass of memories belonging to the period
from his fourth to his seventh year, which I can collate shortly
in view of the traumatic character which recurred monotonously
in them all.

One day in the engine-room he put his finger into the
machinery and was severely injured. Another time he swallowed
a fish-bone and barely escaped choking to death. When his
father beat him he used to run to the water-mill and listen in a
melancholy mood to the water rippling; on one such occasion
he fell into the water and was nearly caught by the mill-wheel.
Once in the open he was badly frightened by a mouse that ran
up his leg; he caught it on his thigh under his knickers (a patent
falsification of memory and screen-memory!). As a boy of six
he often rode bareback without saddle or stirrup; on one occasion his horse shied and bolted into a wood, where his neck
caught in a low bough and he was left hanging. Another time
his horse shied and bolted into a stable and he only escaped by
ducking his head in the nick of time, so as to get through the
low door, and even so his back scraped against the door-jamb
and his throat was pressed tight against the horse's neck. After
this last memory had emerged, the feelings of pressure on his
throat, chest and back disappeared suddenly. While he was

relating this adventure he became very much moved, and suddenly he said with tears: "I wish I was alone in a small dark place now or near some water."

I will not now try to decide how far these recollections represent actual experiences or how far they are the products of fantasy. It is not important for us whether they were actual faulty actions on the part of the child which constantly brought his life into danger, or creations of fantasy: in any case they were the products of his unconscious (faulty actions are also determined by the unconscious). What is conspicuous in all these recollections is the mortal danger and the *form* of the threatened death—*suffocation;* among them are interpolated some memories of the castration type (finger cut off, mouse in knickers, hanging by the neck—the last also a danger of suffocation).

I should like here to refer back to my earlier remarks on the subject of *affective association,* in order to bring in the evidence of these other observations in support of them. Behind the anal and the oral loss of a pleasure-giving part of the body there lies the *first* traumatic experience, the act of birth: the loss of the enveloping womb, accompanied by strangulation in the throat, feelings of pressure on chest and back, and the danger of suffocation. The earliest affective experience of pleasure followed by "pain" through the loss of a part of the body is unquestionably the act of birth, and it is thus suited to express the expectation of castration in the manner of the most primitive level of the unconscious. *The patient's transitory hypochondriacal sensations of pressure were repetitions of the sensations present during the act of birth.* These hypochondriacal sensations were resolved in the analysis partly by memories of faulty acts in childhood dangerous to life entailing similar sensations, and partly by memories of the castration type. Hanging by the neck, falling into water, riding into a small space through a narrow passage in danger of strangulation are clear representations of birth, the last two, indeed, in the reverse direction: representations of a return into the womb.

The double meaning so characteristic of unconscious processes here comes clearly to expression. The meaning of all these transitory bodily sensations, memories, faulty acts, and associations replacing one another is at once incest wish and castration wish, return into the womb and birth. The unconscious equations run: castration = birth, incest wish = return to the womb.[21] The incest wish and the punishment for it are carried through in one and the same process, expressing the compromise between ego and libido with which we are so familiar. Falling into water and being drowned, riding into a small closed space through a narrow passage and thereby being strangled, serve, by their element of suffering, as punishments for the wish which is at the same time symbolized in these performances: the return into the womb = incest.

A few more remarks about the equation "return to the womb = incest."

During coitus a part of the body, which in dreams, as we know, so often stands for the whole personality, presses up against the womb; further, through cell-division the germ-cells, detached particles of the body which also biologically correspond to an extract of the personality—one remembers the fact of heredity—also reach the womb. On the genital level the libido is indeed, speaking biologically, an impulsion to introduce the germ-cells into the uterus. The pressure of the penis against the uterus can in this light be regarded as the symbolic representation of the wish to return to the womb. Reality, however, necessitates two deprivations: the mother is replaced by another woman and the return is accorded only to a part of the organism, to the germ-cells.

On the basis of the compulsion to repetition discovered by him, which seems to be the fundamental fact underlying all mental and biological processes, Freud conceives the sexual instinct to be an impulse toward the re-union of matter which has at some time become divided.[22] I have attempted[23] to equate this division with the cell-splitting which ensues upon

[21] Freud has interpreted the fantasies of re-birth as wishes for incestuous intercourse with the mother. "The re-birth phantasy is probably always a milder form, a euphemism, so to speak, of the phantasy of incestuous intercourse with the mother." "Aus der Geschichte einer infantilen Neurose," *Sammlung kleiner Schriften,* Vierte Folge, S. 693.

[22] Freud, *Beyond the Pleasure Principle.*

[23] Metapsychologische Betrachtungen, *Internationale Zeitschrift für Psychoanalyse,* 1921, Bd. VII, S. 270.

growth, and to identify the impulsion to re-union with the impulsion to re-establishment of the mature state before division. As an act preparatory to the union of the two products of division (the germ-cells) coitus is the first step on the way to this re-establishment of the mature state. The germ-cells and the complete individual are actually the asymmetrical products of cell-division and correspond essentially to the two equal halves of the single-cellular protozoa which reproduces itself by division.

In conclusion, I will sum up the essential points of this paper. In the castration complex two self-injuring tendencies met in one stream: on the one hand, the talion punishment for active castration wishes, out of the father-conflict; on the other hand, the punishment for incest wishes. Further, in this second source the expectation of castration is only *one* manifestation of an expectation of a general narcissistic wound. It is the deposit of an ontogenetic experience—that every pleasure has its outcome in loss, in pain.[24]

The patient's behavior in his marriage now becomes completely comprehensible. His impulsion to give, to pay for every act of intercourse, is a need to give out a substance of narcissistic value and thus a sublimated anal representation of his castration wish, by which he allays his sense of guilt in regard to coitus. In spite of depreciating her by payment the wife remains to him the superior being—the mother. He thus behaves exactly as in his youth when he did penance for his incest-fantasies by his blunders, whose double meaning was at once castration and incest, a guilty impulsion to death by water and by suffocation: to birth and the return into the womb.

The castration wish stood as the central point of his whole character-formation and that is why he was such an unusually

---

[24] The uncanny sense of expectation, often felt by neurotics but also by the healthy, that an indefinite vague misfortune will follow just when great success has been achieved or when life seems for a moment to have granted perfect happiness, also rests upon the affective expectation of a narcissistic wound, deeply imprinted by the affective experiences of ontogenetic development. Polycrates throws his ring into the sea at the moment when he has attained complete happiness, in order to ward off, by this symbolic self-castration, the envy of the gods and the misfortune it brings. This symptomatic act too has its reverse meaning: he throws the ring into the water and thus expresses the wish to return to the womb.

favorable object in which to study this complex. The analytic solution of it led not merely to a complete change in his social character-traits, but also to a change in his sexual character. This change too did not take place without disturbances. The dissolution of the sense of guilt led at first to an unbridled longing for a mother instead of a wife, only later on to be gradually brought into adjustment with reality.

X

The Analytic Interpretation and Treatment of Psychosexual Impotence*

By Sandor Ferenczi

One of the few objective arguments brought against the method of treatment of the psychoneuroses inaugurated by Freud is the criticism that it effects only a symptomatic cure. It is said to cause the pathological manifestations of hysteria to disappear, but not the hysterical disposition itself. In regard to this, Freud quite rightly directs our attention to the fact that the same critics show much more indulgence toward other anti-hysterical procedures, which cannot even effect a *final* cure of one symptom. We may also bring forward against the argument just mentioned the fact that the analysis, penetrating into the depths of mental life (a process which Freud tellingly compares with the excavating work of the archaeologist), not only effects a cure of the symptoms, but also results in such fundamental change in the patient's character that we no longer have any right to call him a sick man.[1] We are the less justified in doing so, in that after the analysis is finished he is well armed also against new psychical conflicts and shocks, pretty much as well as the non-analyzed "healthy persons," who—as we now know with certainty—carry about with them throughout life a multitude of repressed ideational complexes that are at all times

* Chapter I of *Contributions to Psycho-Analysis*, published in the *Psychiatrisch-Neurologische Wochenschrift*, 1908, Jahrg. X.

[1] Jung and Muthmann in their works come to the same conclusion.

ready to increase and exaggerate with their affect-value the pathogenic action of psychical traumata.

Besides this, the burden of proof completely disappears in the cases where our medical task is comprised in the curing of a single symptom. Among these tasks the treatment of psychical impotence has constantly been regarded as one of the most difficult. So many of my patients came with this complaint, and so great have I found the mental misery due to this symptom, that I have been untiring in the application of the most diverse medicinal[2] and suggestive[3] methods of treatment. Now and then I have had success with both of these, but neither of them proved to be reliable. I count myself all the more fortunate to be able now to report much more successful results, for which I have to thank Freud's psychoanalytic method of treatment.[4]

I will first relate, without any theoretical discussion, the cases I have observed, and interpolate my own remarks.

I was consulted by a workman, aged thirty-two, whose apprehensive and almost abject appearance allowed the "sexual neurasthenic" to be recognized even at a distance. My first thought was that he was being tormented by conscience-pangs due to masturbation, but his complaint proved to be a much more serious one. In spite of his age, and in spite of innumerable attempts, he had never been able, so he told me, properly to perform cohabitation; an inadequate erection and *ejaculatio praecox* had always made the *immissio* impossible. He had sought help from various physicians; one of them (a notorious newspaper-advertiser) spoke to him roughly, saying "You have masturbated, that is why you are impotent," and on this the patient, who in fact had indulged in self-gratification from his fifteenth to his eighteenth year, as the result of this consultation went home convinced that the sexual incapacity was the well-deserved and irrevocable consequence of the "sins of his youth." Nevertheless he made further efforts to be cured, and went through among others a long hydriatic and electrical treatment,

[2] Ferenczi, "Arzneimittelschatz des Neurologen," *Gyógyászat,* 1906.
[3] Ferenczi, "Ueber den Heilwert der Hypnose," *Gyógyászat,* 1904.
[4] Freud's works may be referred to in this connection, as well as the following ones by two Vienna physicians: M. Steiner, "Die funktionelle Impotenz des Mannes," Wiener med. Presse, 1907, No. 42, (also *Die psychischen Störungen der männlichen Potenz,* 1913, by the same author: Translator's Note), and W. Stekel, *Nervöse Angstzustände,* 1908.

without success. The patient would already have bowed to the inevitable, but that he had recently become attached to a very suitable girl; the wish to marry her was the motive of his present attempt to be cured.

The case is a very mundane one, nor did the anamnesic exploration and the examination of the patient bring out anything special in addition. It became evident that besides the impotence he suffered from a neurotic symptom-complex: various paraesthesias, auditory hyperaesthesia, pronounced hypochondria, disturbed sleep with unpleasant dreams; altogether, therefore, an anxiety-neurosis in Freud's sense, for which an adequate explanation was to be found in the lack of sexual gratification and the frequent frustrated excitations. The patient, although the coitus-mechanism completely failed at just the critical moment, indulged in fantasies, both when awake and when half-asleep, the content of which was entirely comprised of sexual situations, and during these experienced the most intense erections. This circumstance aroused in me the suspicion that besides the nervous results of the abstinence he might also be suffering from a psychoneurosis, and that the cause of the impotence itself would have to be sought in the inhibiting, interdicting power of an unconscious psychical complex, which became operative just at the moment of the wished-for sexual union. This pathological condition has, under the term "psychical impotence," long been known to us, and we have known that with it the inhibiting action of morbid anxiety and fear makes impossible the otherwise intact sexual reflex-arcs. It was formerly believed, however, that such cases were fully explained by the "cowardice" of the patient or by the conscious memory of a want of success sexually, and our medical activity was confined to calming or encouraging the patient, with successful results in a certain number of cases. With a knowledge of Freud's psychology I could not remain content with such superficial explanations; I had to suppose that not conscious fear, but unconscious mental processes, having an absolutely definite content and taking their origin in infantile memory-traces, probably some childish sexual wish that in the course of the individual cultural development had become not only unobtainable, but even unthinkable, would have to be made responsible for the symptom. I received merely negative answers to the questions put to him along these lines. Nothing special had happened to him in a sexual connection;

his parents and the family had always been very decent and reserved in this respect, and as a child he had not bothered himself in the least about "these matters"; he knew himself to be entirely free of homosexual impulses; the thought of the functioning of "erogenous zones" (anal- and oral-erotism) filled him with repugnance; the doings of exhibitionists, voyeurs, sadists and masochists were almost quite unknown to him. At the most he had, rather unwillingly, to admit a somewhat excessive fondness for the female foot and its covering, without being able to give any information as to the source of this fetishistic partiality. I allowed the patient, of course, to relate exactly how he had gained his knowledge of sexual matters, what his fantasies consisted of during the period of self-gratification, and how the first attempts at cohabitation, unsuccessful from the start, had passed off. Still, even this detailed anamnesis did not elicit anything that I would have been able to accept as an adequate explanation of the psychosexual inhibition. We know, however, since Freud's work that such an account of the illness does not reproduce the real story of the individual's development, even with complete honesty and a keen memory on the part of the person questioned; so cleverly can consciousness "overlook" and "forget" thoughts and memories that have become disagreeable that they can be withdrawn from the repression or made conscious only by laborious analytic work. I did not hesitate, therefore, to apply the analytic method.

In the analysis it soon turned out that suspicion as to the presence of a psychoneurosis was justified. With closer attention the neurotic nature of the paraesthesias mentioned above was recognizable ("pains" and "crackling" in the tendons, "agitation" in the abdominal and crural muscles, etc.), but besides these there appeared a number of undoubtedly obsessive thoughts and feelings: he dared not look people in the eyes; he was a coward; he felt as if he had committed a crime; he was always afraid of being laughed at.

Obsessive ideas and sensations of this kind are typical of sexual impotence. The cowardice of the sexually impotent person is explained by the radiation over the whole individuality of the humiliating consciousness of such an imperfection. Freud speaks very appositely of the "prefigurativeness of sexuality" for the rest of the psychical behavior. The degree of sureness in sexual efficiency becomes the standard for the sureness in

demeanor, in views, and in conduct. The motiveless consciousness of guilt, however, that seemed to play a not inconsiderable
part with our patient, made one suspect the presence of deeper,
suppressed, unconscious thought-processes, which in a certain
sense were really "sinful"; the analysis gradually yielded the
psychical material from which I was able to infer the nature of
this "sin."

It struck me above all that in his sexually colored dreams the
patient occupied himself very frequently with corpulent women
whose faces he never saw, and with whom he was unable to
bring about sexual union even in dreams; on the contrary, instead of an emission occurring, as might have been expected, he
would be overtaken by acute dread and would wake up in alarm
with such thoughts as: "This is impossible!" "This situation is
unthinkable." After such anxiety-dreams he would wake up
exhausted, bathed in sweat, with palpitation, and usually had "a
bad day."

The fact that in the dream he never saw the face of the sexual-
object I had to interpret as a dream-distortion (Freud); it serves
the purpose here of making the person toward whom the
libidinous dream-wish was directed unrecognizable in consciousness. The starting up in alarm signified that it was nevertheless
beginning to dawn in his consciousness how "unthinkable this
situation was" with the woman hinted at by the dream. The
anxiety-attack is the affective reaction of consciousness against a
wish-fulfillment of the unconscious.[5]

The unconscious interdiction of full sexual gratification was
so strict in the patient that even in daydreams, when he indulged
in his sexual fantasies, he had in a terrified way to pull himself
together and somehow divert his thoughts elsewhere in the mo-

[5] The Hungarian poet Ignotus seems to have surmised the existence of
the distortion and censuring of dreams, as is evident from the following
fragment of verse:

". . . A coward's dreams betray the man:
So harshly can Fate ply her flail,
That of safety he dare not even dream."

It had occurred to me long ago (see the article on "Love and Science" in
Gyógyászat, 1901) that for any useful writings on individual-psychology
we have to go not to scientific literature, but to belles-lettres.

ment when he was about to imagine to himself the act of cohabitation.[6]

A certain active cruelty made its appearance several times in his dreams; for instance, he bit someone's finger off, or bit someone's face. It was not hard to recognize the source of these cannibalistic inclinations in the infantile hostility against a brother, twenty years older, who in his time had behaved much too strictly and not at all kindly toward his little brothers. This propensity for cruelty, by the way, also lurked in the waking state behind the patient's "manifest" cowardice. Every time it was discovered in how cowardly a manner he had behaved in regard to this or that person (mostly a superior) he would sink into fantasies that lasted for several minutes, in which he depicted to himself in the greatest detail how he would conduct himself on the next opportunity in a similar situation, what bodily castigations and abusive language he would serve out.[7] This is an expression of the *esprit d'escalier* so frequent among psychoneurotics, or, as Freud terms it, "subsequentness." These high-flown plans, however, remain for the most part otiose fantasy-pictures; dread or fear always paralyzes the patient's hand and tongue again and again in the critical moment. The analysis finds a determining factor of this kind of cowardice in the infantile awe of the parents and older members of the family, which at that time restrained the child's revolt against their rebukes and bodily chastisements.

With the close physiological connection and the ideational association that obtain between the sexual function and the passage of urine I found it intelligible that the patient's inhibi-

[6] Freud first called attention to the frequent occurrence of anxious examination-dreams in those sexually impotent, and I can fully confirm this observation. The dream fantasy of sitting for an examination very often recurs with such people as a "typical dream," and is constantly associated with the unpleasant feeling of not being ready, of making a fool of oneself, etc. This feeling is a dream-displaced affect; it belongs to the consciousness of the sexual incapacity. A synonym of cohabitation that is commonly used in vulgar Hungarian ("to shoot") is probably the reason why in the dreams of impotent patients under my treatment situations so often recur in which the chief part is played by the (mostly clumsy) use of weapons (*e.g.*, rusting of the rifle, missing the target, missing fire in shooting, etc).

[7] In Ibsen's "Pretenders" the figure of the Bishop Nicholas excellently illustrates cowardice and concealed cruelty as the result of sexual impotence.

tion also made its appearance, as it soon turned out, in regard to micturition. He was unable to discharge urine in the presence of a second person. So long as he was quite alone in a public urinal he urinated regularly, and with a good stream; at the moment when anyone entered the flow was "as if cut off," and he became unable to press out even a drop.

From this symptom, as also from his bashfulness in regard to men, I inferred that with the patient, as with most neurotics (Freud), the homosexual component was present in a higher degree than usual. I believed that the infantile source of this was to be sought in his relation to a younger brother, with whom he had slept in the same bed for years, and with whom he had lived in an offensive and defensive league against the elder brother who ill-treated them. With the expression "usual amount of homosexuality" I imply that my psychoanalyses, now quite numerous, support the theory of psycho-bisexuality, according to which there is retained from the original bisexual disposition of man not only anatomical, but also psychosexual rudiments, which under certain circumstances may obtain the supremacy.

On the ground of other similar analyses I suspected that the corpulent woman who recurred in the dreams stood for some near relative of the patient, the mother, or a sister; he indignantly rejected this imputation, however, and triumphantly told me that he had only one corpulent sister, and it was just this one that he couldn't bear; he had always been sullen and gruff toward her. When, however, one has experienced, as I have, how often a sympathy that is burdensome to consciousness is hidden behind an exaggerated harshness and ill-temper, one's suspicion is not lulled by information such as this.[8]

On one of the following days the patient had a peculiar hypnagogic hallucination, which with slight modifications he had already noticed a few times before: in the act of going to sleep he had the feeling as if his feet (which, though naked, appeared to him to have shoes on) were rising in the air, while his head sank deep down; he awakened at once with an intense feeling of dread. Having regard to the already mentioned foot- and shoe-fetishism I submitted afresh to an exact analysis the patient's free associations to this theme, with the result that the following memory-images emerged, which he had long for-

[8] "I hate because I cannot love" (Ibsen).

gotten, and which were most painful to him: The corpulent sister, whom he "couldn't stand," and who was ten years older than the patient, used to undo and do up the shoes of her then three- or four-year-old brother, and it also not infrequently happened that she would let him ride on her naked leg (covered only by a short stocking), whereupon he used to experience a voluptuous sensation in his member. (Since this is obviously a "cover-memory" in Freud's sense, more must have passed between them.) When he wanted to repeat this later on, his sister, now fourteen or fifteen years old, rebuffed him with the reproach that such conduct was improper and indecent.

I was now able to tell the patient of my assured conviction that the psychological ground for his impotence was to be sought in the wish for the repetition of those sexual acts, a wish incompatible with the "cultivated sexual-morality" (V. Ehrenfels, Freud) and hence repressed, but which lived on in the unconscious. The patient, with whom the arguments only half prevailed, adhered to his denial, but his resistance did not last much longer. He came shortly after with the news that he had thought over what I had said to him, and recollected how in his youth (from the fifteenth to the eighteenth year) he would select this infantile experience with his sister as the object of his masturbation fantasies; indeed, it was the dread of his conscience after self-gratification of this kind that had moved him to give up masturbation altogether. Since that time the childhood story had never occurred to his mind till now.

I induced the patient from the beginning to continue during the treatment his attempts at cohabitation. After the dream-analysis related above he came one day with the surprising news that on the day before (for the first time in his life) he had succeeded in this; the erection, the duration of the friction, and the orgasm had given him complete satisfaction, and, with the avidity characteristic of neurotics, he repeated the act twice again on the same evening, each time with a different woman.

I continued with the treatment and began to reduce analytically the other symptoms of his neurosis, but the patient, after he had achieved his chief aim and convinced himself of the durability of the result, lacked the necessary interest for the analysis, and so I discharged him after treating him for two months.

This therapeutic success needs explaining. From Freud's pioneering work on the evolution of sexuality in the individual

(*Drei Abhandlungen*) we learn that the child receives his first sexual impressions from the immediate environment, and that these impressions determine the direction in the later choice of the sexual-object. It may happen, however, that—as a result of constitutional causes or of external favoring factors (for example, spoiling)—the incestuous object-choice becomes fixed. Cultural morality, gradually strengthened by example and education, defends itself energetically against the obtrusion of the improper wishes, and repression of these comes about. This defense to begin with succeeds completely ("Period of successful defense," Freud)—as also in our case—but the suppressed wishes may again become active under the influence of the organic sexual development in puberty, making necessary another corresponding stage in repression. The second repression signified for our patient the beginning of the psychoneurosis, which manifested itself in, among other ways, the psychosexual inhibition and the aversion to the sister. He was incapable of performing the sexual act, since every woman reminded him unconsciously of his sister; and he couldn't endure his sister because, without knowing it, he always saw in her not only the relative, but also the woman. The antipathy was a good means of protection against his becoming conscious of a feeling-stream of the opposite kind.

Still the unconscious (in Freud's sense) is only able to control the mental and bodily being of man until the analysis reveals the content of the thought-processes hidden in it. Once the light of consciousness has illuminated these mental processes there is an end of the tyrannical power of the unconscious complex. The repressed thoughts cease to be heaps and collections of nonabreacted affects; they become links in the ideational chain of normal association. It was, therefore, in our case thanks to the analysis—to a kind of "circumvention of the censor" (Freud)—that the affective energy of the complex was no longer converted into a physical compulsion (inhibition) symptom, but was disintegrated and led off by thought-activity, losing its inadequate[9] significance forever.

That incestuous fixation of the "sexual hunger"[10] is to be recognized not as an exceptional, but as a relatively frequent

---

[9] This word is used in psychopathology to mean "disproportionate." Translator.

[10] This word is used to translate the German "Libido."

cause of psychosexual impotence, is shown by the quite analogous psychoanalyses by Steiner and Stekel. I am also able to
bring forward a second similar case. A psychoneurotic, twenty-
eight years old, (who had been treated by me and at that time
was almost cured), was tormented by anxious obsessions and
obsessive acts, and suffered besides from psychosexual inhibition, just like the patient whose history was related above. This
symptom, however, ceased of itself in the sixth month of the
analysis after we managed to make conscious infantile incest-
thoughts that had been fixed on the person of the mother. When
I mention that this otherwise rather "overmoral" patient also
indulged in hostile fantasies against his father among his unconscious thought-processes, one will recognize in him a typical
personification of the Oedipus myth, the general human significance of which has been revealed by Freud's discoveries.

The libidinous thoughts repressed in childhood, which condition psychical impotence, need not refer to the nearest relatives; it is enough that the infantile sexual-object has been a
so-called "respected person," demanding in one way or another
high consideration. As an example of this I may cite a patient,
aged forty-five, with whom both the tormenting "cardiac anxiety"
(angina pectoris nervosa) and the sexual weakness considerably
improved after he was able to give an account of repressed dis-
respectful fantasies, the object of which was his dead foster-
mother. In this case the incestuous fixation (if this designation
is permitted in regard to people not related in blood) was
furthered by the circumstance that the foster-mother also had
not restrained her child-love within the necessary limits; she let
the boy sleep in her bed till his tenth year, and for a long time
tolerated without contradicting him his demonstrations of affection, which was already plainly tinged with erotism. Children
are often exposed to such dangers and temptations from the side
of their teachers and educators; it is not rare for them to fall a
victim to masked sexual acts on the part of grown-up relatives,
and not only—as might have been supposed—in the slums, but
also among classes of society where the greatest possible care is
lavished on children.[11]

The tragic part that the foster-mother had played in the life

---

[11] See Freud's *Kleine Schriften*, S. 114., and also my article, "Sexual-
Pädagogik," *Budapesti Orvosi Ujság*, 1908.

of this patient was shown by the fact that, when he wanted to marry, a few years ago, the old lady, then over seventy years old, committed suicide in her despair; she threw herself out of the window of the second floor[12] just at the moment that her adopted son left the front door. The patient believed that the motive for this deed was her dissatisfaction with his choice. But his unconscious must have interpreted the suicide more correctly, for about this time appeared the cardiac pains, which one regards as converted (projected into the corporeal sphere) "heart-ache." The sexual weakness had existed with this patient since puberty, and he will perhaps attain full sexual capacity only toward the decline of masculine life.

Steiner distinguishes, besides the cases of functional impotence that are determined by unconscious complexes of infantile origin, two other kinds of psychosexual inhibition; with one of these congenital sexual inferiority, with the other certain injurious influences acting after puberty, are to be regarded as the causative agents. The value of this division is, in my opinion, more a practical than a theoretical one. From the "congenital" cases we have above all to exclude the cases of pseudo-heredity, where neuropathic parents as a result of their complaint treat the children wrongly, train them badly, and may expose them to influences that have as a result a subsequent sexual inhibition, whereas without these influences even the person afflicted through heredity would perhaps not have become sexually impotent.

Freud compares the pathogenesis of the neuroses with that of tuberculosis. The predisposition also plays an important part with the latter, but the real pathogenic agent is none the less only the Bacillus Kochii, and if this could be kept at a distance not a single soul would die of the predisposition alone. Sexual influences of childhood play the same part in the neuroses as bacteria do in infective diseases. And though one must admit that where the predisposition is very marked the ubiquitous, unavoidable impressions may suffice to determine a future functional impotence, one has nevertheless to be absolutely clear that these impressions, and not the unsubstantial "predisposition," are the specific cause (Freud) of the disorder. From this

[12] In America this would be called the fourth floor, in England the third. Translator.

it also follows that even with "congenital sexual inferiority" psychoanalysis is not quite without hopeful possibilities.

The psychosexual impotence that is acquired after puberty also differs, in my opinion, only apparently from that constellated by unconscious complexes. When anyone, after being able for a time properly to perform the act of copulation, loses for a long period his capacity under the impression of special circumstances (for example, fear of infection, of pregnancy, of being detected, too great sexual excitement, etc.), one may be confident that repressed infantile complexes are present in him also, and that the exaggeratedly long or intense, that is, pathological, effect of the present harmful agent is to be ascribed to the affect that has been transferred from such complexes to the current reaction. From a practical point of view Steiner is entirely right when he brings this group into special prominence, for the cases to be reckoned here are often curable by simple tranquilization, suggestive measures, or a quite superficial analysis (which may be equated to the old Breuer-Freud "catharsis" or "abreaction"). Still, this kind of cure has not the prophylactic value of the penetrating psychoanalysis, although one cannot gainsay its advantage in being a much lesser burden to the physician and the patient.

A superficial analysis of this kind restored his *potestas coeundi* to one of my patients, a young man who became impotent from hypochondria after acquiring his first gonorrhea, and also to a second one, who was made impotent with his wife by the sight of her menstrual blood. Simple encouragements and suggestive tranquilization had the same effect with a thirty-six-year-old man who, although he had previously been fairly active sexually, became impotent when he married and it was a question of marital "duty." In this case, however, I continued the analysis after restoring the sexual function, and the result of this was the discovery of the following facts: The patient, the son of a cooper, had in his fourth or fifth year masturbated the genital parts of a girl of the same age; in this he was encouraged by an undoubtedly perverse assistant of his father's, who then got the girl to manipulate the boy's prepuce with a small wooden needle, such as is used for stopping up casks with worm holes in them. In this way the needle happened to bore into the prepuce, and a medical man had to perform an operation to take it away. With all this there was considerable fright, dread, and shame. What depressed him still more, however, was that his comrades got wind of the occurrence and teased him for years with the nickname "needle-prick." He became taciturn and sullen. About the time of puberty he was often frightened that the scar in his prepuce, trivial as it was, would diminish his capacity for the act, but after a little wavering the first attempts succeeded fairly well. Still, the fear of being unable to meet the higher sexual claims of married life entailed an inordinate burden for his sexuality, already weakened through an infantile complex, and after the marriage he was reduced to impotence.

The case is instructive in several respects. It shows that when potency returns after dispersing the current anxious ideas, this does not mean that this fear has been the exclusive cause of the inhibition; it is much likelier that, in this case as in all similar ones, the preconscious dread has only a "transferred field of activity," while the original source of the disorder is hidden in the unconscious. The successful treatment by suggestion would then have only "broken the point" off the symptom—as Freud says—that is, would have so far diminished the total burden of the neuropsychical apparatus that the patient could then manage it alone.

The case also illustrates how, besides infantile incestuous fixation, other experiences of early childhood connected with the affect of pronounced shame may later determine a psychosexual inhibition.

One kind of shame deserves special mention on account of its practical importance, that, namely, which the child feels on being caught masturbating. The feeling of shame on such an occasion is often still more strongly fixed through the child receiving bodily punishment and having the fear of severe illnesses implanted in him; Freud has called our attention to the fact that the way in which the child is weaned from onanism is a typical influence in the later character- and neurosis-formation. It may be asserted with confidence that the tactless behavior of parents, teachers, and physicians in this matter, which is so important for the child, causes more mischief than all the other noxious influences of civilization that are so often blamed. The isolation of children in their sexual exigencies, the resulting exaggerated and false notions on everything that physiologically or ideationally has to do with sexuality, the inordinate strictness in the punishment of sexual habits of childhood, the systematic train-

ing of children to blind obedience and motiveless respect for
their parents: all these are components of a method of education,
unfortunately prevailing today, that might also be called artificial
breeding of neuropaths and sexually impotent people.

I may sum up as follows my view on male psychosexual impotence: 1. Male psychosexual impotence is always a single
manifestation of a psychoneurosis, and accords with Freud's
conception of the genesis of psychoneurotic symptoms. Thus it
is always the symbolic expression of repressed memory-traces of
infantile sexual experiences, of unconscious wishes striving for
the repetition of these, and of the mental conflicts provoked in
this way. These memory-traces and wish-impulses in sexual impotence are always of such a kind, or refer to such personalities,
as to be incompatible with the conscious thought of adult
civilized human beings. The sexual inhibition is thus an interdiction on the part of the unconscious, which really is directed
against a certain variety of sexual activity, but which, for the
better assuring of the repression, becomes extended to sexual
gratification altogether.

2. The sexual experiences of early childhood that determine
the later inhibition may be serious mental traumata. When the
neurotic predisposition is marked however, unavoidable and
apparently harmless childhood impressions may lead to the
same result.

3. Among the pathogenic causes of later psychosexual impotence, incestuous fixation (Freud) and sexual shame in childhood are of specially great significance.

4. The inhibiting effect of the repressed complex may manifest
itself at once in the first attempts at cohabitation, and become
fixed. In slighter cases the inhibition becomes of importance only
later, in cohabitation accompanied by apprehension or by
specially strong sexual excitement. An analysis carried to a
sufficient depth, however, would probably be able in all such
cases to demonstrate beside (or, more correctly, behind), the
current noxious influence that is acting in a depressing way also
repressed infantile sexual memories and unconscious fantasies
related to these.

5. Full comprehension of a case of psychosexual impotence
is only thinkable with the help of Freud's psychoanalysis. By
means of this method cure of the symptom and prophylaxis
against its return is often to be obtained even in severe and

inveterate cases. In mild cases suggestion or a superficial analysis may be successful.

6. The psychoneurosis of which the sexual inhibition is a part manifestation is as a rule complicated by symptoms of an "actual-neurosis" in Freud's sense (neurasthenia, anxiety-neurosis).

TRANSLATOR'S NOTE

The following sentence may be added here, extracted from a short article written some years later by Dr. Ferenczi ("Par-aesthesias of the Genital Region in Impotency", *Internat. Zeitschr. f. Psychoanalyse*, May 1913): "Apart from unconscious (onanistic) incest-fantasies, fears of castration are the most frequent cause of psychical impotence; most often both are the cause (dread of castration on account of incest-wishes)."

XI

Phallic Passivity in Men[*]

BY RUDOLPH LOEWENSTEIN

I

A number of psychoanalytical papers have recently appeared which deal with the evolution of the genital function in men and in women. In particular, its first stage, that is, the phallic phase, has been studied by various psychoanalysts, beginning with Freud and including Marie Bonaparte, Helene Deutsch, Jeanne Lampl-de Groot, Ruth Mack-Brunswick, Ernest Jones, Fenichel, and Radó.

In the course of a conversation Madame Marie Bonaparte informed me of her investigations in connection with "the passive phallic phase in little girls." The notion of such a phase, considered in relation to what we know of the development of the genital function in boys, seems to me to throw light on certain peculiarities in the genital behavior of a large number of men who may or may not suffer from disturbances of potency.

Let us briefly review the facts, beginning with those of a pathological character, for the element of exaggeration in the latter enables their characteristics to be clearly seen.

It is well known that, in many men who suffer from disturbances of potency, inhibitions, such as collapse or total absence of erection, make themselves felt in certain circumstances only. In some cases this occurs whenever the sexual partner makes the

[*] Based on a paper read before the Thirteenth International Psycho-Analytical Congress, Lucerne, August, 1934.

slightest show of resistance, while, in others, coitus is impossible unless the woman not merely consents but takes the initiative.

We know that the inhibition from which these men suffer has its source in the fear of castration and that this fear is associated with episodes in their childhood. In analysis it often transpires that, as boys, they made an attempt to seduce their mother, or a mother-substitute, behavior which called forth a rebuff or a threat. Such attempts at seduction are generally of a childish character, as is natural at that stage of sexual development, and they would hardly be recognized for what they are by adults ignorant of such a possibility. For instance, a little boy may try to take his mother by surprise, when she is undressed, and may sometimes be bold enough to attempt to touch her breasts, her buttocks or even her genitals. A frequent form of attempt seduction is masturbation in the mother's presence, for example, when she is attending to the child's toilet: this maneuver is tantamount to an invitation to her to touch his penis. Or the attempt may assume a paradoxical form, so that at first it escapes recognition: a little boy who has already been forbidden to masturbate nevertheless does so in front of his mother. It is as if his intention were to call forth a fresh prohibition, a threat or even punishment. The meaning of his behavior is this: by causing his mother to catch him in the act and to punish him he forces her nevertheless to take part in his masturbation. The rebuff which he meets and the threat of castration which often accompanies it frequently constitute traumas that help to put an end to his infantile genital activity.

Between these traumas and the genital inhibitions to which I have alluded earlier in this paper there is a certain relation: the adult man seems to wait for the woman's "permission" to have intercourse with her, for the effects of the prohibition imposed in childhood have to be counterbalanced. For some young men suffering from inhibitions it is enough if "permission" be given on one single occasion by a woman who is a substitute for the female "castrator" of their childhood: their genitality is then set free, once and for all, from the "curse" which had fallen on it. But, as a rule, the woman has to repeat her "permission" and even to extend it to important details of the sexual act itself, e.g., to the introduction of the penis by her help. Men to whom such activity on the woman's part is necessary often allege ignorance of the conformation of the female genitals, which they never dare to look at, and they actually "forget" the structure of these organs if they chance to have taken the trouble to study them in a textbook of anatomy. In many cases of impaired potency where the erection collapses at the exact moment of penetration the man's unconscious aversion to the female organs takes the form of a horror of a *vagina dentata*. It is surprising to find that some men, in whom this fear causes erection to subside, can accomplish erection and ejaculation through immission of the penis into an organ which really is set with teeth, namely, the woman's mouth. Sometimes the *selective* nature of this form of impotence—its exclusive relation to the vagina—is emphasized by the following facts. A man who cannot achieve normal penetration and had had recourse to fellatio to restore erection makes another attempt at coitus. Once more the erection collapses and only in response to oral caresses can ejaculation take place. This paradoxical situation, which is of real clinical importance, requires explanation.

One of my patients explained as follows the relatively satis-factory functioning of his automatic genital processes during fellatio and their inhibition at the moment of coitus. "I don't have to do anything: the woman does it all." This peculiar view of the matter derives some support from the fact that the majority of men whose automatic genital processes function correctly in fellatio find that the same thing occurs if they cause themselves to be masturbated by a woman. The inhibition from which they suffer applies to active penetration and to that alone.

It seems, therefore, that in these cases we must distinguish two forms of the genital function: (1) an active form, which ter-minates in penetration and coitus, and (2) a form in which the aim is passive, the man's wish being to receive caresses from without, whether from someone else or from his own hand.

These two aspects of the genital function—active and passive—reflect two phases of its development in childhood.

In every analysis in which the amnesia of childhood has been overcome beyond any possibility of doubt we have, indeed, ob-served that the first manifestations of the phallic phase took the form of tendencies, wishes and acts whose aims were passive: the child desired to look at or touch his own penis or cause it to be touched by someone else. Psychoanalysts are aware that these genital manifestations occur in the earliest period of child-hood. I should like, however, to cite a case which I had an opportunity to observe with my own eyes some years ago. A baby boy, aged five months, used to bend himself back into an opisthotonic attitude, and, so to speak, present his penis to his mother, whenever she was attending to his toilet and her hand approached the region of his genitals. At the same time he uttered little grunts of pleasure, accompanying them with a pantomime the meaning of which was unmistakable. This child is now ten years old and is perfectly normal, both physically and mentally.

In the vast majority of cases which I have been able to analyze, the phallic phase of libidinal development has been characterized by a functioning of the genital organs which was purely passive in aim. The active aim of the genital function, penetration, did not appear until later and often took the form of vague and indefinite fantasies. One form of sexual aim, however, which may be regarded as intermediate between the passive and the active aims, may make its appearance fairly early. I refer to the tendency to rub the penis against inanimate objects or the body of a woman.[1]

In my opinion we shall do well to distinguish two stages in the phallic phase: a passive and an active stage. The passive stage manifests itself first and, according to my own observations, it actually includes the period of the Oedipus complex. Indeed, the sexual aims of the little boy's incestuous wishes are clearly passive, although they may exist side by side with the active aim of penetration which begins to make itself felt at the same period. In some cases the masturbation practiced at puberty begins with purely passive genital acts.[2] Boys of this type like to have their penises handled more or less roughly, and they achieve orgasm without any semblance of a "to and fro" movement or of penetration. Some of these boys develop normally but the majority are likely to remain habitual masturbators, for whom masturbation will always provide a more complete satisfaction than coitus.

---

[1] I know of one case in which this form of masturbation was practised from the age of two and a half right up to manhood.

[2] In her very interesting paper, read before the Thirteenth International Psycho-Analytical Congress at Lucerne, in 1934, Ruth Mack-Brunswick brought forward certain notions with regard to the phallic phase in boys which are entirely in agreement with my own. She, however, holds that the desire to penetrate does not occur until shortly before puberty, whereas I am inclined to date it earlier.

II

The analysis of a man suffering from somewhat serious disturbances of sexual potency provided me with an opportunity of bringing to light the connection between phallic passivity and disturbances in ejaculation. The patient, aged forty, declared that he had two kinds of erection and, until he was analyzed, he did not know which of the two was normal. The one kind (clearly the normal type) was characterized by rigidity of the whole penis and had formerly enabled him, though infrequently, to have fairly prolonged coitus. This sort of erection still sometimes occurred when he was in the presence of a woman. But now, as soon as he attempted coitus (the sexual partners whom he selected being prostitutes) the erection would collapse and was replaced by the other sort, which was characterized by swelling of the glans only, the rest of the penis remaining flaccid. This form of erection, or pseudo-erection, made penetration quite impossible but did not hinder fellatio, to which he generally resorted. By this means the automatic genital process was carried to its conclusion, but there was one important point about it: the ensuing ejaculation was extremely rapid, the semen being discharged continuously, in a single jet. This ejaculation took place at the exact moment at which the automatic process had run its full course, in response to excitations of a purely passive character.

In other cases as well I have noted such purely passive genital excitations produced rapid, continuous ejaculation, with a single jet of seminal fluid, accompanied by rather weak or even slightly difficult orgasm.

I propose to cite only one out of several such cases which I have observed: it is, I think, peculiarly conclusive. In this patient ejaculation and orgasm varied with the nature of the excitations, sometimes being of the "asthenic" type (to use M. St. Higier's term), such as I have just described, while sometimes there would be normal, intermittent ejaculation. He could have the one kind of orgasm or the other: it depended on whether he remained motionless throughout the woman's caresses or whether, as he felt orgasm approaching, he made the to and fro movements which induced normal orgasm.

Now the connection between this type of ejaculatory disturbance and ejaculatio praecox is obvious. As to the latter affection

Abraham's writings clearly demonstrate that it is intimately related to urethral erotism, the "asthenic" ejaculation being unconsciously equated with micturition. Papers by Reich, Fenichel and Ferenczi have established beyond doubt the fact that pregenital phases of the libido leave their impress upon certain disturbances of the genital function.

The influence which pregenital libidinal phases may exert over the development of the genital function and its subsequent disturbances is, in my opinion, due to one special circumstance, namely, that that influence comes into play at a period in which the aims of the genital function are essentially passive. That is to say, in this period of development the little boy's genital organs function in precisely the same way as any other erotogenic zone, such as the nipples of the female or (and this is perhaps a better illustration) the clitoris. These are organs capable, like the little boy's penis, of erection and their erotogenic function is purely passive in its aim, which is to be caressed. This, in my opinion, is the special factor which differentiates the passive from the active stage in the phallic phase. With the appearance of the latter stage the genitals assume their primacy over the extra-genital erotogenic zones.

We have just seen that the to and fro movement of the penis, i.e., the tendency to penetrate, is of great importance for the differentiation of the active and passive forms of the genital function. This fact recalls to our mind the unconscious connection between bodily movement, and especially walking, and the genital function. In a communication which I made in 1924 to the Berlin Psycho-Analytical Society I pointed out that the unconscious mind equates standing, learning to walk, the co-ordination and control of bodily movements with the active, genital function of the male.

It seems possible that as regards the active stage of the phallic phase the unconscious takes as its model the profound modification in a human being's relation to the external world which takes place when he learns to walk. We see how the little creature, as soon as he is capable of moving about and approaching various objects, ceases to be immobile and passive and becomes active. An analogous change, on a different plane, does in fact take place during the transition to the active phallic stage and, more especially, to the phase of genital primacy—a change in the child's libidinal and psychological attitude in relation to his objects.

III

It is advisable to define more precisely the place which we believe to be occupied by the passive phallic stage in the development and disturbances of the libido. The term "passivity," as we have used it, applies to the sexual aims natural to the genital function at this period of life. We must therefore be careful not to confuse "passivity" in our sense of the term with feminine passivity, which is the sense in which the word is commonly used. For the passive phallic stage occurs in boys whose attitude and sexual behavior are none the less masculine and aggressive and who, once their development is completed, will attain normal virility. Phallic passivity, at any rate in boys, appears to be exclusively erotic in character and the behavior of the genital zone in this respect seems to be identical with that of the erotogenic zones in general. But, secondarily, there is a certain interaction between phallic activity and passivity on the one hand and, on the other, aggressive tendencies and masochism. Thus, if aggression be repressed, the genital function will regress in the direction of passivity, now reinforced by the addition of masochism.

Abraham has pointed out the important part played by repressed sadism in the pathogenesis of ejaculatio praecox. It is this factor which accounts for that regression to the passive phallic attitude which characterizes the genital behavior of patients suffering from this disturbance.

In other cases, too, where urethral erotism is much less pronounced and there is therefore no predisposition to ejaculatio praecox, disturbances of potency can also be brought under the heading of regression to genital behavior the aim of which is passive. Indeed, in the vast majority of cases of impaired potency the clinical picture is not simply that of an inhibition of normal genitality: we can discern in it also the persistance of recrudescence of passive forms of genital satisfaction.

Thus, in by far the larger number of cases, the castration complex, which is the main factor in the production of abnormalities in genital activity, appears to operate selectively, inhibiting the normal exercise of the genital function while tolerating it in its passive form.

In conclusion, I would draw your attention to one other result of the division into two distinct stages of the phallic phase in males.

The results of certain analyses suggest that fixation at the passive phallic stage may predispose the individual to a certain type of homosexuality. I refer to the passive homosexuality which is expressed exclusively in terms of genital gratification and in which no anal wish or gratification seems to have a place. The desires of this type of homosexual, who may be described as *passive*, culminate in fantasies on the following lines: his own penis, which is small, is touched by the larger penis of the man whom he loves. Obviously this fantasy has its source in the wishes characteristic of the so-called "inverted" or "passive" Oedipus complex and we shall draw the conclusion that between this form of the complex and phallic passivity a special affinity exists.

XII

The Psychology of Transvestism*

BY OTTO FENICHEL

I

All authors who have dealt with the subject of transvestism are agreed that the mysterious behavior of the victims of this perversion has points of contact with various other perverse practices. It was not until 1910 that this manifestation of *psychopathia sexualis* was, rightly, described by Hirschfeld as a specific form of perversion.[1] Earlier authors had classified cases of the sort on the basis of their points of contact with other perversions. This affinity leads us to hope that the psycho-analytical elucidation of transvestism may contribute something of importance to the explanation of the psychology of perversions in general. Again, in so far as the allied perversions have already been exhaustively studied by analytical methods, the fact that it is akin to them will enable us to understand the phenomenon of transvestism.

The behavior of many transvestists gives an entirely masochistic impression: we call to mind, for instance, the figure which is the ideal of many such perverts—Hercules clothed in woman's garments and serving his mistress, Omphale. We know, too, that many who practice this perversion obtain gratification only when they are seen in the clothes of the opposite sex, that is, strictly speaking, they are exhibitionists. But there are other, far more obvious, points in which transvestism is related to

---

* Read at the Eleventh International Psycho-Analytical Congress, Oxford, July 31, 1929.

[1] M. Hirschfeld. *Die Transvestiten*, Berlin, 1910.

fetishism and homosexuality, and these points have already been the subject of scientific controversy. I refer to the overestimation of clothing and body-linen, and to many purely fetishistic traits in cases of the sort, for example, a particular preference for shoes or earrings. These characteristics have led writers on the subject to conceive of tranvestism as a specific type of fetishism. Hirschfeld[2] and Ellis,[3] on the contrary, rightly emphasize the fact that the transvestist has one characteristic which is foreign to fetishism proper. To him the fetish becomes a fetish only when brought into relation with the person of the patient, not (or at any rate only in a very modified degree) as an object in itself. But transvestists want not only to wear women's clothes but to live together like women; that is, they are effeminate. This fact afforded sufficient reason for their being frequently grouped with passive homosexuals, a view energetically controverted by Hirschfeld, who demonstrated that transvestists in general are erotically attracted exclusively to persons of the opposite sex. Later, he[4] and Näcke[5] classified transvestists according to their sexual aim as the heterosexual, homosexual, narcissistic and asexual types. To psychoanalysts there is no meaning in such a classification, because it is based solely on the manifest expressions of instinct and completely disregards the unconscious instinctual processes. In this connection Stekel[6] is of opinion that transvestism should be construed simply as a mask for homosexuality. But the problem which then confronts us is to find out under what conditions this mask in particular is selected.

To sum up: the point which the transvestist has in common with the fetishist is the overestimation of feminine clothes and body-linen, while he shares with the passive homosexual (and the feminine masochist) the feminine psychic attitude. The point of difference between him and both these other types of perverts lies in his specific sexual wish to assume the dress of the opposite sex. Psychoanalysts will suspect that where there is

---

[2] *Loc. cit.*

[3] "Eonism," *Studies in the Psychology of Sex*, Vol. VII, Philadelphia, 1928.

[4] *Jahrbuch für sexuelle Zwischenstufen*, 1923.

[5] "Zum Kapitel der Transvestiten," *Archiv. für Kriminalanthropologie*, Bd. XVII.

[6] Compare "Der Fetichismus" and "Onanie und Homosexualität."

this manifest agreement, there will be a corresponding resemblance in the fundamental unconscious mechanisms. And the
analysis of transvestists entirely confirms this suspicion.

Fetishism and passive homosexuality in men have been so
exhaustively studied analytically that the results of the investigation can be reduced to certain short formulae. According to
Freud[7] castration-anxiety prevents the fetishist from accepting
the fact of the lack of the penis in women, and he can love only
when he has supplied his female love-object with an illusory
penis. The cause of the feminine homosexual's abnormality is,
likewise, castration-anxiety. He is incapable of loving a being
who lacks the penis; castration-anxiety (and, of course, also constitutional factors) have led him to solve his Oedipus complex
by substituting identification with his mother for his love of her.
He is now himself the mother, the woman, and in this role he
seeks for new objects, whether it be the father or a representative of himself.[8] The transvestist, who is akin to both these types
of pervert, seems to be the one to whom both formulae
simultaneously apply: he has not been able to give up his belief in the phallic nature of women and, in addition, he has
identified himself with the woman having the penis. Identification with the woman, as a substitute for, or side by side with,
love for her, is so plain in the manifest clinical picture that Ellis,
as we shall hear presently, regarded it as the essence of transvestism.[9] But the woman with whom the transvestist identifies himself is conceived of by him as phallic, and *this* is the essential
feature in the situation—a feature which, since it is unconscious,
could not have been discovered but for psychoanalysis.

In the act of tranvestism both object-love and identification
are present, the forms in which each manifests itself being
modified by the castration-complex and the patient's obstinate
retention of his belief in the woman's possession of the phallus.
The act has a twofold significance: (1) object-erotic (fetishistic),
and (2) narcissistic (homosexual). (1) Instead of coitus with
the mother or her substitute the patient enters into fetishistic
relations with her clothes, which he brings into as close contact

---

[7] Freud, "Fetishism," *International Journal of Psycho-Analysis*, Vol. IX,
p. 161.

[8] Compare, for instance, "Drei Abhandlungen zur Sexualtheorie," *Ges.
Sch.*, Bd. V, S. 18, footnote.

[9] *Loc. cit.*

as he can with his own person, and particularly with his genital organs. This is the explanation of the "condition of love," frequently met with, that the garments or body-linen in question should have been used and, if possible, should still retain something of the warmth and odor of the woman's body. This intercourse is conceived of in typically sadistic terms. (2) The patient himself represents a woman with a penis. A woman: he shouts that abroad. A woman *with a penis:* that is revealed by analysis. Here we have a twofold representation of the penis: (*a*) in the patient's genital, actually present under the woman's clothes (one transvestist had recurrent fantasies of the amazement of a lover who, approaching him under the impression that he was a woman, discovered the penis when the woman's clothes were removed); (*b*) in the garment, which is a symbolic substitute for the penis and which the transvestist (even if he indulges his passion only secretly and onanistically) always wants to display— a form of displaced exhibitionism which, like true exhibitionism, is designed to refute the idea of castration. In order to make the clinical picture of transvestism intelligible in terms of psychoanalysis we must expand these formulae by a description of the way in which the transvestist, like the homosexual, proceeds to fresh object-choices, having completed his identification with the woman. In these choices we shall again find an element both of narcissism and of object-erotism. With regard to the former we must note that only in a subject of a peculiarly narcissistic disposition is it possible for object-love to be so extensively replaced by identification. It is a fact that the narcissistic regression manifested in this identification goes far beyond that which we are accustomed to observe in homosexuals. Love for the subject's own self—fantasies that the masculine element in his nature can have intercourse with the feminine (that is, with himself) are not uncommon. Love for the phallic mother is often transformed into love for the ego in which a change has been wrought by identification with her. This is a feature in the psychic picture which has struck even non-analytical writers, who have described a narcissistic type of transvestist besides the heterosexual and homosexual types.

On the other hand, patients are influenced by their feminine identification in their choice even of real objects; they want to be looked upon and loved as women or, alternatively, where the primal sadism has been turned against the ego, to suffer masochistic tortures. (Here again we note in the passive sexual aim, which, in spite of the phallic character of the illusory woman, dominates the picture, the introduction of the narcissistic factor.) Analysis demonstrates that this object-tendency of the transvestist is directed (1) in the deeper mental strata toward the *father*. In this point the transvestist resembles the passive homosexual, but the former is seldom conscious of the homosexual character of this object-choice. He says in effect to the father: "Love me, I am just as beautiful (in the phallic sense) as my mother." Or, more correctly: "Love me as you love my mother; it is not true that this wish of mine places my penis in jeopardy!" But the tendency of which we are speaking is also directed (2) toward the mother. This is the more superficial and obvious relation, and it was this which justified Hirschfeld, who did not include the unconscious in his purview, in denying the homosexuality of the transvestist. Perverts of this type consciously take a special interest in feminine homosexuality; they want to be loved as women by women, to be in the relation of the slave to her mistress. The analytical explanation is to be found in the most important accidental factor in transvestism, namely, that, as a rule, contemporaneously with the identification with the mother, there exists in another, more superficial, psychic stratum, a similar identification with *a little girl*. This is designed to secure for the subject all the advantages of a regression into early childhood. (For example, a patient of this type who had handled a female infant during the day, dreamed the following night that he put on women's clothes and during the dream he wet his bed.) This second process of identification may occur when, as seems often to be the case, a sister has at an early period to a great extent become a mother-substitute. Then the transvestist not only addresses the father as we have already described, but at the same time says to the mother: "Love me, I am just as beautiful (in the phallic sense) as my sister." Or, more correctly: "Love me as you love my sister! It is not true that this wish of mine places my penis in jeopardy."

II

I think it now behooves me to cite some analytical material in proof of these propositions. I will confine myself to putting before you the most important points in a case which was subjected to a thorough analysis, and I hope that they will illustrate the meaning of transvestism as I have tried to present it to you.

The patient was a married man forty years old, who, in spite of his neurosis, was successful in his professional life and was the father of several children. He suffered from obsessional neurosis and hypochondria with certain paranoid symptoms. He loved his wife deeply and was very considerate and affectionate to her, but sexual intercourse with her left him unsatisfied. He could obtain gratification only in onanism; this he practiced with the accompaniment either of transvestist fantasies, or, more often, of actual transvestist behavior—dressing himself in his wife's clothes. The content of the accompanying fantasy was simply: "I am a woman." Of the details which he communicated in analysis I may mention the following: he indulged in an additional important fantasy, whose content was: "And I am seen to be a woman," and, further, gratification was conditional upon the wearing of women's clothes being a matter of everyday occurrence that is, he experienced the most lively excitation when he imagined that he was putting on women's clothes not for the purpose of stimulation but because it was natural for him to be dressed so. He had, in addition, various masochistic fantasies of the type in which the female slave serves her mistress, and he entertained the desire to be a woman, quite apart from any actual sexual situation.

From the history of the patient's childhood I may communicate the following facts. His mother died early and his father soon married again. His father was a man of a petty, fault-finding, anal character, while the stepmother was domineering, quarrelsome and very strict with the children. Evidently there must have existed a very strong sensual (probably passive-anal) bond between the father and the stepmother, but at the same time the former kept up a kind of cult of the memory of his first wife. In everything the stepmother ruled the house (here we have the type of "the feeble father"), so that the patient had plenty of opportunity to believe in her phallic nature. His attitude to her was ambivalent throughout, but in both his hatred (fear) and his love he remained entirely passive. There emanated from her a strong atmosphere of prohibition; the castrating figures in his dreams proved to be screen-figures standing for her. When the patient was a little boy, she had forced him to wear gloves and had bound his hands to prevent his practicing masturbation (or possibly to prevent his scratching himself at a time when he was being treated for worms). (This binding gave rise later to masochistic fantasies.) Moreover, as a little boy he suffered from prolapse of the rectum and, every time he defecated, she pressed back the rectum with her finger. In analysis the patient could still recall the tremendously pleasurable feeling which this gave him.

His principal sexual object in childhood was a sister three years older than himself, with whom he indulged in all manner of sexual games, mutual masturbation, etc. Probably this elder sister originally played the part of seducer, and this seduction caused a similar disturbance in his sexual development as is recorded in that of the Wolf-man.[10] There certainly was a period in which he assumed the active role in their mutual relations; for example, he remembered that on one occasion he had purposely wet her with urine. This relation, like his relation with his stepmother, was highly ambivalent. He not only loved his sister, but hated her as a rival. This hatred combined with the sensual element to produce a markedly sadistic attitude (possibly to cancel the seduction). One day this attitude vanished, and the patient became purely passive in his relation to his sister. We shall return to the question of this later passive attitude, and discuss when it developed and why. During analysis it was still recognizable in a certain apprehensiveness of an obsessional nature and, further, in an important screen-memory in which the patient professed to have pulled one of his sister's arms from its socket. Otherwise, the passive attitude was repressed, and the underlying tendency, having been diverted toward the subject's ego, had been converted into masochism.

It was from his relation to his sister that the patient developed his transvestism. His sister used to play at "dressing dolls," and she would dress up the living doll—her little brother—putting clothes of her own on him. This used to happen when the patient was about four years old, and at first he disliked it, because it degraded him into a doll. After some repetitions, however, he began to enjoy the game, because he derived sexual pleasure from the smell of his sister, which clung to things she wore, especially to her hair-ribbon and pinafore. In his eighth

[10] Freud, "The History of an Infantile Neurosis," *Collected Papers*, Vol. III.

and tenth years the children used to act little plays, in which they changed clothes with one another. They went on doing this in their games, and the patient, when he imagined he was a girl and especially that others regarded him as a girl, experienced pleasure which was unquestionably sexual, and was accompanied by sensations resembling orgasm. Presently his sister became bored with the game, and he had to be more and more artful in persuading her to play it. Finally he took to putting on her clothes in secret, when he was alone, and the pleasure this gave him roused a lively sense of guilt. At the age of about thirteen he forgot this game, but in his seventeenth year he recollected it and began it again with unmistakable sexual excitation. From that time on, dressing up in women's clothes became associated with manual masturbation, and the beginning of the perversion dates from this. It is noteworthy that for a long time the patient made use of his *sister's* clothes and, later, those of sister-substitutes. The idea of putting on garments belonging to his stepmother or to women resembling her did not stimulate his imagination in the least.

What then is the meaning of this perversion? The object-erotic factor is the easier and simpler to understand from the case-history. The pleasure which the patient derived proceeded in the first instance from the smell of the clothes: a hair-ribbon and, above all, a pinafore, represented parts of the body of his sister, with whom he was in the habit of masturbating. This practice sometimes took the form of his sister's sitting on his knee and sliding backward and forward. When he wore her pinafore he used to move it about in a similar way. The pinafore represented his sister's body. Later, when he made use of her clothes instead of her person, he had the advantage of ceasing to be dependent, for his sexual enjoyment, on the caprices of his sister, who was not always inclined to gratify him. Another circumstance was that, originally, using the same bed or the same bathwater as she, had the same significance as wearing her clothes. How came it about that the sister herself gradually lost her sexual significance for him, while "symbols" (her clothes) were substituted for her? Analysis revealed the answer unmistakably. It was because the brother discovered that she had no penis. We mentioned the remarkable screen-memory of his pulling his sister's arm from its socket. This memory "screened" their mutual onanism and especially the patient's sadism. Once, when he and his sister were having a bath together in the bath-room, he caught sight of her genitals, and this reactivated a still earlier, repressed recollection of his stepmother's genitals. It happened that at the same period his sister was having electric treatment for enuresis (the patient himself used for a time to wet his bed) and used to scream dreadfully when the treatment was in process. There could then, he reasoned, be only two possibilities: either the electric treatment was the punishment by castration for sexual naughtiness; in that case he was threatened with it, after his sister. Or it was a medical remedy for the lack of the penis, which had fallen a victim to his own sadism. In that case it was but just that the talion punishment of castration should await him. In this anxiety he desisted alto-gether from his sadistic behavior and turned the tendency against himself. He wanted to have nothing more to do with his sister, who reminded him of the mischief he had done, and he sub-stituted for her her clothes, which did away with the dreadful nakedness. The bath (and, later, water in general) remained a situation of terror. We shall have to discuss the fact that his anxiety took the form that the water in running out might carry off one of his fingers or his whole body and that the dread be-came displaced to the watercloset, where the flush might wash away the whole child as well as his bowel movement. So far, the patient's mental processes followed the scheme which Freud has worked out for fetishism.

The patient, however, became a transvestist because his re-tention of the idea of the female penis was reinforced by his identification with the woman. In later years it became trans-parently clear that he himself was enacting the role of the sister, whom he desired to *be*. In imagination he lived her life, and in the same way, after his marriage, he would feel unwell during his wife's period of menstruation. This has a significance in connection with the question of punishment. It meant: I harbored the wish to do my sister an injury, so now I am forced to be-come like her, so as to submit to suffering. From the point of view of his instinctual life he had sufficient reason to envy his sister. She was the elder, and both parents evidently made a favorite of her. He was especially jealous of her relation to their stepmother, who talked "feminine secrets" with her. Later he developed a neurosis, when his parents were about to arrange a marriage for his sister. Analysis revealed the jealous thought:

"Why do they arrange for her to marry and not for me?" The patient had also a recollection, important in connection with the deeper mental strata, of a fit of envy which overtook him one Christmas, when his mother with much ceremony presented his sister with a particularly beautiful doll. Such ambivalent feelings indicated that, in obedience to the inner prohibition by which his castration-anxiety prevented his entering into an object-relation with his sister, he had regressed to identification.

Now this identification with the girl was bound to come into direct opposition to the most intense castration-anxiety. The influence of this made itself felt in the aim which the patient set before him: "I want to be my sister and yet to retain my penis." When indulging in his perverse pactices, it was his custom, as soon as ejaculation had taken place, to tear the borrowed clothes off as quickly as possible. In connection with this he had the association that he had been warned that, if one made faces and the clock struck, one's face would stay so. Thus he was afraid that he might actually "remain stuck" in his feminine role, and this would involve his forfeiting his penis. His transvestist behavior was designed to counter his castration-anxiety. We have evidence of this in a recollection that, when on one occasion he caught sight of a crippled boy, he felt an impulse to change clothes with him. The implication was a denial that the boy really was a cripple. The patient combined his femininity with a naïve, narcissistic love for his own penis, upon which he bestowed a number of pet names, as though it were a child. Moreover, the girl's name, which he chose to be known by when enacting the role of a girl, had a striking resemblance to one pet name for the penis. The first time he had sexual intercourse with a woman, he did not know where to find the vagina and looked for it on the upper part of her thigh. Even at the time when I knew him, he always had a feeling during coitus that he must look for something which he could not find. At one of the dramatic performances, in which he acted the part of a girl, he represented an Easter hare. He recollected being troubled because he thought the hare's ears and tail were not stiff enough. Here we have a proof of the phallic nature of the woman whose role he assumed—a matter which becomes more intelligible to us when we picture the overwhelming castration-anxiety under which the patient labored. We have mentioned that his step-mother represented to his mind the person who castrates. From the innumerable screen-memories connected with the idea of castration I will quote a single example. An obsessive action of the patient's was that of clutching at his penis (analytically interpreted: to see if it was still there) and of counting his toes (to see that none was missing). Analysis revealed that he had dreaded that his mother, in pressing back the prolapsed rectum, might rob him of the intestine, and at that time he was haunted by the fear that it might fall into the lavatory-pan. The uncanny thing about the watercloset and the bath was that the feces and the water simply disappeared—were no longer there— just so, he feared, had his sister's penis vanished. Further, this idea of being "gone" was his conception of death. And in his mind the whole terrifying mystery of castration was intertwined with the terrifying mystery of his mother's death. The content of his unconscious anxiety was not simply: "My sister's penis vanished because of some sexual act," but also, "My own mother died because of some sexual act." Accordingly, particularly during the period of his subsequent hypochondria, the patient suffered from the most intense dread of death (and especially the dread of infection, as I will show later). Detailed analysis of this anxiety led us first of all to ideas about the color "black" and of "hair." (As a child he himself had long hair and dreaded its being cut. He treasured up the locks which were cut off. His stepmother wore false hair, that is, hair which could be taken off. The hair of the head stood for pubic hair.) These ideas led back to dreams of the primal scene and to occasions, long before his experiences with his sister, when, with anxiety and a feeling of protest, he became aware of the nature of his mother's genitals.[11]

Thus, the patient's transvestism was evidently an attempt to allay these various anxieties. The content of the perversion was: "Phallic girls do exist; I myself am one."

Let us now examine his search for fresh love-objects, when once the identification had been completed, and let us consider the relation to the mother which underlay that to the sister.

[11] The female genital, when thus caught sight of, becomes an object of fear not simply because of the lack of the penis but because it is regarded as a menacing weapon. (The waste-pipes of the watercloset and the bath are thought of as devouring mouths.) Compare my article: "Zur Angst vor dem Gefressenwerden," *Internationale Zeitschrift für Psychoanalyse*, Bd. XIV, 1928, S. 404.

The factor of narcissism was transparently clear. Not only did he love himself in the role of a girl (acting a woman in plays, posturings before the mirror, a preference for a girl's long hair), but this love took an *active* form, such as he longed for from his sister. Thus he dreamt that he was embracing a little boy, saying to him tenderly: "My little brother!" In passing on to consider his actual choice of new love-objects, we will again begin with a dream. This was as follows: "My wife had a disease of the lungs. A stout woman stabbed her in the back from behind. Thereupon I found myself in a theater, with the upper part of my body naked." The exhibition-situation at the end prepares us for the fact that the dream relates to tranvestism. Actually the patient, who was a hypochondriac, suffered from a dread of lung affections. In the dream, he is the woman whom another woman stabs from the rear. His associations to this stab were as follows: the uvula, fantasies of poisoning by way of the anus and, finally, enemas which his stepmother had given him as a child. Before going to sleep on the night of this dream, the patient had indulged in his perverse practices. Hence we arrive at the interpretation: "When I am in women's clothes I should like my stepmother to stick something into my 'behind,' but at the same time I dread it." The passive-anal desires implied in the patient's femininity had become abundantly clear: the recollections of enemas and the prolapsed rectum showed that these wishes had reference to the mother whom he conceived of as phallic. This is where the fantasies of the female slaves come in, the meaning being: "I want my stepmother to treat me like a little girl, but there is no need for me to fear castration." In correspondence with this wish the patient cherished in his mind two types of female imagos between which he strictly differentiated: the "little girl" and the "Amazon," that is, the sister and the step-mother. The women whose clothes he desired to put on belonged to the first type only; on the other hand, he wished to enter into masochistic relations only with women of the second, masculine type.

Having discovered this anal dependence on women it seemed obvious to reason as follows: The patient's Oedipus complex was normal in so far as he, like other males, wished to take his father's place with his mother. Only, the real father's attitude to his second wife was of a passive-anal nature; similarly, the patient wished to enter into a passive-anal relation to the phallic mother. In actual fact the stepmother tended the father in connection with his anal functions and this did really rouse in the patient the wish that his father would die.

But the child had not always seen his father in such a helpless and passive guise. Once he too had been strong and active, and it was to him that in the deepest mental strata the patient's feminine attitude had reference.

Analysis of his social inhibitions revealed that his passivity and anxiety related, fundamentally, not to women but to men. Again, his exhibitionist tendency—the craving to be admired as a woman by people in general—had reference to men. When we were investigating this subject of the father of his infantile days, the first thing that emerged in his memory was a long-forgotten figure which was a "screen-figure" for his father: a carpenter, who had done some work in the patient's home and whose admiration he had solicited. Next, he felt an urgent impulse to change into women's clothes in front of his father's portrait. Finally, there came recollections of excitation, obviously sexual and accompanied by anxiety, which he experienced when lying in bed with his father. But the most striking thing about this part of the analysis was the way in which the patient suddenly grasped the meaning of many inhibitions from which he suffered in his real relations with men! The picture was then blurred once more by a recollection of his later childhood: "I wanted to thrust something into my father's 'behind.'" We found that this implied: "I want to love you, father, in just the same way as my stepmother does." But we were obliged to conjecture that, before he felt the desire to stick something into his father, he must have wished to stick something into *him*. Quite in accordance with this interpretation was the fact that he had *not* identified himself with his stepmother; on the contrary, behind the identification with his sister lay the first identification of all— that with his own mother. His heart cried out to his father: "Do not put away the memory of your first wife. Remember her; she lives still, in me. Love me, your first wife, more than my stepmother!" And the content of the fearful anxiety which came into conflict with these wishes was this: "Did not death overtake my mother because she let my father love her? Then I, too, shall have to die." It now becomes clear that the overwhelming castration-anxiety, which the transvestism was designed to eliminate, was at bottom a dread of impregnation by the father. This was the meaning of the dread of infection, poison and water and also of a number of screen-memories in which the patient envied the act of parturition. As a child he must have fantasied that his mother perished through pregnancy and must have evolved the theory that having children meant losing the penis. In his transvestism he was trying to repudiate this dread also, saying to himself: "I may wish to be a woman and capable of bearing children—and yet keep my penis!"[12]

III

We have adduced analytical material in proof of all the hypotheses we put forward in Section I. If, now, we are in search of a pathognomonic etiology of the patient's transvestism, we are obliged to admit that we have not discovered one. We must in any case assume that he had a special bisexual disposition, for otherwise the desire to bear children, for example, could never have acquired such importance. But we do not know whether, if life had brought him different experiences, his strong sadism might not have enabled his masculine side to develop satisfactorily. But this mental make-up is common to homosexual and transvestist alike. Again, the series of experiences: the primal scene—castration-anxiety—flight into femininity, based on narcissism, occurs in other clinical pictures, and we do not know what circumstances cause the belief in the phallic woman to be retained with the specific perversion of transvestism, since the above series is present in other forms of nervous disease as well. It is true that we frequently find transvestism combined with precisely these diseases: narcissistic neuroses, hypochondria (compare the case quoted by Alexander[13]) and other perversions. Over and above all this, the case we are examining seems to have been determined by

[12] Deeper analysis of the narcissistic mental strata finally revealed that the identification with his dead mother (her "spirit") was performed by means of introjection (inhaling) and that in the unconscious the introjected mother was equated with his own penis. Thus we arrived at the following symbolic equation: patient in women's clothes = the mother with a penis = the penis in general. We recollect the similarity between the girl's name by which he so much wished to be called and his pet name for the penis.

[13] Alexander, *Psycho-analyse der Gesamtpersönlichkeit*, VII Vorlesung.

specific environmental factors: the characters of his father, mother and sister, and their interplay, seem to have thrust the patient's role upon him. But, again, similar specific environmental conditions appear by no means rare, for all writers on the subject tell us of transvestists whose mothers had a very great desire for a daughter! Ellis goes so far as to cite this circumstance as a proof of the purely hereditary etiology of transvestism, but in this he is in error.

Such communications about this perversion as are to be found in analytical literature bear a remarkable resemblance to our own conclusions. It is only thanks to the writings of Freud which have appeared since Sadger[14] and Boehm[15] discussed the question that it has been possible for me to give a greater coherence to my account. Sadger evolved the following formula as summing up the transvestist's train of thought: "As a female I should be loved more by my mother and, indeed, by everyone. When I put on my mother's dress I feel as if I were she herself and so could arouse sexual feeling in my father and possibly supplant her with him. And, finally, a third person derives as much pleasure from a woman's clothes as from herself and looks on the putting on of her frock as a sexual act." This formula is correct, but in my opinion it leaves out the phallic factor, which is so important and which Sadger does mention accidentally elsewhere, though there are yet other passages in which he contradicts this by asserting that it is the vulva which is the fetish. Boehm, again, lays stress in isolated instances on precisely this phallic character of the transvestist's perversion ("In the clothes which they put on they represent the mother with the penis"),[16] and on the sadistic nature of the wishes which originally related to the mother. Stekel contents himself with the incomplete statement that transvestism is based on homosexuality and mother-fixation. Pre-analytic literature gives but a meager account of the matter to analysts, nevertheless, even the manifest

---

[14] Sadger, *Die Lehre von Geschlechtsverirrungen*, Vienna, 1921.
[15] Boehm, "Bemerkungen zum Transvestitismus," *Internationale Zeitschrift für Psychoanalyse*, Bd. IX, S. 497.
[16] Dr. Boehm has been kind enough to tell me that further analyses of transvestists have confirmed this view. He had one patient who used to turn a bottle upside down on his penis and then to put on women's clothes and dance in front of a looking-glass and so, finally, to masturbate.

material of such cases as are described in it contains all sorts of data which go to prove our hypothesis. We note, side by side with the transvestism, fetishistic, masochistic and exhibitionistic tendencies, narcissism, fantasies of the mistress and the female slave, identification with the mother, histories of seduction by elder sisters, aversion from physical sexuality and especially from nakedness, the naked female body and from homosexuality, the *"retour a l'enfance"* (Ellis), but also a passion for women of a masculine type (Hirschfeld). One of Hirschfeld's cases gave rein to his transvestist tendencies by joining in a display of trick-shooting in the guise of a woman, thus publicly courting admiration as an "armed woman."[17] Ellis quotes one case which seems to contradict our view, because the patient's sexual aim was quite obviously castration, but this same man used to put on women's shoes and earrings, which indicates that, although he wished for castration, he was always impelled to cancel it again.[18] Cases of actual self-castration by transvestists or of disgust felt by them for the male genital and longing for that of the female would have to be examined analytically before we could make any pronouncement about them. Ellis' theory is as follows: All normal love contains an element of identification; in the perversion of transvestism this element is hypertrophied—"He has put too much of 'me' into the 'you' that attracts him."[19] This theory is, in our view, correct but incomplete. We think that we have been able to predicate something about the nature and causes of this identification. Just as correct and just as incomplete is Ellis' formula about the relation of transvestism to homosexuality; they are, he says, "two allotropic modifications of bisexuality." But it is possible to differentiate the characteristics of these modifications.

IV

We have recognized that the specific factor in the perversion of transvestism is its relation to the castration-complex. It remains for us to ask whether this conclusion contributes anything to our understanding of the psychology of the perversions in general.

[17] *Die Transvestiten,* Case V.
[18] *Loc. cit.,* Ss. 63 *et seq.*
[19] *Loc cit.,* S. 108.

Sachs, in an article in which he examines the latter question, demonstrates that what characterizes the pervert is his capacity to transfer part of his infantile sexuality over to the ego, to permit himself to indulge it and by this very means to hold in repression those infantile sexual impulses which still remain (that is, the Oedipus complex).[20] The riddle we have to solve is how this process is possible, under what conditions can perverse component instincts retain or acquire the capacity to produce orgasm. As we now know that *all* perversions, including transvestism, are so intimately connected with the castration-complex, we can at least reply with the following hypothesis: Normally, what conditions the disappearance of infantile sexuality (the passing of the Oedipus complex) is the dread of castration.[21] Now the homosexual has no regard for any human being who lacks the penis, the fetishist denies that such beings exist, while the exhibitionist, the scoptophiliac and the transvestist try incessantly to refute the fact. Thus we see that these perverts are endeavoring to master their anxiety by denying its cause. In so far as they succeed in maintaining the illusion that there is no such thing as a lack of the penis, they save themselves anxiety and can indulge in infantile sexual practices *because,* just in proportion as they can effectively deny the grounds for it, their castration-anxiety, which otherwise would act as a check on such sexual behavior, is diminished. We must, however, qualify this statement by saying that this process succeeds only up to a certain point. That is to say, such infantile activities are bound up with a simultaneous, incessantly renewed denial of the reason for anxiety, and it is this denial which is represented in the perverse practice. The behavior of the pervert implies: "You have no need to be afraid" and, so long as he believes himself, his infantile sexual activities can produce orgasm, which signifies the gratification of his Oedipus wishes.

It is true that this hypothesis makes the feminine perversions and the whole subject of the castration-complex in women all the more problematic. Indeed, one does receive the impression that they are to some extent different in character from, though

[20] "Zur Genese der Perversionen," *Internationale Zeitschrift für Psychoanalyse,* Bd. IX, S. 172.

[21] Freud, "The Passing of the Oedipus Complex," *Collected Papers,* Vol. II.

akin to, perversions in men. This strikes us, for instance, when we think of female exhibitionists and recall Hárnik's work on the differences between masculine and feminine narcissism.[22] Female fetishists are extremely rare, and female transvestists seem to be simply women who covet the penis and, out of desire to possess it, have identified themselves with men.

[22] Hárnik, "The Various Developments Undergone by Narcissism in Men and in Women," *International Journal of Psycho-Analysis*, Vol. V, p. 66.

XIII

Fetishism*

By Robert C. Bak

Fetishism, as Freud (6) has shown, is a special solution of the castration threat. This solution is carried out by the mechanism of the denial of a part of reality consisting of the refusal to acknowledge the lack of a penis in women. Thus, the fetish is a substitute for the female penis (that is, of the mother). It may be a symbol of the penis or it may represent the object of "last moment in which the woman could still be regarded as phallic." The choice of the fetish often is influenced by the return of repressed coprophilic smell desires (3). The main significance of the fetish is due to its protective values as a "safeguard against the danger of castration." The reality of this danger is recognized at the sight of the female genital but it is repudiated simultaneously and the two conflicting perceptions in the denial constitute a split in the ego (7). Freud emphasized throughout that the core of the problem lies in the horror of the female genital and he also posed the question why the trauma of the sight of penislessness is overcome in the majority of cases but in some it leads to fetishism or homosexuality.

In what follows we shall make an attempt to contribute to this problem. Freud had indicated that the decisive screen memories of fetishists usually date not earlier than from the

* Reprinted from *Journal of the American Psychoanalytic Association*, Vol. I, No. 2, April, 1953, pp. 285-98.

Read before the Meeting of the American Psychoanalytic Association, Atlantic City, N. J., May 9, 1952.

ages of five or six. Therefore, earlier experiences must determine the choice of the fetish. In other words, whereas the fetishistic defense of castration anxiety emerges in the phallic phase, it is predetermined by prephallic experiences. The constitutional predisposition, according to Freud, consists of the "executive weakness of the sexual apparatus," which may account for the easy deflection from the normal aim by accidental intimidation.

In the development of fetishism we will emphasize the following points:

1. Weakness of the ego structure that may be inherent, or may come about secondarily through physiological dysfunctions or through disturbances in the mother-child relationship that threaten survival. This may account for the inordinate separation anxiety that results in increased clinging (11) to the mother totally, or to a substitute part of her as a *pars pro toto,* leaving behind erotization of the hands and predilection for touching.

2. Fixation in pregenital phases, especially anal eroticism and smelling (1) in the service of maintaining mother-child unity, wherein respiratory introjection plays an important role (Fenichel, 2; Greenacre, 8), besides scoptophilia.

3. The symbolic significance of the fetish corresponds to pregenital phases and thus may represent separately or in condensation: breast-skin, buttocks-feces, and female phallus.

4. Simultaneous and alternating identification with the phallic and penisless mother, corresponding to the "split of the ego" (Freud).

5. The identification with the penisless mother (14) leads to the wish for giving the penis up, creating marked intrastructural conflict. Historically, the pregenital identification with the phallic mother cannot be given up in the phallic phase in spite of the new reality (penislessness) because separation from the mother is experienced as an equal, if not greater, danger than the loss of the penis. Both phases of danger, that is, of separation and castration, are defended by the fetishistic compromise (biphasic).

The triad—fetishism, transvestitism, homosexuality—represents different phases of the compromise between the simultaneous identification with the mother. The apparent insistence on the maternal phallus is a protection against the id wish of shedding the penis in order to maintain identity with the mother. The various degrees of identification with the mother, resulting in homosexuality and fetishism, were stressed by Lorand (14).

First Case. A young man in his early twenties was seeking psychiatric help for his homosexual feelings. He had not engaged in overt homosexual activities, but both his emotional and physical desires were directed toward men from the beginning of puberty. The objects of his attraction were boys of the same age or somewhat older and they had to conform in their appearance to certain specifications. Among these the most important role was given to the buttocks. The buttocks had to have a narrow, compact, boyish shape and the trousers had to fit tightly. There was an almost irresistible desire to fondle the buttocks of these men, to finger the creases of the cloth over the buttocks, and above all, to put his head and nose between the hemispheres. The buttocks should not smell of feces and there was anxiety lest they would. Other fetishes were: boots, both rubber and leather, rubber raincoats and clothes of gabardine material frequently used for riding breeches. Men clothed in these garments excited him sexually. He followed them without even having seen their faces. Sexual gratification was achieved by masturbation, by putting on boots or some of these garments in front of the mirror. Additional excitement was provided by the smell of the rubber or of perspiration.

The patient was raised in a small village, in the milieu of the landed gentry and county officials. He had a brother, four years his senior. There were feeding difficulties from the beginning: he could not take the milk from the breast, also vomited the formula and went through near-starvation in infancy. As a small boy he had to have special food because of his allergies and could not eat outside of the home. He recalled many stories of how he had to be protected because he was so "sensitive." His delicate build and smooth skin were praised by both mother and grandmother; also that he was gentle and nice—like a girl.

Habit training was greatly delayed. He remained enuretic until his early teens and soiled even during the latter part of the latency period. The mother showed considerable interest in his anal activities. Her patience and indulgence with his daily soiling was inexhaustible. "Come and I'll take care of my darling—there is nothing I would not do for you." She washed him with the "facecloth" in the bathroom, to the great satisfaction of the patient who also watched her rinse it out in the sink. He fantasied that the "facecloth" would be used again on her face. This then became the epitome of the expression of the love between him and his mother. Later he planned to cut out a square piece of cloth from the seat of pants in order to use it as a fetish. This "complete" fetish he never realized. He only smelled the stained underwear of his mother and his own whenever he could. The mother fingered the cloth and put her nose to the front and to the back of his trousers to find out whether he had wet or soiled his pants. If so, she showed a sort of mock horror, undressed and washed him, and at the end kissed his buttocks. The patient loved to go after his mother into the bathroom to inhale the odor of her feces. He also very often asked his mother, in baby talk, for enemas. Naturally, he enjoyed his soiling a great deal, withheld feces, then "bit a piece off" and delighted in the sensation of the falling skybalum and carried it in his knickers.[1] The entire family participated in anal amusements. The mother flatulated openly to the delight of the children. The brothers played flatus games and competed in flatulence. Even though the pleasure in these fecal activities was great, the older brother was held up as an example of cleanliness, as the one who "never had his pants stained."

Sexual curiosity was uninhibited at first. Around the age of five he explored the genital of his girl friend courageously, putting the handle of a spoon into her "slit." He was discovered and severely reprimanded, but the object of his main interest remained his mother whom he watched frequently undressing or insufficiently clad. He recalled seeing his mother in bloomers and especially the rubber apron that she wore on her back under the skirt to protect it from creases. He loved to crawl under it, smelling his mother and the rubber. When following her into the bathroom he wondered why she sat down to urinate and decided that probably she thought she would defecate, but only urinated. He did not consciously identify his mother's genital with that of his girl friend but around the same age he de-

---

[1] Romm's (16) case of a hair fetishist manifests behavior patterns of coprophagic origin (eating and smearing nasal secreta, eating dandruff and scabs), resembling the "grooming" ceremonies of monkeys and apes, interpreted by Hermann (10) as a re-establishment of mother-child unity, also indicated in her case in the "complete circle" of autofellatio and Christ fantasy.

veloped great curiosity about his mother's drawers, closets, and pocketbook. The discovery of a big tube with a rubber ball was considered the most interesting find and he showed it in secret to his girl friend. Somewhat later he became fascinated by her dresses, went into her wardrobe, smelled the dresses, put his face on the silk and fur. He also asked mother to give him the dresses she did not wear anymore. He changed them and put them on. Sometimes he had two or three dresses in his closet and dressed up in high-heeled shoes with jewelry and makeup. This was encouraged by mother and grandmother and he was told repeatedly how much he looked like his mother. The disgust of his father and older brother did not create a great impression at that time, only much later. In the same way, his playing with girls only and his attachment to the home were encouraged. It was not so, however, with any genital activity. He was warned very early and very anxiously not to play with his "little bottom." (This expression combined both the buttocks and the penis.) He did not welcome at all the heralds of sexual maturity and he was horrified to see the hair growing on his body as he did not wish to become that bearded, crude ruffian—his father and brother. He despised his growing penis and hid it between his thighs. He was horse-playing with his mother in bed up to the age of sixteen when he recalled distinctly how he had to lie in bed with his mother, frozen motionless, lest he get an erection.[2] He was dimly aware of his father's disapproval.

The relationship with the older brother, after a start of love and closeness, changed into hatred and murderous rivalry. Up to adult age he maintained a fantasy that a younger brother could not become a man and if he could, he surely did not have a father or his father must have died early. The brother bullied and teased him, called him a sissy and told him his behind looked like a girl's. Father and brother refused to take him along on their manly pursuits, shooting, jumping. The father obviously favored the older boy and for the mother too, the older one was "the boy" and the patient was "sonny." He felt there was a division in the family, his brother belonging to his father, whereas he belonged to his mother and grandmother. He had passionate interests in girls at this age; also around the age of

[2] Lorand stated that the realization of sex difference would *eo ipso* put an end to all sex play with the mother.

thirteen he was passionately in love with his music teacher and had a compulsive drive to kiss her. The sudden change to overt homosexuality occurred around the age of fourteen, at the onset of puberty and when his brother left home to volunteer in an elegant Hussar regiment. He fell in love with a boy of the same first name as his brother's. The boy had one crippled foot that was covered by the boots he wore. This boy was also pointed out as an example to him. These tender homosexual relationships with only masturbatory satisfaction continued up to the time of treatment.

In the homosexual fantasies and in their acting out later, this patient dramatized his pregenital relationships with his mother. The objects were his idealized self modeled on the older brother while he himself played the role of his mother, literally repeating the same caressing words to the object as he used to hear them from his mother. This re-enactment not only repeated the pleasurable childhood situation but also undid the unsuccessful rivalry with the brother who became his ego ideal. In the act of sucking and inhaling the object he incorporated him. "If my brother loves me and I can be one with him, I become a man." The unconscious goal of the homosexual act was to achieve manhood, identity with the brother and unification with the phallic mother. The homosexual act also contained aggression and revenge against the "two-timing mother" and the denial of hate toward the rival brother. The main meaning of the mother identification was: "I don't need you. You cannot abandon me. I am the same as you and love my brother." During treatment the main resistance centered around his wish for revenge against the mother by remaining ill, by making her feel guilty. Once, after a performance of *Othello*, he developed considerable anxiety about the murder of Desdemona.[3]

[3] J. Glover (9) was the first to stress the sadism of the fetishist and the revenge motives in his case. In our patient the homosexual act, per se, is revenge against the mother who said to him, "If you won't get over this [meaning homosexuality], I don't want to live." However, the content of the act is complete denial of sadism against mother and brother. Kronold's and Sterba's (13) first case shows ambivalence toward the fetish in the form of temporary discarding, expressing ambivalence toward the mother and the attempt at separation as reaction formation to the clinging (see our second case). In their case the disturbed mother-child relationship is evident. The patient was an illegitimate child and after some days was separated from the mother.

The fetishes at first were clearly related to the mother. Her dresses and smell, and especially the rubber aprons that she wore in front and back, the facecloth, became the fetishes with minor alterations. They provided substitutes for tactile sensations of her skin, of her body smell and of the smell of her feces and ultimately of her penis. The mother appeared in dreams with "long rubber hose between her legs" and in other dreams he was "going home looking for something in the attic and while crawling under some shelves ejaculated from the smell of the rubber boots." In the fetishes mother's skin, feces and penis are condensed as if the various phases of pregenital relationship were telescoped into one symbol.

Freud mentioned that the fetish creates an independence from the love object. We would rather say that the fetish undoes the separation from the mother through clinging to the symbolic substitute. The fetishist behaves similarly to the infant who holds onto the mother or to her clothing when falling asleep. It is obvious that the pregenital identifications with the mother through clinging, warmth, feeding and smell inhaling do not entail the threat of castration. The discovery of her genital does. However, the fetishist seems to have remained undecided. He does know that the mother has no penis and therefore to be one with her would mean giving up his penis. This wish is not abandoned by the fetishist. In our patient it remained almost without conflict until the time he wanted to take over his brother's place. A dream demonstrates the two phases of this development.

I am dancing around with the lower part of a silk dress on me. Later I take it off and when coming back I either have riding boots on or have a big whip in my hand.

Three dreams during one night demonstrate the way he attempts to resolve and undo the castration resulting from his identification with the women in the family.

First dream: Grandmother looked like a young woman, smooth skin, blonde hair. My mother, her sister, grandmother and myself, went to the hunting lodge. While going up the stairs I noticed that grandmother had her face lifted. I noticed a scar on her cheek. We are supposed to sleep in a tremendous room with two beds. I felt I should not sleep there as I felt that Dr. K. would disapprove of my sleeping in the same room with mother.

Second dream: Mother was lying in bed and as I was about to crawl in with her I noticed two small garter snakes which frightened me away. I then saw her sitting in bed with a book on her lap. Lying in the open book was the head segment of a huge snake which had apparently been cut off. She was using it as a bookmark. Although it was dead, it opened its jaws and instead of fangs there was a set of human teeth. I didn't know for sure whether it was a snake's or a cat's head. There seemed to be characteristics of both.

Third dream: A row of houses were, or had been, remodeled. My family's and a neighbor's. Both had elaborate additions on the front—columnar porches. Our neighbor's house became top-heavy and fell forward over an embankment. My father, in riding boots, pulls out a tremendous horsewhip, puts it to the edge of the house and pushes it back into place.

In the first dream the wish to sleep in the same room with the women is realized though their injury is noticed. In the second dream, closeness with the mother and seeing her is frightening and the dreamer cannot deny the injury in the image of the cut-off snake, even though there is the attempt at uncertainty as to the nature of the seen object (snake or cat?). Finally, in the third dream an attempt is made at "remodeling" through the father's gigantic penis.[4]

This patient throughout his life was desperately engaged in the endeavor to prove to his mother than he was as good as his brother. All these attempts failed even though in reality he did surpass his brother in many respects. Disappointment which related to this sphere mobilized the fetishistic urges. When he felt abandoned or derided by his mother, the irresistible desire turned up to "mother" other men, to hold them in his arms. He could not be convinced of the love of a woman and fantasied that he could not compare with the brother or father of the beloved woman. The slightest doubt of not preferring him exclusively mobilized the fetishistic urges. When some heterosexual potency was established, it became clear that through coitus he became a woman. Fantasies of intercourse with big-breasted women,

[4] According to Payne (15), the potency of these patients depends on the unconscious belief of introjected father's or brother's penis.

with large buttocks, created the feeling of manliness in him. It meant that he would make the grade with women like his mother. Also, by equating breast with penis he acquired manhood through identification.[5] The orgastic sensation created the fear that the thrusting penis would be torn off. After coitus the need to regain the penis by homosexual acts increased.

Second Case. A twenty-three-year-old man sought psychiatric help after his discharge from the army. Overseas he related poorly to his comrades, was incapable of studying and failed in O.C.S., was terrified that his testicles would be shot away. Even though he had the burning ambition to mow down the Germans with his rifle, he got his feet frozen and received a neuropsychiatric discharge before he even fired a shot. For the young man whose ideal was General Patton, this meant the ultimate in failure and resulted in depression.

This patient has been shy and inhibited from childhood on. He was somewhat retarded in his intellectual accomplishments and could not complete college. For this he earned the contempt of his father.

Before the start of treatment this patient had no sexual relations and confided his fetishistic symptoms only after a year. This patient also was a horseman, preoccupied with horses and riding, but especially with riding clothes. He was excited by women wearing jodhpurs, especially if the calves of the legs were well protruding and even more if they wore boots. Added excitement was produced if the pants were cut to have a strongly bulging appearance on the sides and if the insides of the knees had a patch of suede lining. In riding pants, he masturbated in front of the mirror. He also had the compulsive drive to buy these pants and at some times collected half a dozen. When concerned about being discovered, he wrapped up a couple and surreptitiously disposed of them in some abandoned part of the city. He had a great interest in leather goods, guns and revolvers and of course, cars. Besides the riding-pants fetishism, there was

[5] Hermann (12) emphasized the child's image of the parents, experiencing them as giants; especially the pelvic region of mother or father must seem gigantic. Out of the image of largeness the child forms the image of a phallus, not as an erroneous perception but as an inner lie. Holding on to this child-parent ratio is characteristic in my cases and reappears in relation to the own body and in displacement to various tasks that appear "enormous."

a compulsive wish to stroke silky hair. His female ideal was a long-haired, blonde, slender, "Park Avenue girl," Gentile and unreachable. The patient's childhood for a good part was spent in Scandinavia. His most outstanding memory dates from the age of four when his parents were going abroad and left him behind. Soon after their return he got a younger brother about whom he had practically no memories before the age of ten. The shock of being abandoned and the birth of the younger brother must have been great because the little boy was greatly attached to his mother before that age. Between two and three years of age he had great difficulty parting from his mother, sleeping alone, and insisted on going to bed with a piece of velvet which he stroked and put to his cheeks before falling asleep. This the patient did not remember. It was partly a reconstruction, later verified by his parents. This fetish of infancy underwent a change in the interest in fabrics and was worked into the suede patch of the breeches. Similar tactile sensations were created by the stroking of hair about which he remembered the long hair of his mother and his own long blond hair from childhood pictures. Up to the age of four he was dressed like a girl and had long, blond, silky hair. From early puberty he had a recurrent fantasy in which he was dancing naked with long hair in front of his father and the lower part of his body was indistinct. Around the age of five or six, during vacation in Scandinavia, he suffered a shock at seeing the female genital. The mother and aunt were arriving on horseback in riding clothes at the lake shore and were undressing in a bathhouse. He had opportunity to watch them and recalled the anxiety-filled curiosity of these experiences. What stood out especially in his memory was the moment of throwing off the boots and the jodhpurs, how they changed suddenly in the bathing suits when they went for a swim. He was then especially fascinated by the pants bulging at the sides and remembered asking his aunt many times what made them stick out. When he had opportunity, he sniffed around and inhaled the odor of the riding clothes. Following this he developed a phobia of going into the water and feared being bitten by the fish. He was encouraged in vain by being told that the fish were smaller than he. He could not venture into the water. Dreams of big sharks swimming toward him in the water were frequent, also in adult-

hood. Memories of the smell of his feces and of being afraid to
see them disappear were recalled and also the unwillingness to
use the outhouse in the country because of the fear that something might emerge from the dark hole and injure him. He experienced this part of his childhood as if he were a worm among
giants. These childhood experiences appeared in some dreams
from which I mention a few images.

I was standing at the edge of a great pine forest. As I stood
there a tremendous horned creature, like a giant moose or elk,
came thundering out of the forest and rushed toward the
precipice, paused ever so slightly and then, sprouting wings,
soared off into space with the smoothness of an airplane. And
this great creature was immediately followed by another and
another and another—a whole rushingness of them into my
view (as I stood there feeling insignificant and awe-struck)
and then away they all went soaring off into the sky with the
power and swiftness of great planes and my whole consciousness was thrilled and inspired by them and also I was afraid.
But they didn't even notice me. These creatures were at least
partially clothed in military-like uniforms and wearing the
old U. S. Army campaign hats. They made me feel very insignificant and unimportant. I wanted to be like them but
didn't seem to stand a chance.

Part of another dream: I was in an enormous barbaric and
Germanic-looking banquet hall. Utterly and completely pagan
and savage is the impression it created upon me and the
enormous jovial and terrifying beings in there were more like
monstrous, shaggy animals. Nobody was chasing me or anything like that but I felt that if I didn't keep out of the way I
might get hurt. I stayed in partial concealment behind an iron
door that had barbaric carvings on it. Then there was a tremendous tumult and roaring that shook the whole vast hall
and the whole world with it. The hall was the world and then
there suddenly came thundering right by me down the bottom
end of a ski jump slope which must have started in the endless
night of infinity, a gigantic, shaggy, furry, wild bear of truly
epic proportions, in an upright position, maybe on skis, wearing more brilliant Germanic armor than all the rest in the great
gathering and with a splash of color across his chest (probably
campaign ribbons and similar citations), and also some sort of
weapon. He was closely followed by two or three other giants
of a similar type. It is impossible for me to describe the deafen-

ing cheer and applause that greeted these tremendous, monstrous heroes who came down that ski slide into that pagan and barbaric hall. How much I envied them. I was like a crumb on the floor.

The perception of the parents' genitals was also in such gigantic proportions when at the age of thirteen, on account of learning difficulties he saw a school psychiatrist, he mentioned his hatred for his father's enormous red penis. Up to late puberty, however, he remained true to his mother's ambition and wanted to carve out for himself an artistic career. Only in puberty was the artistic career evaluated as feminine and had to be abandoned. Ambitions to follow the father or some of the gigantic uncles of childhood were discouraged by the father's hostility to the underendowed, disappointing son. In his outward behavior this poor young man used all the accessories to appear like a man. The gait, the holding of the head, big moustache, pipe, rough clothing, way of speech, were superimposed on the fantasy of the long-haired, blond, little boy with indistinct genitals. Needless to say, it is his own childhood image that returns in his object choice in the Park Avenue girl. The preference for Gentiles derives from the identification with the mother who herself, through her rustic, Scandinavian background, was experienced as Gentile. This patient was not spared from homosexual object choice either, and later on had the compulsive urge to walk on the street in jodhpurs, to be picked up by men. His heterosexual choice was finally a woman, a commercial artist, intellectually far his superior, domineering and polio-stricken in one leg.

The phallic quality of these fetishes is obvious but it seems also justified to say that the prephallic fetishes representing the mother's skin and smell are condensed into them. This fetish also represents the "last minute object" which still preserves the woman as phallic but we cannot fail to see the identification with the penisless mother in his fantasies and object choice. The fetishist's wish to be one with the penisless mother becomes just as much reality as the identification with the phallic mother. In spite of his constant preoccupation and fear of cripples which sometimes prevented him from picking up his check because he had to talk or go through contact with a mutilated veteran, he chose a crippled woman. It is frequently said that the fetishist also wants to make sure that the woman is castrated and has no penis. However, one may consider that this is not to prove his manhood but, on the contrary, to find the object identical with his own penisless state.

The anxiety at being abandoned mobilized also in this patient the fetishistic and transvestitic ceremonies. The threat of being left by the loved woman, her leaving him in the house alone after an angry scene, made him feel compelled to put on her clothes.

Leaving now the specialized problems of perversion, one may consider more general implications. Freud (4) stated that the giving up of object relationship results mostly in identification. Perhaps we should reopen the question of how it is possible for the boy to abandon his incestuous object without identification. Freud's answer was clear. The attachment to the mother is given up due to the fear of castration, and Freud finally considered the danger as coming entirely from the outside (5). We are inclined to think that besides the factor of outside threat, the intensity of the castration fear may also depend on the inner wish of identity with the mother. In any renewed contact with the love object the wish for identity with her may renew the threat from within.

REFERENCES

1. K. Abraham, "Remarks on the Psycho-Analysis of a Case of Foot and Corset Fetishism," *Selected Papers on Psycho-Analysis*, Hogarth Press, London, 1927.

2. O. Fenichel, "Über respiratorische Introjektion," *Int. Ztschr. f. Psa.*, Vol. XVII, 1931, pp. 234-55.

3. S. Freud, (1904), "Three Contributions to the Theory of Sex," *J. Nerv. and Ment. Dis. Monogr.*, 1910, pp. 198-205.

4. S. Freud, (1923), *The Ego and the Id*, Hogarth Press, London, 1927.

5. S. Freud, (1926), *The Problem of Anxiety*, Norton, New York, 1936.

6. S. Freud, (1927), Fetishism, *Coll. Papers*, V, Hogarth Press, London, 1951.

7. S. Freud, (1938), "Split of the Ego in the Defensive Process," *Coll. Papers*, V, Hogarth Press, London, 1951.

8. P. Greenacre, *Trauma, Growth and Personality*, Norton, New York, 1952.

9. J. Glover, "Notes on an Unusual Form of Perversion," *Int. J. Psa.*, Vol. VIII, 1927, pp. 10-24.

10. I. Hermann, "Zur Psychologie der Chimpanzen," *Int. Ztschr. f. Psa.*, Vol. IX, 1923, pp. 80-87.

11. I. Hermann, "Sich Anklammern—Auf Suche Gehen," *Int. Ztschr. f. Psa.*, Vol. XXIII, 1936, p. 22.

12. I. Hermann, "The Giant Mother, the Phallic Mother, Obscenity," *Psa. Rev.*, Vol. XXXVI, 1949, pp. 302-306.

13. E. Kronold, and R. Sterba, "Two Cases of Fetishism," *Psa. Quart.*, Vol. V, 1936, pp. 63-70.

14. S. Lorand, "Fetishism in Statu Nascendi," *Int. J. Psa.*, Vol. XI, 1930, pp. 419-27.

15. S. M. Payne, "Some Observations on the Ego Development of the Fetishist," *Int. J. Psa.*, Vol. XX, 1939, pp. 161-70.

16. M. Romm, "Some Dynamics in Fetishism," *Psa. Quart.*, Vol. XVIII, 1949, p. 137.

XIV

Foreskin Fetishism and Its Relation to Ego Pathology in a Male Homosexual*

By M. Masud R. Khan

Introduction

In psychoanalytic literature the fetish has been discussed exclusively as an auxiliary object or device in the service of heterosexual gratification, and as a defense against perversions proper, particularly homosexuality. Freud (1927) had derived the etiology of fetishism from castration anxiety relating to the phallic phase. He had established the psychic contents of the fetish as denial of castration and had stated: "The fetish is a substitute for the woman's (mother's) penis that the boy once believed in and does not want to give up." By his emphasis on the singular importance of the mechanisms of denial (disavowal) and splitting in the ego's attempt to deal with the castration threat, Freud (1927, 1938) had also established the beginnings of researches into ego pathology and its relation to perversions which have since enlarged extensively the etiology of fetishism to include: (a) primary pre-Oedipal relation to the (breast) mother (Lorand, 1930; Wulff, 1946; Buxbaum, 1960); (b)

* Presented at a Scientific Meeting of the British Psycho-Analytical Society on 20 January 1965. Earlier versions were presented to the Philadelphia Association for Psychoanalysis and to the Los Angeles Psychoanalytic Society in April 1964. I am grateful to Dr. John D. Sutherland, Dr. Robert Waelder, and Dr. Ralph Greenson for their helpful suggestions and criticisms.

internal objects and early ego development (Payne, 1939; Gillespie, 1940, 1964; Hunter, 1954); (c) transitional object phenomena and primitive mental functioning (Winnicott, 1953; Lacan and Granoff, 1956; Fraser, 1963); (d) separation anxiety and the dread of abandonment (Bak, 1953; Weissman, 1957); (e) pathological body-ego development and threat of disintegration from disturbed mother-child relationship (Greenacre, 1953, 1960; Mittelmann, 1955); (f) bisexual primary identifications with the mother and the wish to bear a child (Kronengold and Sterba, 1936; Kestenberg, 1956; van der Leeuw, 1958; Socarides, 1960); (g) flight from incest (Romm, 1949); and (h) a defense against archaic anxiety affects which threaten the relation to reality with the accompanying dread of breakdown into psychotic states (Glover, 1932, 1933, 1949; Socarides, 1959; Katan, 1964).

In the literature, to my knowledge, there is only one case, reported by Bak (1953), where the patient indulged masturbatory practices with fetishistic homosexual fantasies relating to boys with buttocks of a certain shape and smoothness. I shall here present material from an overt male homosexual whose sexual interest and activities were exclusively centered round a fetishistic relation to the foreskins of uncircumcised youths. I shall try to detail the psychodynamics of this foreskin fetish and its defensive self-protection role in relation to the severe latent ego-pathology which derived from a grossly disturbed and intimate relation to his mother in his childhood.

PATIENT'S EARLY HISTORY

The patient, a man of forty years of age, was one of four children. He had an elder brother and a sister two-and-a-half years younger. The parents had divorced when he was seven and the mother had married again soon afterwards; another boy followed within a year. Both marriages of the mother had been passionately, noisily and hysterically unhappy and she had intimately involved the patient in all her woes and emotional tantrums. She was a beautiful and ambitious girl who had miscalculated both times. According to her later insistent confessions to the patient, she had never loved her first husband whom she had reviled after divorce as a dirty man with nasty sexual habits. She had made out that the three sons (the youngest after the marriage) had all been her second husband's children, and to establish this fact she had their surname changed to his. The daughter she had conceived from another person. Her second husband was much older than she, and a rich and respectable citizen, who, however, lost all his wealth within a year of marrying her. This had exaggerated her terror of poverty and disease and the children were made witnesses of her eloquent complaints and grievances against fate and the husbands. Instead of improving her economic status she had, in fact, to do with a humble existence now. She was, however, very devoted to the patient who idealized her as a person throughout his childhood, and he had a profound attachment of love and affection to her right up to his adolescence.

The patient, who had been circumcised at birth, had a curiously vivid memory of isolated events as well as of fantasies from his childhood which he produced schematically in the first week of his treatment. They mostly belonged to the period between three years and six years of age. Briefly they were:

Memories from age about 3:

1. Sitting on a china egg and imagining he had laid it; feeling very disappointed on discovering it was not real.
2. Being very interested in the penis of geldings and imagining himself united to them via the urethra. (This fantasy stayed with him till 14 or 15 years of age and had become absorbed into his masturbation fantasies.)
3. Tasting milk direct from a cow's teats during milking time and disliking it intensely.
4. He has been told, though personally had no direct memory of it, that one day his parents found that all the rhubarb plants had been nibbled and bitten at the root. First they had thought it was the work of rats and then discovered it was he who had done it.
5. He and his brother began going to the parents' bed in the morning and he started to entertain a compulsive wish to suck his father's penis and wished his mother were not in the way. Once he tried tentatively and was rebuffed. When he was seven, and both the mother and her new husband had started to revile the father as a man of nasty habits, he had confessed to his mother that he had actually sucked his father's penis and she had readily believed it.

6. His only other memory of his father was of the latter's once by mistake piercing the patient's foot with a prong while digging potatoes in the garden. Apart from this he had only the vaguest notion of his father and thought he had been a kindly person.

7. He remembers playing with his newborn sister by the fire and setting the blanket on fire. He burnt his hand and the nanny soaked it with the baby's wet diaper. He was very attached to this nanny. She had been sacked when the mother remarried because she had told the children that it was not their father who had been a nasty man but their mother who had loose morals.

8. His most vivid memory of his mother was of being tickled by her throughout his childhood, especially on the soles of his feet, and being reduced to ravished helplessness.

Memories from age 5:

9. Of his mother's singing about fishermen lost at sea and his crying.

Memories from about 8 onward:

10. Of his mother's bitter complaints against her first husband's sexual habits and her grievances against her second husband, with the patient always taking her side.

11. Of his mother's painfully congested breasts after her last child and his offering to suck them and being very relieved when refused.

12. Feeling terrified of his stepfather on their first meeting and wishing he would go away and leave them alone. (He never got to know him well.)

13. Acute unhappiness when mother went on her honeymoon and starting sexual games with his brother and later threatening to tell on him.

14. It was also during this period (mother went away for six weeks) that he began noticing that his circumcised penis was different in shape from some boys'.

15. When he was eight, his parents moved to another country. From the period of his mother's divorce, remarriage, and move from home, started his obsession with foreskins. At first he had thought that the boys who had foreskins had an abnormality. At 10 he wrote anonymously to the father of a boy in his class,

advising him to have his son circumcised as his foreskin was abnormal. He was found out but not punished.

16. Of mother having an abortion done in the house, when he was ten, and seeing the nurse and pans full of blood and other material.

17. His first masturbation activities started while he was listening to the hysterical rows between his mother and stepfather, at the age of 11.

18. When he was nineteen, his mother returned to the home country with her husband and left him at college. From this period his pruritis ani started and it persisted to the time of this analysis.

The patient presented these memories somewhat flamboyantly. Though he claimed to have a very good memory of his childhood, in fact there was very little else that he was able to produce during the first sixteen months of this analysis. Greenacre (1955) has pointed out the limited nature of the fantasies of the fetishist and this was true of this patient as well. He had almost no recall of any relationships to people other than his mother, brother, and father from his childhood and adolescence and all his masturbatory fantasying from puberty onwards had been almost adhesively centered on this foreskin fetish. Later in the discussion of his ego pathology, it will be seen how much this blank affectless image of his own youth screened an extremely disturbed and crippled ego development as well as his incapacity for object relationships (cf. Khan, 1964a).

Psychodynamics of the Foreskin Fetish

The patient had sought treatment because of what he had ironically phrased "a theoretical dislike of homosexuality." By this he had meant that he did not wish to become or be regarded as "a queer," meaning a socialized overt homosexual. He had described in a euphoric way his current existence as dedicated to sexual love and the sexual seduction of young men with foreskins. The search for foreskins on beautiful youthful male bodies had become his chief private and personal preoccupation, although he had successfully integrated it with a sophisticated professional life. He was an educated person, well-groomed, slick and elegant of speech, and fastidiously polished in his manners. I have described the sexual cravings and pursuits of this patient and their relation to his identity diffusion during the first sixteen months of his analysis in my paper, "Homosexuality and the Sexual Nursing of Self and Object" (1965). Here I shall detail the phenomenology of his specific sexual wish and activity: to find a youth with foreskin, perform fellatio on him, and then masturbate into the foreskin. The first phase of his analysis was filled up by euphoric and exhibitionistic accounts of his night-prowls in search of his accomplices. I have used the word "accomplices" deliberately because he never once coerced a youth into sexual intimacy who had not been looking for a similar type of experience. There was also very little overtly nasty or sadistic or even unpleasant in his relation to his sexual object. The whole search for the suitable sexual object, the technique of seduction and the relation to the person of his sexual gratification were obsessionally ritualized. He had a compulsion to search for the foreskin object and if he failed, which was most infrequent, he was then reduced to masturbation. To this he always reacted with disgust, apathy, acute loss of self-esteem, and a sense of futility.

When the patient started the analysis his sexual activities had reached a crescendo of orgiastic excessiveness. He was fully aware of the dangers entailed (socially and legally) and early in his analysis had, as it were, reassured me by informing me that he had sufficient supply of poison should he find himself trapped, either through blackmail or police action. This type of splitting and denial was typical of him. Though he did his professional work efficiently and conscientiously he was concerned that he had lost all ambition and was living a day-to-day existence, without any real interest in his future.

The patient had had some sixteen months of analytic treatment in another country and it was during this previous analysis that he had acted out into real shared sexual experiences what had been till then merely obsessive private sexual ruminations with compulsive bouts of masturbation, which always left him disgusted with himself. Once he had started on his sexual adventures he had discovered his talent for such activities and when he came to me for treatment he could boast with some justice that there was not a youth he would wish to seduce who could resist him.

Though he had presented me with his stock of memories there

was little material in the sessions during the first phase that one could relate to his childhood experiences with any clinical cogency. Of course his manic, perfervid, and impassioned sexual pursuit of the youths, his lyrical accounts of their beauty and his greedy consumption of their semen could be all too easily translated into patterns of childhood experiences with mother and father; but for me, at least, it was important not to be seduced into this type of intellectual analysis. I had also the fate of his first analysis as a good cautionary tale to guide my work. What had impressed me most from the start was that he had created for himself an ahistorical, as-if, screen identity in terms of his practices and pursuits relating to the foreskin fetishistic object. I have discussed theoretically this aspect of his behavior in my paper, "The Function of Intimacy and Acting Out in Perversions" (1964c). During the first sixteen months analytic work had been concentrated on weakening his manic defense (Winnicott, 1935) as it operated through the sexual practices and on enabling him to bear minor anxiety-states without taking recourse to automatic defensive maneuvers of the erotic or obsessional kind (Khan, 1964b). It was when the patient began to relax his hectic and furious pursuit of sexual adventures that it became possible to examine in detail the psychic and affective contents of his foreskin fetishism. At this stage he became regressed in mood, apathetic and depressive in affect, and more dependent on his relation to me and the analytic situation.

Greenacre (1953) in her definition of the fetish has stressed that "in some instances it is not only the possession of the object but a ritualistic use of it which is essential." The ritual in relation to the person carrying the foreskin fetish was most revealing in the behavior of this patient. Equally important was the affective inner climate which would compel him into night prowling and searching for the foreskin fetish. This affective inner climate was an amorphous and confused state of excitement, anxiety bordering on psychically indecipherable terror, and a dread of collapse into total inertia and negativity (cf. Khan, 1964b).

I am now condensing details which were laboriously culled together clinically over a very long period of time. The fetishistic reverie and pursuit organized this larval confused agitated affectivity into an alert and active state of elation. Hence the fetishistic search for an object both organized the patient's amorphous affectivity and, by transforming the latter into an active modality of behavior, rescued him from apathy and inertia. The nourishing aspect of this type of acting out into reality as flight from an endopsychic crisis that the patient could not deal with had a definite self-protective role. How abjectly helpless and paralyzed he could be would occasionally become visible in the early phases when he had to stay indoors due to weather conditions and was reduced to masturbatory discharge activities.

RELATIONSHIP TO THE FETISHISTIC OBJECT

I shall differentiate the total fetishistic practices of this patient into two component parts: (a) his ego-relation to the fetishistic object, i.e., the uncircumcised youths with foreskins, and (b) the intimate physical sexual relation to the fetish proper, i.e., the foreskin itself. The patient himself was fully aware of this duality in his experience of, and relation to, the youth and his foreskin. He had always idealized and boasted about the nature of his concern for, and appreciation of, these youths as persons, whereas he regarded his activities with the foreskin as in the nature of "childish and absurd games." It became quite clear to me very early in his analysis that the type of affects and defense mechanisms involved in his relation to the fetishistic object were quite different from those expressed in his sexual play with the foreskin. The meaning and psychic content of the latter became possible only through analysis of the first and enabling the patient to see *himself* in the fetishistic object.

I have mentioned the amorphous mood of agitation and latent excitement mixed with anxiety and apathy from which the patient would launch himself on his night-adventures. This form of acting out of endopsychic crisis enabled his ego to use objectifying and anticipating functions (Hartmann, 1956). Instead of a phobic negativistic state of apathy the search for the fetishistic would mobilize a selective range of ego-functions. This patient had been crippled throughout his latency, adolescence, and earlier youth by an intense form of apathy and phobic-paranoid withdrawal into himself, in which state his only gratifications were the immediate discharge activities of masturbation with their stereotyped fetishistic fantasies about foreskins. The search after, and the relationship to, the youths had enabled him to sense himself as a living, active, and effective human being. This had led gradually to an almost manic state of over-weening self-confidence and exaggerated self-regard. He now considered himself an omnipotent person, imperturbable and dedicated to the rescuing and nursing of beautiful abandoned youths. He felt not only in touch with reality but also omnip-otently munificent towards it. His argument was that he helped these young men to become more conscious of their in-nate dignity and superiority and so enhanced their self-esteem.

He selected a very special type of youth for his fetishistic object: he had to be uncircumcised and, in physique, strong and beautiful. In mood he should be listless, depressed, at a loose end and searching for sympathetic contact. The fetishistic object should not be an avowedly practicing homosexual, i.e., the youth should not have accepted homosexual relationships as an ego-syntonic mode of sexual gratification. On the contrary, he should profess an overt dislike of such practices. If the patient felt that the youth was in himself excited and looking for homosexual gratification he would drop him immediately. This mixture of confused unease, apathy, and negativity in the mood of the youth was important for the patient because this alone established (unconsciously) the identity of the youth as one like himself. This type of projective identification as the vehicle of object relationship I consider inherent in the ego-pathology of the pervert. Socarides (1959) has presented some very interesting clinical material exemplifying the role of projective identification in the pedophilic perversion in a male homosexual.[1]

Once he had established the significant and essential attributes in the object (the foreskin and the effective mood) he would then involve them in a verbal relationship. The youths he picked

---

[1] Anticipating my discussion of this patient's ego-pathology I would like to comment here that to designate this type of relationship as projective identification is somewhat of a misnomer. This type of ego interest and ego-cathexis of another person is more in the nature of a transitional state between relationship to the self and the relationship to the object, where neither the self nor the object are as yet fully differentiated as separate entities. I think we should use the concept of projective identification to designate an affective relationship where an internal object-representation is being displaced on to an external object and which further denies this object his own psychic and existential reality. For my patient the existential reality of the external object and its empathic perception were of vital importance.

up were invariably "lost souls" who felt abandoned, angry, suspicious, and ill-treated by life and worthy of a better deal. They were also as a rule grossly illiterate and quite often uncouth. The first task that he set himself in relation to the fetishistic object was to mellow the latter's mood and change it from negativity and suspiciousness into one of trust and cooperativeness. He always succeeded with remarkable ease and rapidity. That his successes were largely due to the simple fact that he had encountered the youths in an explicitly sexual situation and that sexual urgency goaded them into compliance he denied for a very long time. When eventually he had to accept this fact it drove him to bleak despair and he gradually gave up the adventures. He always tried to convince them of two things: (a) that they were uniquely valuable persons, and (b) that they should treat themselves with dignity, reserve, and reverence, and expect this of others in relation to themselves as well. I need hardly say that this is precisely what the patient wanted for himself. In order to promote this quality of narcissistic self-regard in them he would volunteer to teach them the proper use of language, good manners, and other cultural attributes. He would also feed them and show them the necessity of body-hygiene. The youths were generally unkempt, dirty, and undernourished. He would also give them a little money. All this in a matter of hours. This would invariably lead to physical intimacy, but before I discuss that I will make a few comments on the meaning of this type of relation to the fetishistic object.

That the fetishistic object represented the aspects of the patient himself as a forlorn, deprived, and abandoned, as well as idealized and special, person is obvious. What was significant for the patient was that the acted-out relationship enabled him to make a restitution towards his own ego as well as to the external object. This was in marked contrast to his inner hopeless relation to himself and his equally futile relation to his mother throughout his childhood. Furthermore, in his role as a provider of comfort and nourishment he was identified with the primary good mother: active, omnipotent, and full of nurture (cf. van der Leeuw, 1958). It is my contention that this type of relation to the fetishistic object enabled this patient to resurrect a good early relation to his mother which had got lost through the vicissitudes of his family life from about four years of age onwards. Winnicott (1956) has postulated that behind the anti-social tendency there is a *memory* of a good (maternal) relationship that was present and got lost and the compulsion behind the anti-social tendency is to get back to this point and recover it. The patient in his relation to the fetishistic object was actively the good parent nursing the abandoned ideal child (youth).

The fetishistic object was also a whole person: intact and separate. The capacity to relate to him created the hope that not all was lost forever. The illusional value of this type of relationship as a defense against a psychotic type of depression, apathy, and despair cannot be exaggerated. The relationship further established concretely the reality of the patient's identification with the good mother. He became and was the good parent (mother) in the transient expanse of such a relationship. It is possible to postulate here that in this type of patient the earliest relation to the mother has not been internalized. It is available only in terms of identifications and not as a stable internal representation of the good mother. Hence, when the patient was not operative in such an identificatory manner his sense of his self was one of bleak and morbid vacuity. The ego's incapacity to internalize the experience is also visible in the necessity to live through compulsive repetitions. The failure in his childhood development of a sustained good relation to the mother was dramatically repeated in the regressive breakdown in each encounter of the ego-cathexis in the fetishistic object as a person into the archaic and primitive sexual practices with the foreskin fetish.

Freud (1927) has stressed the mixture of affection for and hostility to the fetish. Aggression toward the fetishistic object took a very peculiar form in this patient, namely that of exciting deviously and indirectly the youths to a pitch of sexual tension in which they would crave for discharge-relief. This was done so subtly that it is difficult to recount it. Through his verbal pattern and narcissistic boosting of these youths' self-regard he managed to get them "sexually overheated" (to use the patient's phrase). To deny the operation of this factor in the early phase of the activities was important. In fact verbally a psychic resistance was built up in the youths against sexual intimacy. The aggression expressed took the form of gaining a complete mastery over the excited state of the youth. This excitement was not allowed to be personalized. It was engineered furtively and obliquely. The youths had to experience it in a dissociated way: responding to his ego-solicitations their narcissistic self-regard was heightened and they had then to treat their excitement as a foreign body in their experience of self and treat it with casual cynicism. That they were used to sexual exploitation by their "patrons" was adamantly denied, by him on purpose, and by them through collusion with his technique of relationship. So they invariably protested when he changed the direction of the episode from ego-support to sexual seduction. He knew precisely at what point their excitement had reached its peak. The role of sight and seeing was imperative here. He scanned every nuance of feeling and tension in their face and posture until he had worked up a "colossal erection" in them. At this point his sense of achievement, triumph over, and mastery of the fetishistic object would be complete. He would now solicitously and compassionately offer to suck them and/or masturbate them. The excited helplessness of these uncouth, strong, aggressive youths had a specially pleasurable impact on the patient. Here a distinctly aggressive-sadistic element entered into his relation to them. He would secretly gloat over them: they were in his power. The more they got excited and frenzied with their sexual tension the more imperturbably quiet and gentle he became in his manner. He would often compel them to watch and see him masturbate them and make them ejaculate. He always swallowed the semen. The youth in the state of congested erection was both the mother and the excited self. At this point the inner status and psychic value of the object changed for him. He was the baby-person nourishing himself from the excited breast-penis of the youth (mother). He always had a guilty apprehension that this state of sexual excitement was not pleasurable for the youths. Here the identification of the youths with erection and the mother with painfully congested breast was complete. The youth with erection was also the phallic-breast mother. He had to hold tightly onto them while masturbating or sucking them. He could never cling hard enough and was forever disappointed that this clinging grasping fervor in him meant so little to them. Here the disillusionment about the fetishistic object would already set in. He was also deeply aware of their humiliation and abject passive role in the masturbatory activity. Since he had first encouraged them to boast of their heterosexual inclinations and virility the situation of finding themselves homosexually seduced was negated by the youths through a rough and cynical attitude toward the whole activity. This would mortify the patient. Never could he get them to acknowledge it as a good experience and this caused him both sorrow and pain. On the other hand, whenever someone did become excitedly eager and involved in the masturbatory experience he would lose interest and become frightened and withdrawn. The dread of the excited and exciting object was intense in him. The excited state in the fetishistic object had to be an encapsulated and localized one and under his control (cf. A. Freud, 1952).

After the youth had ejaculated, the relation to the fetish itself would come into full operation, although this is not strictly accurate, because the relation to the foreskin was biphasic: as a property of the erect penis and as a sac into which he masturbated. The total fetishistic event can be differentiated into three stages: (i) ego-relation to the fetishistic object as a person, (ii) sexual passive oral and manual relation to the erect penis and the foreskin, and (iii) active intrusive ejaculatory relation to the foreskin as a receptacle.

Before examining the psychic contents of the foreskin fetish proper I would like to emphasize the importance for this patient of the relation to the fetishistic object. In heterosexual fetishism the fetish functions as a reassurance against the (castration) anxieties relating to the female sexual object and sexual organs. In my patient the ego-relation to the homosexual fetishistic object operated as a reassurance against the archaic and regressive nature of the relation to the fetish itself. Gradually it became quite clear to the patient and me that he had sought treatment because of the inner threat to his ego and personality from the chaotic and archaic feelings and excitements of the foreskin fetish practices. During the first year and more of his analysis, his idealized and ecstatic pursuit of the fetishistic objects screened his dread of what was happening in the sexual practices themselves. He tended breezily to slur over them and described his frenzied sexual activities as "cure through exhaustion." The elation and greed experienced in relation to the foreskin fetish was truly frightening for him. His dreams in the earlier stages of analysis were barely cloaked primitive wish-fulfillment of the wish to suck the penis with the foreskin and swallow the semen. That he never experienced any real gratification was hidden from himself and vigorously denied in the narratives of his sexual exploits.

PSYCHODYNAMICS OF THE FORESKIN FETISH

I shall first schematically detail the meaning of the foreskin-penis in the state of erection and the patient's relation to it. He attributed a very special magical significance to the foreskin-penis in such a state. To him it represented the ideal breast-penis from the first oral stage. It filled him with a sense of awe, fascination and excruciating excitement. By the time he had brought the foreskin-penis into this stage of congested aliveness he felt it to be his "creation" and treated it as such. Sight, touch, and smell played a significant part in his relation to it. He could never fully digest the pleasurable possibilities of the situation. He wanted to fuse and merge with it. It was nearer to a hallucinatory imago than a perception of a separate organ on another person or as a symbolic vehicle of relationship. Lacan and Granoff (1956) in their discussion of the role of the symbolic, the imaginary, and the real in fetishism have discussed this point in an intriguing manner. This regressive mode of relationship to the foreskin-penis fetish involved the breakdown of symbolic and secondary process mental activity. The patient felt he had *created* this magical object and through visual and manual touch and oral incorporation *became* it. This meant to him refinding and recreating concretely the original unity with the omnipotent nourishing breast-mother. Nunberg (1947) in his study "Circumcision and Problems of Bisexuality" has established the fact that circumcision can mean loss of mother and has further detailed the meaning of the foreskin as symbolic of vagina, rectum, and femininity. The wish to suck father's penis had arisen in this patient following his younger sister's birth. He had always felt his own circumcised state a deficient, inadequate, maimed gender identity (cf. Greenson, 1964: Stoller, 1964). The fusion with the foreskin-penis re-established the lost omnipotent unity between the infantile pleasure-ego and the breast-penis-mother. It also served the function of denying the later traumatic separation from the mother through her marriage as well as negating his discovery that she was a castrated penisless object. Nunberg (1947) has discussed his patient's fantasy that the female labia are a sort of foreskin that hide and protect the female penis. In my patient's fantasy and image this was true of the foreskin-penis. It was the ideal bisexual organ composed of the glans penis and foreskin-vagina united in inseparable (non-castrative) oneness. Hence his extreme delight and pleasure in it. The glans penis protected by the foreskin, which he could manipulate without injuring, meant also the primitive infant-self of the patient in the ideal protective nurturing ambience of the mother (foreskin), safely and pleasurably held by it.

The oral craving to fuse with the foreskin-penis and his idealization of a trance-like state of bliss that he experienced bear out the hypotheses offered by Greenacre (1953), Bak (1953) and Socarides (1960) that separation anxiety and the fear of abandonment are the primary anxiety affects in the fetishist. In this patient the repetitive recreation of this illusional oneness with the mother through the concrete and physical idiom of his oral and manual relation to the foreskin denied the separation from her and at the same time established a new transient *event* that was its own reality and negated the affects related to the (internal) maternal imago. This capacity to carry contradictory affects and motivations seems to make the fetish-istic practices particularly effective in the ego's defensive maneuver against primitive and archaic emotional needs. The temporal element plays an important part here. The foreknowl-edge that the whole engineered event would last a short while and would be terminated by discharge (ejaculation) lessened the threat from the eruption of the very primitive body needs and experiences with their traumatic genetic associations. The element of pleasure through gratification, the transcience in time and the as-if make-believe of the whole fetishistic sexual game enabled the ego to split: thus if one part was involved another looked on with bemused objectivity. This dissociation defeated, however, the regressive motivation to fuse with breast-mother and in retrospect the patient had no internalized satisfactory image of the whole experience available.

Just as the attempts to boost the narcissistic self-regard of the fetishistic object (the youths) ended in compelling them to sub-mit to the sexual orgy and thus experience humiliation, the oral-manual relation to the foreskin-penis with its exaggerated and idealized excitement and fervor also ended in a collapse (detumescence) of the omnipotent organ through ejaculation. The patient always felt sorry and apologetic towards the youths and had a sense of them as having suffered a pain and an injury. The unconscious intention cannibalistically to murder the loved object in an excited frenzy was clear here (cf. Payne, 1939).

Before I detail the third phase of the total fetishistic activity, i.e., the intrusive (aggressive) relation with the foreskin, I would like to single out the importance for this patient of swallowing the semen. He had a distinct notion of it as a very powerful substance with magical attributes and constituting the very essence of the vigor and beauty of the youths. It was both comic and pathetic the way he always tried to make them promise not to let their girl friends perform fellatio on them. The rationalization he offered was (and this neatly betrayed the sadistic greedy and hostile intent in his behavior) that the girls would not respect them afterwards. The patient had at one time talked of his greedy compulsion to swallow semen as an addiction. An addiction it was too. It had the unconscious significance of incorporating a good substance which would neutralize his bad inner substances. We shall see later its magical curative value as a defense against hypochondriacal states. Glover (1932) has pointed out how transitory fetishistic phenomena appear when an alcoholic gives up his compulsive drinking. Here we see an addiction introduced into the very structure of a fetishistic practice. The infinite complexity of archaic body processes, pregenital impulses, archaic primary process mentation and affect which the fetishist can tolerate in an unorganized state is a remarkable phenomenon that still needs proper explanation.

It was only after the youth had ejaculated and detumescence had set in that the third phase started and the patient moved from a passive-oral relation to an active intrusive phallic one. His wish was always to penetrate the sac of the foreskin with his penis. This was another variant of symbiotic fusion, but at a phallic level. And here he experienced his most painful mortifications because the youths never reciprocated his feelings. He wanted to be held tight and to be loved, and they were generally bored and aloof by this time. So his penis was never appraised as a good object and it ended in a mere discharge gratification for him, which left him sad and disconsolate. One important fantasy involved was the wish to enter the womb of the mother, to be engulfed and enveloped. The submergence of his penis into the foreskin was both a wish-fulfillment and a defense against it. There was a profound dread in him of his passive masochistic desire to submit to the phallic-omnipotent mother, as represented by the foreskin. This was borne out by his dreams in which claustrophobic anxiety played a prominent part and he felt trapped or asphyxiated.

His ejaculation brought the fetishistic activities to an end in a dismal bleak way because he never experienced pleasure in his orgasm and had a sense of disgust about his own semen. The termination of the excited events in this meager way was counteracted by a ritualistic nursing of the fetishistic object. He would wash and clean the youths, reassure them that nothing deleterious had happened, and through speech and conversation create a sort of benign amnesia about the whole episode. He rarely repeated these experiences with the same person. The person who became his first stable, social, and affectionate love-object was a circumcised youth, and by then his fetishistic manic pursuits had given way to a depressive hypochondriacal withdrawn state where the true nature and extent of his ego-pathology became fully visible. Before I discuss this I shall summarize the three main motifs that were enacted in myriad, amorphous, and fragmented ways in the relation to the fetishistic object and the foreskin fetish: (i) the wish to have a baby, i.e., give birth; (ii) the erotization and control of rage and murderous impulses regarding the mother, father, and siblings; (iii) the craving for, and dread of, a passive masochistic sexual surrender, which was the most potent unconscious wish and also a threat to the unity and existence of the ego.

The wish for a baby in the male child and its specific importance for fetishism has been discussed by Kestenberg (1956), van der Leeuw (1958), and Socarides (1960). They have further related it to Winnicott's (1953) concept of the transitional object. Van der Leeuw has postulated that "the transitional object is not only breast and phallus, but also the child made by the mother." In my patient's ego-relation to the fetishistic objects there was the expression of the wish for a baby in terms of endowing the youths with a new identity and sense of self, and facilitating "a psychological birth" in them. They were for him, in the context of the excited interchange, his *creations*, his babies: his own ideal self born through his psychological actions and activities in their shape and contour. The identification with the procreative, active and omnipotent mother was obvious here. But also present was the knowledge of its impossibility, hence rage and sadistic attack. This expressed itself through the compulsion to break down the identity of the whole fetishistic object into the regressive part-object, the foreskin fetish. The psychologically enhanced self-esteem of the "created" youth was "murdered" through sexual attack on it. The same theme expressed itself in the relation to the foreskin fetish: the mouth-manual-cannibalistic relation to the glans penis was the vehicle of the wish for oral impregnation. The unconscious fantasies behind making the glans penis emerge and submerge in the foreskin and making the youth look at it, as well as making the glans penis enter and retract from his own mouth (vagina), were all variations on the theme of giving birth to the self and the youth, symbolized by the penis. It also served the function of reassurance against being devoured. One element of castration anxiety in this patient was the dread of being eaten up (overwhelmed) by the mother.

This also ended in a fiasco through ejaculation, and here the sadistic delight in their helplessness at the point of orgasm and the consequent detumescence of the penis were in his unconscious fantasy an attack on the pregnant mother and her baby-phallus. The swallowing of the semen now endowed him with the magical power to impregnate and the use of the foreskin as (vaginal-mouth) sac for his "intercourse" was a wish both to impregnate and to be born from this foreskin-uterus. This also ended in discharge-futility, and was followed by psychological nursing of the fetishistic objects and the need to reassure them as well as to re-establish psychic mental distance between the self and the object. The third element, that of the masochistic passive wish for total surrender and the dread of it, we see in his coercive stimulating the youths to a pitch of intolerable sexual excitement. Their egos, and not his, experienced the abandon to excitement. This way of splitting off the masochistic passive wish, projecting it onto the youth and then making them *live* it through his kindly sexual ministrations was one of the self-protective functions of the fetishistic practices (cf. Khan, 1962, 1964c).

Klein (1932) has detailed the complexity of the boy's fantasies in the "feminine phase" of development. She has designated it as "the period of maximal sadism." She postulated: "In this phase the boy has oral-sucking fixation on his father's penis, just as the girl has. This fixation is, I consider, the basis of true homosexuality in him." In the fetishistic fantasies and practices of my patient the regression from the phallic phase of this feminine phase is explicitly clear, with all its omnipotent sadistic wishes to enter and possess the father's penis, as well as to attack the body-contents of the mother's inside. One consequence of this regressive intensification of the "feminine phase" fantasies and part-object relations was the dissolution of his emergent phallic identity. Payne (1939) stated in her discussion of fetishism: "The weakness of ego development is one aspect of the weakness of genitality and denotes interference with the libidinization, formation, and integration of the body ego, especially of the *penis imago*. This brings about an exaggeration of the first mechanisms and an exaggerated dependence on the introjected objects, but no sustained identification with any."

The regression from phallic strivings in my patient led to a basic diffusion of the *penis imago* as a narcissistic model of self and the collusive sexual relationship with youths was an attempt to seek reassurance against the disintegration of the *penis imago*. In this aspect relation to the fetishistic whole-object was a defense against the persecutory anxieties inherent in the fantasies belonging to the foreskin fetishism. Sight of the whole-object as a sexualized phallic object also reassured against anxieties relating to sensations of the changing size of the phallus in sexual behavior (cf. Greenacre, 1953).

EGO PATHOLOGY AND THE DISTURBED MOTHER-CHILD RELATIONSHIP

The analytic work of the first sixteen months had gradually enabled the patient to tolerate his inner panicky anxiety states without immediate flight into the idealized and erotic reassurance of the sexual practices with the foreskin fetish. Correspondingly, he began to be disillusioned about his relation to the fetishistic objects. They were not such ideal and lovable human beings after all. He could now see that his program to provide love for the "outcasts for whom life had made no provision" had not succeeded, for three reasons: (i) his inability to love, (ii) their inability to receive love, and (iii) his choice of youths who had psychopathic, delinquent personalities, verging on the criminal. It was very humiliating for him to acknowledge that they had never cared for him, had stolen his money and goods, and treated him with scorn and derision.

He could now say that he did not want anyone to be dependent on him. He wanted to be dependent himself and be loved and taken care of. In this mood he began to search for a more human and what he had described as a "personable" relationship. He met a youth and started a relationship which was neither fetishistic nor compulsively sexual (Khan, 1965). The youth was circumcised and quite a decent person. It was this relationship that revealed the true nature of his ego-pathology and the extent of his identifications with his mother. Soon after starting this relationship he found himself delusionally jealous and hysterically emotional all the time about the activities of the youth. He lived in a nightmare state of anguish when the youth was away, compulsively imagining the latter being seduced by someone else. His state of imperturbability gave way to fits of raging jealousy and a crazy sort of possessiveness. He would question the youth, endlessly row with him, search his underwear for signs of sexual activity, etc. Meantime he himself was furtively faithless to the youth with others—as his mother had been.

He now began to realize this was exactly how he had seen his mother behave to her second husband. She felt wronged, betrayed, jealous, and inconsolable. The patient had been her chief confidant and had shared all her moods and sympathized with her grievances. His stepfather had often remarked to him that he should not take every statement of his mother's as if it were God's written word.

The relation to this youth had led to the recurrence of his two old symptoms: anal itching and nightmares. He scratched himself furiously at night and could not sleep because of ghastly nightmares which frightened him so much that he could never remember them. They had mostly to do with a physical sense of body-dismemberment and/or fantastic enlargement of certain limbs. These latter he could experience in fleeting sensations during wakefulness as well (Greenacre, 1953).

Here we were able to identify another motif in fetishistic practices with the foreskin: the sadistic wish to dig into another's body and discover the truth—to rob it of its precious contents which were his right and were being withheld from him. His anal itching also led to a general state of hypochondria. Gillespie (1940) and Greenacre (1953) have stressed the importance of hypochondriacal states in fetishistic perversion. In this patient the hypochondriacal states could be divided into two distinct moods: (a) those relating to acute sense of personal unworthiness and loss of self-esteem, and (b) those relating to a disgust with the personal body and its secretions. They were intrinsically related to his jealous fits of rage about his new friend and his dread of being abandoned. This dread of abandonment was also a recurrent theme of his mother's emotionality. She had two terrors that ruled her life: (a) of being deserted by her husbands, and (b) of poverty, of being left destitute.

The history of his relation to his mother as we reconstructed it now from his memories, his acting out, and his transference relation can be presented schematically as follows.

His mother, a beautiful young woman, had started on her adult life rather traumatically. Her father had committed suicide and the ambitious girl had decided to make a rich and secure marriage. She had married an affluent farmer but had been unfaithful to him throughout (by her own confession). When the patient was 2½ years old she had conceived extramaritally and this had led to overt discord between her husband and herself. She had dealt with the guilt and anxieties about her pregnancy by turning passionately to her youngest child (my patient) and had taken over from the nanny who had looked after him till then. The nanny had stayed on till the divorce four years later when she had been sacked for telling the children that it was not their father who was a nasty man but their mother who had been a fickle wife with loose morals.

It was in this context that the three memories of the wish to suck his father's penis, the wish for union with the urethra of the geldings, and his sitting on eggs imagining he had laid them began to be integrated into a more meaningful pattern. We could see how the young child had reached the beginnings of the phallic phase. The parental discord and mother's pregnancy had a traumatic effect on him. He had reacted to it (a) with the wish to be like his mother and have a baby from father; (b) the dread of father's penis and rage at it (and the baby as father's penis) expressed in his biting the rhubarb plants; (c) the response to the sudden influx of insecurity in the mother and her involving him with it by flight to a magical fantasy of being united to the urethra of the geldings. Here the urethra meant the father's penis as a hollow womb-like secure place as well as the safe inside of the mother.

The patient as a child had made repeated observations of his mother's body and his younger sister's genitals. His mother had kept up a curious myth of the innocence of childhood and had exposed herself frequently, though inadvertently, right up to his eleventh year. She had stopped when one day she suspected he had started to masturbate and had then volunteered to tell him how if boys rub their penis a white fluid comes out. The relation of all these elements of his childhood experiences with the mother to his fetishistic practices was clearly established in his treatment.

His current relation to the youth settled down to a relatively stable and affectionate bond between them. He also had to accept that the youth helped him more than he helped the youth. Here the futility of his childhood efforts to help the mother, soothe her impassioned hysterical states, reassure her against her dread of abandonment and poverty all came to the fore. We could now see how the restitutive element of providing sexual pleasure to the fetishistic object was a great asset to him. He had grown up feeling and seeing that people only traumatize and hurt each other and are inconsolable.

In the treatment he now started to sink gradually into total apathy, inertia, and a helpless state of bleak withdrawal. All his phobias returned as well. He felt he could not face people and had an excruciating sense of his inadequacy and poverty of being. He could not go to work and took two years' unpaid leave, which was granted him. He now contacted his father whom he had not seen for over thirty years and who agreed to pay his living expenses.

The patient's state became one of a deep regressive dependence, in which the only thing that kept him going was his treatment. This phase lasted for nearly a year. It repeated in all essential elements the way he had lived his youth before his sexual acting-out had started. Once he had left home and gone to boarding school he had become a shy, timid, withdrawn boy. He had made no friends; lived by his fetishistic reveries and masturbation. Even though he had done well at the university and got a good degree he had not felt up to the rigors of a competitive professional life. After his college life he had felt so frightened of going mad that he had decided to become a laborer and worked in a coal mine till the war started. Soon afterwards he had been called up and was taken a prisoner of war. He had survived the frightfully arduous and dismal existence in a Japanese camp without much sense of the dangers involved—at one time he had said how to him it had felt like being in a lunatic asylum and no more. The grim reality of the Japanese prisoner-of-war camp rationalized his worst terrors. His apathetic mood and mechanical obedience saved him from being victimized by the Japanese soldiers. After the war, when he returned home, he had been given a good job and advised to have psychiatric treatment. This had led him to his first analysis and the acting out of his fetishistic masturbatory fantasies into actual relationships.

In his regressive illness in analysis the patient again decided to become a laborer because he could not bear the emptiness of his life, and it was indeed most painful to watch him live it. This alone, however, enabled us to work through the traumata of his relation to his mother.

We could now see how his mother's seduction of him as a child, which he had passionately reciprocated, had made no allowance for his emotional and developmental needs. He had felt unloved, abandoned, and terribly frightened. Added to this was the weight of the mother's hysterical emotionality. He had dealt with it by surrender to her moods and seduction on the one hand and a secret splitting off of his personal self into the masturbatory fetishistic reveries on the other. This had constituted the only private life his mother had no access to or control over. I cannot detail here the complexity of the material and analytic work involved in this phase. At the depth of his depressive apathy, phobic withdrawal, and feeling of total collapse the patient had the following dream which tells the whole story very vividly:

> On a table is a rectangular bowl three to four inches high, generally used for fruit or flowers. It is full of turds that look like sausages and bananas. He feels an acute sense of apprehension that at any time the pretense will break and they will be visible for what they are. There is a bit leaning over the edge of the bowl and from its soggy consistency he fears it will break off and fall. He takes it with a silver spoon to save it from falling on the tablecloth. Pretending it is a sausage, he puts it into his mouth, discovers it is shit and spits it out.

This dream succinctly portrays the patient's inner emotional perception of his relation to his mother (the spoon in the dream had been the one given by his mother) and to the foreskin fetish. Here we see behind the idealizations and denial the true picture of the depressed deprived child's feelings of despair (cf. Spitz and Wolf, 1949).

This dream, which is from the middle of his fourth year of analysis, led to the discussion of his attitude of *negativity*. He now described himself as an *un-person,* someone who has never existed, never really experienced anything. All his life he had merely precipitated events and had remained aloof and dissociated from them—an onlooker, neither nourishing nor nourished. Another theme parallel to this attitude of negativity was his secret sense of being special, that inside he had a very precious something which he could never share, hence could not experience himself either. One cannot exaggerate the life-saving value of this illusion for this patient. It enabled him to survive his adolescence and the regressive depressive apathy in analysis. He had often felt quite objectively that there was no point in his going on living, but he could not kill himself. He was external to this ideal inner self and he had no right to destroy it.

This led to his anxieties about

(a) over-stimulation through identification with the mother, the castrated sexual mother;

(b) fear of being emptied out, left totally vacant like a shell, and abandoned, i.e., being robbed of primary self and breast-mother;

(c) dread of his own wish to surrender to the sadistic mother and an acute anxiety about passive annihilation;

(d) dread of males and an archaic form of castration anxiety.

The fetishistic practices had reversed these fears. It gradually became quite clear to the patient that his passionate love of his mother in his childhood had been very shallow. Basically he had sealed himself off and lived a pseudo-existence through identification with her moods. This in turn had made masculine-phallic development impossible. He had not really participated. Very early on he had split off into two persons: the clinging phobic anxious child intimately tied to the mother and the negativistic withdrawn boy fixated on his fetishistic internal objects. His attitude to everyone had been one of phobia and paranoid suspicion. He had later added to this a cunning use of language which cancelled all relationships through verbal badinage.

This patient as a child had reacted to the ugly discord between his parents with a regression to a very private and encapsulated state of fantasy. His schematic memories witnessed this and his fetishistic practices enacted it. What characterized these fantasy states was an unintegrated mixture of the most archaic feelings, part-object relations, and excessive erotization. Payne (1939) and Gillespie (1940) have emphasized the importance of sadism and introjection-projection mechanisms. Gillespie (1940) has further stressed the admixture of incorporative tendencies with phallic strivings. In the contents of my patient's fetishistic fantasies all these elements were grossly and flagrantly present. In fact, I consider that one of the primary functions of his creation of fetishistic fantasies regarding the foreskin was to encapsulate and control these very primitive and sadistic impulses. What constitutes the specific threat to the fetishist's ego is the regressive fusion of phallic stage strivings with oral and anal impulses and part-object relationships. In my patient's childhood the mother's overt hostility toward, and devaluation of, the father, and the sudden and violent break-up of the home led to the child's:

(i) identification with the mother, both as a source of security and a denial of castration threat from the father;

(ii) feminine identification with mother as a way of maintaining internal possession of father (penis);

(iii) regression to part-object aspects of the parents (father as penis, mother as vagina-foreskin) and the attempt to concoct a parental couple through an amalgam of these two part-objects in one foreskin-penis;

(iv) collusion with mother's passionate emotionality, the over-stimulation from this leading to excessive sexualization of these fetishistic reverie states.

The anxiety states which this patient had experienced in childhood were diffuse and acute, verging on panic all the time and yet without much psychic content to them. He could all too easily feel depersonalized and terror-stricken, to which he reacted with either apathetic depression or acting out, or hypochondria. He felt a threat of disintegration and annihilation was forever nagging at him inwardly. It was this type of anxiety state which had exaggerated castration anxiety. In the fetishist, as Greenacre (1953), Payne (1939), and Gillespie (1952) have emphasized, it is the more archaic anxiety-states that overload castration anxiety at the phallic phase. This patient's ego had reacted to it by dissociations. These dissociations in the ego were maintained through denial, omnipotent idealization of mother, regressive use of incorporative mechanisms and their sexualization and the total suppression of sadistic-aggressive behavior.

Payne (1939) has singled out the specific importance of sadism and the failure to integrate it to sexuality and ego-process in the fetishist. She stated that the sexual aim in the fetishist is to kill the love-object. I have shown earlier how in the fetishistic practice the ejaculation of the partner and consequent detumescence were experienced unconsciously by the patient as "sexual murder" of the penis. The awareness of this murderous wish then led to attempts at undoing through tender nursing and care. In this the fetishist's ego is very like the obsessional's: it continuously oscillates between an archaic wish for sexual fusion and a murderous attack on the object. Both processes intensify the ego's need for self-protection. It is this that leads to exploitation of phobic attitudes and deadening of affectivity in the fetishist. The fetishist's relation to his object is more a sexualized ego-interest than an instinctual investment and love. Gillespie (1939) has pertinently remarked that in the fetishist "the theme of satisfaction is dependent on frustration, or rather a sort of partial frustration," and that one of the safeguards needed by the fetishist is "just that he should be frustrated." In my patient there was never once an experience of full sexual satisfaction. Satisfaction meant extinction and annihilation. It entailed either the ego's surrender to a masochistic archaic wish for total incorporation or a sadistic annihilation of the object in the excited state. Sexuality was exploited only for erotization of defenses and archaic frightening part-object relationships. What Anna Freud (1952) has described as negativism and dread of emotional surrender in the pervert is a further aspect of this threat of annihilation.

In this patient the separation from the father and the involvement with mother's emotionality sabotaged the phallic strivings and development and over the course of his childhood and adolescence led to fixations on fetishistic reveries and diffusion of his identity both as a male and as a person.

CONCLUSIONS

I have discussed material from the treatment and life history of a male homosexual patient who had suffered acute ego-distortion from a pathogenic involvement with his mother's mood and personality from the age of 3 onwards. The questions I want to ask are:

(i) why the patient as a child did not develop a severe psychotic illness?

(ii) what enabled him to create so early a fetishistic inner reverie state that protected him against total surrender to the mother's pathological intrusions upon his personality?

I think it is feasible to answer that the ego's capacity to dissociate and create a fetishistic reverie protected it from total submergence in mother's pathology. The libidinization from the mother also facilitated the stabilization of the fetish. The fetishistic reveries protected the ego against psychotic breakdown. What had compelled the patient to seek treatment was the unconscious knowledge of the threat to his ego through acting out of the fetishistic fantasies. The question as to what enables a child to create a fetish is not so easy to answer. In my patient there was certainly a good early feeding relation to the (breast) mother and to a stable healthy nanny. It was around the beginnings of the phallic phase that the traumata began to happen. The emergent Oedipal (negative and positive) relations were disrupted by these traumata and a collusive pre-Oedipal regressive relation to the mother materialized instead. The maturational processes and growth enabled the ego, however, to fight a defensive self-protective battle through dissociation and regression. I have tried to show how the fetishistic object and the foreskin fetish comprised the early infantile self and the primary object (mother). The fetish is built like a collage: it envelops complex and archaic affects, psychic processes, and internal part-object relations and manages to sustain them in an unintegrated state.[2] I am inclined to say that in the capacity to

[2] Dr. Hanna Segal in her discussion pertinently pointed out that it might be more accurate to define the fetish as a portmanteau. In this patient the fetish (as a reverie state and object) was a container of very archaic and primitive psychic and sexual processes.

create a fetish we see the inherent strength of the infant-child ego and its capacity to save itself from total collapse and disintegration. The capacity to create a fetish presupposes that maturationally the ego has access to its synthetic functions. The basic mechanisms involved are: splitting, denial, isolation, idealization, somatization, objectivation, and sexualization. The primary affects relate to dread of surrender to excitement and the exciting object, sadism, and threat of body-dissolution, and annihilation and being abandoned. The fetish is both a phobic and a counterphobic phenomenon. This duality of the fetishistic phenomena relates them closely to obsessional states. Through the fetish the ego tries to find a way out of its negativity and paranoid withdrawal and through the process of sexualization tries to bind the aggressive, sadistic, and uncontrollable rage impulses. The fetish enables ego functioning and object relationships, the extreme obverse of which is autistic withdrawal.

The interplay of two distinct types of psychic processes are prominent in this patient: one related to his ego-functions and the other to sexual excitement. The ego-functioning had been crippled by a severely apathetic, phobic attitude throughout the childhood, adolescence, and youth of this patient. During this period he had maintained a highly organized excitement and emotionality in which masturbatory fantasies about the foreskin-penis were the dominant integrating factor. The case-history shows how the patient as a child had reached a rudimentary phallic phase of psychosexual development. These intense phallic-genital excitements had been both sponsored and encouraged by the contemporary care-taking environment and object-relations. The breakdown of the parental environment had led to a chaotic regression to pregenital modes of oral-anal incorporative fantasies, but the penis-imago had been retained throughout these vicissitudes, though in a pathologically dissociated precarious state. Henceforth the most striking feature of this patient's internal reality was the intense and amorphous excitement that this foreskin-imago could mobilize in him. I have also suggested that these phallic excited states operated as a manic defense (Winnicott, 1935) and were exploited as a defense against acknowledgment of the disruptive upheavals of his childhood and the consequent threat of ego-disintegration, despair and dissolution of personality. He had later found a way out to reality and object relationships through acting out this encapsulated phallic-cum-pregenital amalgam of internal excitement and sexual frenzy. This had enabled him to achieve a pathological ego-mastery over his impulses and the object as well as to force his ego out of its phobic-paranoid attitude of apathetic mistrust. But if this acting out had served the function of a rescue operation, it had also threatened him with a total loss of self through surrender to sexual impulses and the object. He had sought treatment because of his amorphous state of lack of identity and purpose in life. I am proposing here that this type of internal anxiety-situation constitutes the basic predicament for the fetishist. Fetishism is a state of omnipotently, but precariously, controlled mania. Hence it is at once intensely pleasurable and frightfully vulnerable. What the patient had sought from his treatment was the assimilation of this manic sexual fetishistic excitement and affectivity into an ego-capacity that could be related to the self, the object, and the environment. This he has certainly achieved through his analysis. During the past ten years since his analysis, the patient has lived an active and creative professional, social, and intellectual life as a member of his own culture, doing good work in an atmosphere of social belongingness.

Freud from the very beginning had stressed the crucial role of castration anxiety in the genesis of fetishism. Researches since then, particularly those of Glover, Payne, Gillespie, and Greenacre, have emphasized the role of early internalized anxiety-situations, object-relations, and vicissitudes of body-ego development which characterize the peculiar intensity of the fetishist's castration anxiety. In my case-material all these factors are vividly present. This case history tries to show how these early anxiety-states and excitatory experiences reinforce the castration threat in the fetishist. Furthermore, it is possible to point out from where the as-if adult quality of the fetishist's sexual exploits and behavior derives its ego-syntonicity. It is the phallic-genital excitement that holds the dynamic clue (cf. Katan, 1964). At the point of childhood traumata both the ego and psychosexual development have achieved phallic status though they are not stabilized as yet. The regressive process brings with it an influx of pregenital impulses and archaic psychic functioning. This regressive process is collusively reinforced by the mother's behavior in many subtle ways (cf. Greenacre, 1960). Hence the bizarre, hopeful, and absurd nature of all fetishistic phenomena. The mutative factor, however, remains the intensity of phallic affective excitement and the regressive intrusion of pregenital part-object relationships in the fetishist. The omnipotent control of the object to discharge this manic phallic excitement is a most characteristic feature of the fetishist personality. Through it the archaic part-object relationships are held in control. This does not reduce the threat to ego-stability in any way. In fact, it exaggerates it. The very media by which the fetishist is compelled by his internal anxieties and impulses to seek reassurance, through collusion with external objects and reality, expose the ego to severe and persistent danger situations. Hence the acuteness of the threat of castration (annihilation) and ego-collapse in the fetishist. The ego is never in full mastery of the internal crises or external objects. The exploitation of primitive mechanisms, like splitting, projection, incorporation, and idealization by the ego, in order to create the illusion of omnipotent control interferes with its normal functioning. The fetishist achieves his sense of security, self-esteem and well-being entirely through his manipulation of the agitated excitability of the penis-imago and the complex archaic pregenital impulses and object-relations inherent in it. This exploitation increases the threat of overstimulation to the ego and faces it with the predicament of either total exhaustion and annihilation or masochistic surrender to the object. The failure to neutralize sadistic impulses and their fusion with libidinal strivings without modification of murderous intent exaggerates further the threat to the object and the retaliatory threat to the self (Payne, 1939).

It is in this internal constellation of pregenital sexual impulses, primitive object-relations, and affectivity that we can fully decipher the necessity of the maternal imago as a phallic object for the fetishist. Freud (1927) had explicitly stated that the psychic content of fetishistic practices is the fixation on the phallic mother-imago: "the fetish is a substitute for a woman's (the mother's) penis that the little boy once believed in and—for reasons familiar to us—does not want to give up." My case material suggests that the phallic mother imago upon which the fetishist is fixated is composed from sensations derived from the self-phallus in the excited states and the maternal object toward whom these are directed. Also involved are passive longings for the father's penis. Through a *tour de force* of psychic functioning the fetishist in his childhood creates a unitary imago from experiences and characteristics that belong to two different persons: the self and the object. I have shown how the foreskin fetish in my patient had attributes both of the self and the mother as well as of the father. Once these features have been coalesced they are dissociated from reality-testing *vis-à-vis* the external object. It is at this stage that denial plays such an important role in the psychodynamics of fetishism. It is this that relates fetishistic phenomena specifically to transitional object type of psychic functioning (cf. Winnicott, 1953). The instinctual regression is reinforced by ego-regression to more archaic and magical forms of psychic functioning. The fetish is created out of the sensations of self-body and object-perceptions. The threat to the body-ego from anxiety of annihilation (castration) is averted by projecting the penis-imago to the mother, who is then incorporated as a phallic omnipotent object. This has the added advantage that not only is the threatened penis-imago rendered safe but the archaic bond of security with the mother is also re-established. Similarly, the father's penis is internalized as a magical food-object. The maintenance of this complex affectivity and psychic functioning entails severe curtailment of the ego's growth and development. Hence the fetishist is a person deluded by the certainty that he has access to, and omnipotent possession and control of, a magical object.

The fixation on the internal magical object interferes with the neutralization of aggressive and sexual impulses in the fetishist. The specific ego-pathology in the fetishist thus relates to the failure to establish "secondary autonomy." Hartmann (1964) has defined his concept of "secondary autonomy" as:

> . . . many, though not all, ego activities can be traced genetically to determinants in the id or to conflicts between ego and id. In the course of development, however, they normally acquire a certain amount of autonomy from these genetic factors. The ego's achievements may under some circumstances be reversible, but it is important to know that in normal conditions many of them are not. The degree to which its activities have become functionally independent from their origins is essential for the undisturbed functioning of the ego, and so is the degree to which they are protected against regression and instinctualization. We speak of the degrees of this independence of the ego as the degrees of secondary autonomy. (Hartmann, 1964, p. xi.)

In Hartmann's idiom we could postulate that fetishism is a pathological substitute for "secondary autonomy." It is this specific type of ego-pathology that accounts for the complexity and bizarre qualities of the fetishistic phenomena.

REFERENCES

BAK, R. C. (1953). "Fetishism." *J. Amer. Psychoanal. Assoc.*, Vol. 1.

BIRD, B. (1958). "A study of the bisexual meaning of the foreskin." *J. Amer. Psychoanal. Assoc.*, Vol. 6.

BUXBAUM, E. (1960). "Hair pulling and fetishism." *Psychoanal. Study Child*, Vol. 15.

FRASER, A. W. (1963). "A relationship between transitional objects and preconscious mental processes." In: *Modern Perspectives in Child Development*, eds. Solnit and Provence. (New York: Int. Univ. Press.)

FREUD, A. (1952). "A connection between the states of negativism and of emotional surrender." *Int. J. Psycho-Anal.*, Vol. 33, p. 265.

FREUD, S. (1927). "Fetishism." *S.E.*, Vol. 21.

———— (1940). "Splitting of the ego in the process of defence." *S.E.*, Vol. 23.

GILLESPIE, W. H. (1940). "A contribution to the study of fetishism." *Int. J. Psycho-Anal.*, Vol. 21.

———— (1952). "Notes on the analysis of sexual perversions." *Int. J. Psycho-Anal.*, Vol. 33.

———— (1964). "The psycho-analytic theory of sexual deviation with special reference to fetishism." In: *The Pathology and Treatment of Sexual Deviation*. ed. I. Rosen (London: Oxford Univ. Press.)

GLOVER, E. (1932). "On the aetiology of drug-addiction." *Int. J. Psycho-Anal.*, Vol. 13.

———— (1933). "The relation of perversion-formation to the development of reality-sense." *Int. J. Psycho-Anal.*, Vol. 14.

———— (1949). *Psycho-analysis.* (London: Staples.)

GREENACRE, P. (1953). "Certain relationships between fetishism and faulty development of the body image." *Psychoanal. Study Child*, Vol. 8.

———— (1955). "Further considerations regarding fetishism." *Psychoanal. Study Child*, Vol. 10.

———— (1960). "Further notes on fetishism." *Psychoanal. Study Child*, Vol. 15.

GREENSON, R. (1964). "On homosexuality and gender identity." *Int. J. Psycho-Anal.*, Vol. 45.

HARTMANN, H. (1956). "Notes on the reality principle." In: Hartmann (1964).

—— (1964). *Essays on Ego Psychology* (London: Hogarth; New York: Int. Univ. Press.)

HUNTER, D. (1954). "Object-relation changes in the analysis of a fetishist." *Int. J. Psycho-Anal.*, Vol. 35.

KATAN, M. (1964). "Fetishism, splitting of the ego, and denial." *Int. J. Psycho-Anal.*, Vol. 45.

KESTENBERG, J. (1956). "On the development of maternal feelings in early childhood." *Psychoanal. Study Child*, Vol. 11.

KHAN, M. M. R. (1962). "The role of polymorph-perverse body-experiences and object-relations in ego-integration." *Brit. J. med. Psychol.*, Vol. 35.

—— (1963). "Ego ideal, excitement and the threat of annihilation." *J. Hillside Hosp.*, Vol. 12.

—— (1964a). "The role of infantile sexuality and early object relations in female homosexuality." In: *The Pathology and Treatment of Sexual Deviation*. ed. I. Rosen. (London: Oxford Univ. Press.)

—— (1964b). "Ego deviation, cumulative trauma and the role of reconstruction in the analytic process." *Int. J. Psycho-Anal.*, Vol. 45.

—— (1964c). "The function of intimacy and acting out in perversions." In: *Sexual Behavior and the Law*. ed. R. Slovenko (Springfield: Thomas.)

—— (1965). "Homosexuality and the sexual nursing of self and object." (in press.)

KLEIN, M. (1932). *Psycho-Analysis of Children* (London: Hogarth.)

KRONENGOLD, E. and STERBA, R. (1936). "Two cases of fetishism." *Psychoanal. Quart.*, Vol. 5.

LACAN, J. and GRANOFF, V. (1956). "Fetishism: the symbolic, the imaginary and the real." In: *Perversions*. eds. Lorand and Balint. (New York: Random House.)

VAN DER LEEUW, P. J. (1958). "The preoedipal phase of the male." *Psychoanal. Study Child*, Vol. 13.

LORAND, S. (1930). "Fetishism in statu nascendi." *Int. J. Psycho-Anal.*, Vol. 11.

MITTELMANN, B. (1955). "Motor patterns and genital behavior: fetishism." *Psychoanal. Study Child*, Vol. 10.

NUNBERG, H. (1947). "Circumcision and problems of bisexuality." *Int. J. Psycho-Anal.*, Vol. 28.

PAYNE, S. M. (1939). "Some observations on the ego development of the fetishist." *Int. J. Psycho-Anal.*, Vol. 20.

Romm, M. E. (1949). "Some dynamics of fetishism." *Psychoanal. Quart.*, Vol. 18.

Socarides, C. W. (1959). "Meaning and content of a pedophiliac perversion." *J. Amer. Psychoanal. Assoc.*, Vol. 7.

Spitz, R. and Wolf, K. (1949). "Autoerotism: some empirical findings and hypotheses on three of its manifestations in the first year of life." *Psychoanal. Study Child*, Vols. 3-4.

Stoller, R. (1964). "A contribution to the study of gender identity." *Int. J. Psycho-Anal.*, Vol. 45.

Weissman, P. (1957). "Some aspects of sexual activity in a fetishist." *Psychoanal. Quart.*, Vol. 26.

Winnicott, D. W. (1935). "The manic defence." In: *Collected Papers* (London: Tavistock; New York: Basic Books, 1958.)

———— (1953). "Transitional objects and transitional phenomena." *ibid.*

———— (1956). "The antisocial tendency." *ibid.*

Wulff, M. (1946). "Fetishism and object choice in early childhood." *Psychoanal. Quart.*, Vol. 15.